BOLLYWOOD

'Bollywood' is the dominant global term to refer to the prolific Hindi language film industry in Bombay (renamed Mumbai in 1995). Characterized by music, dance routines, melodrama, lavish production values and an emphasis on stars and spectacle, Bollywood films have met with box-office success and enthusiastic audiences from India to West Africa to Russia, and throughout the English-speaking world.

In *Bollywood*, anthropologist and film scholar Tejaswini Ganti provides a guide to the cultural, social and political significance of Hindi cinema, outlining the history and structure of the Bombay film industry, and the development of popular filmmaking since the 1930s. Providing information and commentary on the key players in Bollywood, including composers, directors and stars, as well as material from current filmmakers themselves, areas covered in *Bollywood* include:

- History of Indian cinema
- Main themes and characteristics of Hindi cinema
- Significant films, directors, and stars
- Production and distribution of Bollywood films
- Interviews with actors, directors, and screenwriters

ROUTLEDGE FILM GUIDEBOOKS

Bollywood: a Guidebook to Popular Hindi Cinema
Tejaswini Ganti

Jane Campion
Deb Verhoeven

James Cameron
Alexandra Keller

BOLLYWOOD

A GUIDEBOOK TO
POPULAR HINDI CINEMA

TEJASWINI GANTI

Routledge
Taylor & Francis Group

NEW YORK AND LONDON

First published 2004
Simultaneously published in the UK, USA, and Canada
by Routledge
29 West 35th Street, New York, NY 10001
and
Routledge
11 New Fetter Lane, London EC4P 4EE

Routledge is an imprint of the Taylor & Francis Group

© 2004 Tejaswini Ganti

Typeset in Joanna by Florence Production Ltd, Stoodleigh, Devon

Printed and bound in Great Britain by TJ International Ltd, Padstow, Cornwall

Library of Congress Cataloging in Publication Data
A catalog record for this title has been requested

British Library Cataloguing in Publication Data
A catalogue record for this book is available from the British Library

ISBN 0–415–28853–3 (hbk)
ISBN 0–415–28854–1 (pbk)

CONTENTS

FIGURES

Tables

ACKNOWLEDGEMENTS

I would like to thank Vipul Agrawal, Maris Gillette, James Gulick, Amardeep Singh, and Christine Walley for their feedback, advice, and input during the writing process. I benefited greatly from my discussions with them regarding the format, content, and structure of this book. I would like to thank Richard Ball, associate professor in the economics department at Haverford College, for introducing me to the World Bank's online database and for helping me with some calculations in chapter 2. Aliya Curmally helped me with the painstaking task of interview transcriptions for which I am very grateful. I would like to express my appreciation for Haverford College, especially its Magill Library, where much of the task of writing this book was carried out.

Space does not permit me to list everyone I met in Bombay who helped make my research possible. I would like to thank them all for their generosity, hospitality, and kindness – for taking me into their homes and work spaces, for their patience and willingness to put up with my endless questioning, and for the enthusiasm with which they received my research project. I am especially grateful to the following individuals: Javed Akhtar, Shabana Azmi, Ritha

Bhaduri, Pooja Bhatt, Vikram Bhatt, Sachin Bhaumick, Aditya Chopra, Madhuri Dixit, Subhash Ghai, Sutanu Gupta, Ravi Gupta, Rumi Jaffrey, Ayesha Jhulka, Shammi Kapoor, Shashi Kapoor, Aamir Khan, Shahrukh Khan, Punkej Kharabanda, Anjum Rajabali, Rakesh Roshan, Sharmishta Roy, and Ramesh Sippy for the interviews and communications which I have excerpted in the book.

A special thanks to Nasreen Munni Kabir of Hyphen Films Ltd. for her help in obtaining permissions for the use of some of the film stills, as well as the expeditious manner in which she managed to obtain the permission for the poster used as the book's cover. I would also like to thank Mr. Shaukat Khan of Mehboob Productions, Pvt. Ltd for graciously granting permission to use the *Mother India* poster. The majority of the film stills are courtesy of the Hyphen Films Collection. I would like to thank Joy Roy of Bimal Roy Productions, Arun Dutt of Guru Dutt Films Pvt. Ltd., Tajdar Amrohi of Mahal Pictures, Iqbal and Shaukat Khan of Mehboob Productions Pvt. Ltd., Ketan Desai of MKD Films, Subhash Ghai of Mukta Arts, Dev Anand of Navketan Films, Randhir Kapoor of R.K. Films, Vinod Chopra of Vinod Chopra Productions, and Yash Chopra of Yashraj Films for their kind permission to use photographs from their films in this book.

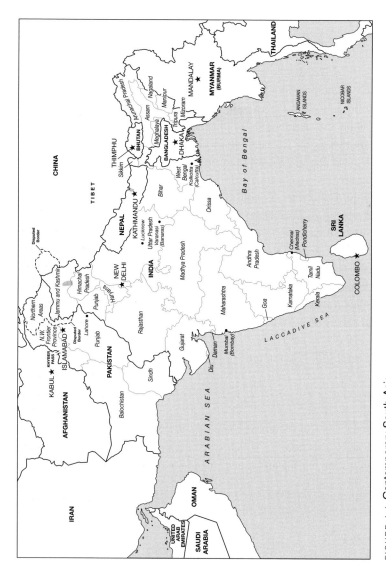

FIGURE 1.1 Contemporary South Asia

1

INTRODUCTION

"Okay, five-six-seven-eight!" a woman shouts into a microphone and blows a whistle to signal to the sound engineer on the other side of the room. As soon as the music begins, a man in a white chef's uniform starts dancing and juggling vegetables, while long-legged waitresses in black T-shirts, miniskirts, and white aprons pass behind him. Once the song starts, the man begins to mouth the words so perfectly that he appears to be singing it himself. Men crouching toward the ground slowly push a trolley with the cameraman and movie camera toward the performer. With a sound of the whistle, and a "Cut it!" the music stops, as does the action. The woman goes over to the man in the chef's outfit and demonstrates a few dance steps. After watching her, the man mimics her exact movements. "Okay, one more rehearsal, and then we'll do a take." The woman blows the whistle and the whole sequence starts all over again.[1]

The above scene is not the shooting of a television commercial or a music video in New York or Los Angeles, but the shooting of a song sequence for a Hindi film in Bombay, better known as a "Bollywood" film. From Baz Luhrmann to Andrew Lloyd Webber, from Channel Four to Turner Classic Movies, from Macy's to

Selfridge's, from the Oscars to Cannes, from Philips to Verizon,[2] the Western world has "discovered" Bollywood, a filmmaking tradition that has been entertaining millions of viewers around the globe for decades. The word "Bollywood," derived by combining Bombay with Hollywood, has even entered the English lexicon. The *Oxford English Dictionary* has had an entry for the term since 2001.

WHAT IS "BOLLYWOOD"?

"Bollywood" – a tongue-in-cheek term created by the English-language press in India in the late 1970s – has now become the dominant global term to refer to the prolific and box-office oriented Hindi language film industry located in Bombay (renamed Mumbai in 1995). The Bombay film industry is aesthetically and culturally distinct from Hollywood, but as prolific and ubiquitous in its production and circulation of narratives and images. As the domi-

FIGURE 1.2 Film billboards near Juhu Beach, Bombay
© Pankaj Rishi Kumar, 2000. Reproduced by permission of Pankaj Rishi Kumar and Tejaswini Ganti

nant media institution within India, the Bombay film industry plays an important role in constructing and defining dichotomies like "traditional/modern," "global/local," "Western/Eastern" and categories such as "culture," "nation," and "Indian" (Ganti 2000).

The most frequent factual error perpetuated by the international and Indian press is that the Bombay film industry produces 800–1,000 films a year. The Bombay industry actually produces about 150–200 films a year. Feature films are produced in approximately 20 languages in India and there are multiple film industries whose total output makes India the largest feature film-producing country in the world.[3] The cities of Madras and Hyderabad are home to the Tamil and Telugu language film industries which are as, or more prolific than the Bombay industry in terms of the number of films made per year.

However, Hindi films, though comprising approximately 20 percent of total production, are the ones that circulate nationally and internationally, dominate the discourse about Indian cinema, and are regarded as the standard or archetype to follow or oppose. Outside India, the category "popular Indian cinema" tends to denote Hindi films produced in Bombay. The distinctive features of popular Hindi cinema – song and dance, melodrama, lavish production values, emphasis upon stars and spectacle – are common to films made in the southern Indian industries as well. Thus, "Bollywood" has become a shorthand reference not only to a specific industry, but also to a specific style of filmmaking within the industry which is aggressively oriented toward box-office success and broad audience appeal.

Cinema in India encompasses a great deal more diversity and has a longer history than the Bombay film industry. Even as a British colony, India was the third largest producer of films in the world.[4] This book will not attempt to introduce "Indian cinema," but will focus on Hindi cinema produced in post-independence India. World War II and independence from Britain in 1947, ushered in social, economic, and political changes that also changed the nature of filmmaking. The antecedents for the contemporary Bombay film industry emerge from this era.

STRUCTURE AND ORGANIZATION OF THIS BOOK

This book introduces popular Hindi cinema and the Bombay film industry and its production practices to readers who wish to understand the form, history, and socio-cultural context of this filmmaking tradition. Written from the point of view of an anthropologist rather than a film critic, this book does not undertake qualitative judgments. Much of the book is based on fieldwork in Bombay, observing the filmmaking process, carrying out interviews with filmmakers, and having long discussions about Hindi cinema with a variety of informants within and outside the film industry. Rather than listing the "best" or "greatest" films, actors, or directors, the book tries to discuss significant developments in Hindi filmmaking from the point of view of the Bombay film industry, mainstream Indian press, and film audiences. There will be some who disagree with the choices of films and personalities represented in the book, but as the title suggests, this book is meant to serve as a guide into the world of popular Hindi cinema. As readers become more familiar with this world, they will easily discover the people and films not covered in this book, as well as form their own evaluations, based on personal tastes and preferences.

This introductory chapter provides the context and history with which to understand the remainder of the book. It presents a brief history of filmmaking in India from its origins, through the silent, early talkie, and studio eras until World War II. The chapter then goes on to discuss Hindi filmmaking since India's independence from British rule in 1947. The chapter concludes by outlining the Indian state's attitudes toward cinema and its historically ambivalent relationship with the Bombay film industry, which is important for understanding the broader context of Hindi film production.

Chapter 2 describes the structure of the Bombay film industry and its production and distribution practices. The chapter includes an in-depth treatment of the most distinctive feature of popular Indian cinema – the ubiquitous song and dance sequences. It describes the production process of film songs, their narrative functions, and their economic importance within the film industry.

Chapters 3 and 4 are intended as resources for readers to familiarize themselves with Hindi films and filmmakers. Chapter 3 introduces some general features of the social world of the Bombay film industry and then provides brief biographical sketches along with short filmographies of some of the noteworthy directors, actors, and composers of the industry.

Chapter 4 makes sense of the other characteristics of popular Hindi cinema such as narrative form, visual style, and the seeming lack of genres that frequently bewilder and perplex uninitiated viewers. It then describes 26 Hindi films which are significant for a variety of reasons: whether it is for unparalleled commercial success, having changed the norms of filmmaking in its time, redefining the roles of the protagonists, technical and aesthetic innovation, narrative ingenuity, or serving as social documents, each of these films provides a glimpse of the development of popular Hindi filmmaking from the 1940s until the present.

Chapter 5 presents excerpts from interviews conducted by the author with a variety of members from the Bombay film industry. The excerpts pertain to the topics raised in the previous sections so that readers have an opportunity to learn about filmmakers' perspectives on these issues. They are divided into statements about the form and style of Hindi cinema, the characteristics of the Bombay film industry, and the relationship between Hindi cinema and Indian society.

Chapter 6 presents a chronology of significant dates, films, events, and trends pertaining to filmmaking in India from 1896 onwards, with an emphasis on Hindi cinema and the Bombay industry in post-independence India. The Suggestions for Further Reading at the end lists some of the key scholarly works on popular Hindi cinema and is meant to aid readers interested in undertaking a more in-depth study.

ORIGINS AND GROWTH OF CINEMA IN INDIA: 1896–1947[5]

Early cinema

Cinema in India has a history that is relatively coterminous with film-making in the West. This is due to the existence of a technological, aesthetic, creative, and entrepreneurial infrastructure that allowed for the easy incorporation of motion pictures into Indian life and society. The most immediate antecedent to motion picture technology was photography. Photography was first used in India in 1840, a few months after its development had been announced in Europe and was taken up with willingness by amateurs, aspiring professionals, individuals with "scientific" agendas and within 20 years by the colonial state. Many Indians started studios in the mid-1850s in cities like Bombay and Calcutta, and 20–30 years later, hundreds of photo studios had sprung up all over the country.

Motion picture technology was introduced in the subcontinent on July 7, 1896, when Marius Sestier, a representative of the Paris-based Lumière brothers, presented the first cinematographe show at the Watson's Hotel in Bombay, a few months after its premier showing in Paris. The show was advertised in the *Times of India* newspaper as "The marvel of the century; the wonder of the world" and only Europeans attended the first screening since the hotel barred entry to Indians. This screening was part of a global moment, where audiences in Africa, Asia, Australia, Europe, North and South America witnessed moving pictures within months of its first demonstration in Paris on December 28, 1895. For example, on the day of the screening in Bombay, another Lumière representative screened the cinematographe in St Petersburg. On July 14, shows open to Indians began at the Novelty Theatre in Bombay. The invention was enthusiastically received by Indian photographers who purchased cameras and started filming shorts which were shown in tents, playgrounds, and public halls in Bombay, Calcutta, and Madras.

In addition to being the site of the first screenings of motion pictures in India, Bombay was also the site of one of the first films made in India – a wrestling match shot in the city's Hanging Gardens.[6] Bombay's development into the center of film production in India is integrally connected to its history as a colonial city and based on its position as the main center of commerce and manufacturing in British India. Bombay was not an indigenous city, but established by the British East India Company in the seventeenth century as a gateway for commerce and trade (Dwivedi and Mehrotra 1995).[7] Bombay served as an entry point for the exploitation of the Indian mainland, and the point through which resources were transferred to Britain. Bombay's connections to the world market determined the influx of certain groups – merchants, artisans, laborers – to the city, as well as the education of a class of clerks and petty officials – leading to the cultural, linguistic, religious, and regional diversity that became the hallmark of the city (Patel and Thorner 1995a). By the mid-nineteenth century, textile mills were established, marking a new phase in Bombay's life, as an industrial center.

The economic base of Bombay allowed for film technology to take root and flourish as capital from other industrial and commercial activity flowed into filmmaking. In addition to having the necessary capital base for filmmaking, Bombay possessed the creative infrastructure as it was also the center of Parsi Theater, a commercial theater movement originating in the mid-nineteenth century sponsored by the Parsi traders who were the dominant business community in the Bombay Presidency. Parsis practice the ancient religion of Zoroastrianism and migrated from Persia to western India – what today would be considered the state of Gujarat – over a millennium ago.[8] Parsis were traditionally involved in shipping and ship building and accrued a great deal of wealth by the early nineteenth century. By the mid-nineteenth century, they diversified into banking and established the Bombay Chamber of Commerce. Parsis played a crucial role in the economic and cultural development of Bombay.

The Parsi theater groups provided the initial pool of performers and writers as nearly all of them switched to film. With its assimilation of diverse influences – Shakespeare, Persian lyric poetry, Indian folk traditions, and Sanskrit drama; an operatic structure integrating songs into the narrative; dominant genres being the historical, mythological, and romantic melodrama; and use of the Urdu language, Parsi Theater was the immediate aesthetic and cultural antecedent of popular Hindi cinema (Garga 1996; Rajadhyaksha and Willemen 1999). In fact Parsi capital supported the film industry in India until the 1930s and had a significant role to play in the early film distribution infrastructure and three major silent and sound studios: Imperial Film, Minerva Movietone, and Wadia Movietone.

Phalke and the silent era

One of the early pioneers in Indian cinema is Dhundiraj Govind Phalke (1870–1944), more commonly referred to as Dadasaheb Phalke, who has been bestowed the title "Father of Indian cinema" by the Indian state, the Bombay film industry, and the popular press.[9] Phalke was interested in a variety of visual arts and technologies. His academic training was in fine art and architecture, but he also learned photography, photolithography, and ceramics. Before his career as a filmmaker, he worked as a portrait photographer, stage makeup man, magician, and as an assistant to a German illusionist. He started Phalke's Art Printing and Engraving Works in 1908 and did photolithographic transfers of Ravi Varma's oleographs, which are lithographic prints textured to resemble oil paintings. Varma was a very popular nineteenth-century painter who greatly influenced the iconography and style of popular painting and early Indian cinema.

Phalke's interest in film was sparked when he saw the *Life of Christ* in a Bombay theater in 1910. He wrote about his experience in the Marathi language journal *Navyug* in December 1917.[10] He described it as transformative,

> While the life of Christ was rolling fast before my physical eyes I was mentally visualising the Gods, Shri Krishna, Shri Ramachandra, their Gokul and Ayodhya. I was gripped by a strange spell. I bought another ticket and saw the film again. This time I felt my imagination taking shape on the screen. Could this really happen? Could we, the sons of India, ever be able to see Indian images on the screen? The whole night passed in this mental agony.
>
> (*Phalke Dossier* in Shoesmith 1988)

Phalke's socio-political context was significantly shaped by anti-colonial struggles against the British. Phalke himself had very nationalist intentions as evident in his concerns for an indigenous film industry. He made explicit the links between filmmaking, politics, and Indian statehood, asserting that "India was unfit to claim Home Rule" if filmmaking did not gain the support of Indian business and political leaders.

Phalke raised finance from a photographic equipment dealer with a short film, *Birth of a Pea Plant*, shooting one frame a day to show a plant growing. He then went to London in February 1912, to familiarize himself with film technology and acquire equipment. Upon his return that year, he established Phalke Films in Bombay for which he made five films. His initial capital came from a loan against his insurance policy and the company was staffed by his family and friends. In 1913 the company moved to Nashik, an ancient pilgrimage town 200 kilometers east of Bombay, for easier access to locations that Phalke thought were necessary for filmmaking such as rivers, mountains, and several famous shrines.

Phalke's first film, *Raja Harischandra* (King Harischandra), commonly regarded as the first Indian feature film, made its debut in Bombay's Coronation Cinematograph Theatre in 1913. While the play *Pundalik* was filmed in its entirety in 1912, it is usually not accorded the status of the first feature because it was a stage play rather than a production created specifically for the screen. Phalke's film was advertised as "the first film of Indian manufacture," and was based on a story from the epic poem, *Mahabharata*. The story of an honest king who loses his family and kingdom and undergoes severe trials and tribulations, *Raja Harischandra* was a success, running in Bombay for a month, when at that time films normally ran for less than a week. With his film, Phalke initiated an enduring and popular genre in Indian cinema known as "mythologicals," which bring to life popular stories of Hindu gods and goddesses. During the early years of cinema in India, films were frequently based on well-known Hindu epics and myths, thus helping to make the experience of cinema familiar and less alien to audiences. While a few mythological films still get produced, it is a genre which has been flourishing on Indian television in a serialized format since 1987.

Phalke went to England again in 1914, to organize trade shows. When he returned to India with new equipment, he closed down Phalke films and set up Hindustan Cinema Films Company in 1918, which was the first purely indigenous film studio with corporate backing. While Phalke was its main filmmaker, there were at least six other directors who made films under its auspices. It was also the first studio to have its own distribution operation with offices in Bombay and Madras. The studio produced approximately 44 silent features, several shorts and one talkie. Though its last film in 1932 was post-synchronised for sound, the studio failed in 1933. Phalke died in 1944, penniless and forgotten. His contributions to cinema in India were only recognized decades after his death when the Dadasaheb Phalke Lifetime Achievement Awards were instituted in 1966 to honor pioneering accomplishments in cinema.

The increased profitability of the cinema enabled filmmakers to reinvest their gains in new productions and additional infrastructure such as studios, laboratories, theaters, and by 1925 Bombay had already become India's cinema capital (Gangar 1995). By the early 1930s, the film industry was competing with the textile industry as the most important local industry in Bombay – bypassing it soon after with over 60 percent of India's film production units in the 1930s located in the city (Dwivedi and Mehrotra 1995).

The arrival of sound

Sound as well as music arrived in Indian cinema in 1931, with the release of the Hindi film, *Alam Ara* (Beauty of the World), on March 14, at the Majestic Theatre in Bombay. Advertised as an "all-talking, all-singing, all-dancing film," this production by Ardeshir Irani, with its seven songs, established music, song, and dance as staples of Indian cinema. Others sought to emulate its success and the number of songs proliferated in films during the early sound era – reaching as many as 70 in the 1932 film *Indrasabha* (Indra's Court). N.R. Desai, a distributor in the 1930s, remarked, "With the coming of the talkies, the Indian motion picture came into its own as a definite and distinctive piece of creation. This was achieved by music . . . it gives us musical entertainment which even the best of Hollywood pictures cannot" (in Garga 1996: 80). Within a decade of the advent of sound, the ratio of foreign films being screened in India dropped to less than 10 percent, and the film industries in Bombay, Calcutta, Madras, Lahore, and Pune grew at a rapid rate without import barriers or state supports.

Sound, however, brought new complications into filmmaking. The most immediate one was that of language. With so many languages spoken in India, and the fact that Bombay itself was a poly-glot city, the question before Bombay filmmakers was which language should their productions be in? Hindi offered the largest markets since a large proportion of the population spoke some version of it.[11] An associated dilemma was which type of Hindi? There was no one Hindi, as it varied according to region. Filmmakers finally settled on a type of spoken Hindi known as Hindustani – a mixture of Hindi and Urdu – a language associated with bazaars and trading that served as a lingua franca across northern and central India.[12] This led to a peculiarity – Bombay became the only city where the language of the film industry was not congruent with the language of the region; Gujarati and Marathi being the dominant languages of the region. The fact that cinema in the Hindi language developed in multi-lingual Bombay, rather than in the Hindi-speaking north, disassociated Hindi films from any regional identification, imbuing them with a more "national" character. As a result of circulating in a national market, Hindi cinema also developed its own idiom and style, which is frequently credited by filmmakers with spreading the knowledge of Hindi throughout India. The language in the films does not necessarily correspond to any particular regional variant of Hindi.

The other consequence of sound was that filmmakers needed actors and actresses who could speak the specific language as well as know how to sing, which meant that the Anglo-Indian women and the wrestlers who had dominated early cinema were no longer viable. In the very early days of cinema when Phalke was beginning to make films, women were not willing to act due to the stigma attached to public performance. Acting, singing, or dancing for an audience was associated with prostitutes and courtesans, and thus outside the boundaries of decent society. The public nature of the filmic image appeared to violate the dominant norms of feminine modesty. Within Hindu and Muslim communities, women bear the burden of representing the family or community's status and respectability which traditionally has been associated with limiting women's movement outside the home. Even prostitutes were unwilling to act in films since that would appear as a public disclosure of their occupation, so in Phalke's first film, *Raja Harischandra*, the role of Queen Taramati was played by a young man. This was not such an unusual occurrence, since in many folk performance traditions in India the parts of women were played by men. Phalke frequently cast his own family members in his films to solve the problem of the lack of willing actors. When women began to act in films by the 1920s, many were from mixed British or European and Indian parentage, frequently Christian or Jewish backgrounds, who were commonly referred to as Anglo-Indians. Due to their hybrid ethnic and cultural heritage these women were already deemed separate from the pale of "normal" society and hence less bound to social conventions concerning respectability.[13]

With the introduction of sound, theater became a logical source of acting talent. Another source of talent, specifically dance and music, came from the male and female descendants of the courtesan tradition in India. Courtesans in the subcontinent had existed for centuries and were traditionally an influential female elite in kingdoms, under the patronage of kings or other ruling nobility. These women were often the exponents of high culture in the courts, performing classical music and dance in their salons for royal patrons. Viewing them as cultured and refined women, nobility would frequently send their sons to the best-known courtesans for training in etiquette, manners, the art of conversation, and the appreciation of literature, poetry, and other arts. Unlike prostitutes, a courtesan had more control over her body and sexual activity and often entered into a monogamous relationship with her patron. The patron would provide for any children he had with his courtesan, and the children would carry on the profession into the next generation – boys being trained as accompanying musicians and the girls in all of the arts of their mother.

The British played an instrumental role in the decline of courtesan culture in nineteenth-century India. As women holding property and wealth, courtesans were seen as an integral part of the ruling elite whom the British were trying to displace. Many of the native rulers in India were portrayed by the British as decadent and unable to govern properly. The British waged campaigns against courtesans to reduce their influence by taking over their property, discrediting their patrons as immoral and debauched, and using many of the women as prostitutes for British soldiers, thereby stripping the women of their cultural function and exposing them to sexually transmitted diseases (Oldenburg 1991).

Though courtesans continued their establishments in more attenuated circumstances even after Indian independence, they had lost their main source of wealth and patronage with the end of monarchy. Their association with classical dance and music was also a source of unease for the political and cultural leadership of the newly independent nation which went to great pains to fashion a sanitized classical tradition that could be deemed "respectable," according to Indian middle-class norms. These norms reflected the colonial Victorian criticisms of the courtesan institution as depraved, decadent, and immoral. Today however, courtesans exist as characters in Hindi cinema, which has had a longstanding fascination

FIGURE 1.3 Madhuri Dixit as the courtesan, Chandramukhi, in *Devdas* (dir. Sanjay Leela Bhansali, 2002)
Kobal collection

with this institution. Stories about courtesans have been popular throughout the history of Hindi cinema, and many actresses have made their dramatic impact by playing one.

When the technique of "playback singing" – recording a song in advance and having the actor lip-synch the lyrics – was introduced in 1935, it revolutionized the nature of film production in India. Actors and actresses no longer needed to be able to sing; the visualization of song sequences was liberated from having to record the song simultaneously with the picture; and it provided a way of publicizing a film as its songs could be released prior to the opening. Playback singing quickly became an accepted practice, giving rise to another distinctive institution of Indian cinema – the autonomous playback singer. By the late 1940s, a division of labor developed in the Bombay film industry where a handful of singers rendered the songs for all of the actors on-screen. These singers became well-known stars in their own right. For almost four decades, the male vocalists Mukesh, Mohammad Rafi, and Kishore Kumar and the female vocalists Lata Mangeshkar and Asha Bhonsle dominated Hindi film music.

The studio era

Film production in the 1920s and 1930s was organized along lines similar to Hollywood where a studio bore the entire cost of a film's production and had technicians and actors as full-time contracted employees. Studios became known for specializing in specific genres of films. However, unlike Hollywood, a handful of studios did not succeed in monopolizing the film business and the majority of Indian studios did not control distribution and exhibition like their Hollywood counterparts. The lack of integration between production, distribution, and exhibition accounted for the high mortality rates of studios where a series of commercial failures or even one major disaster frequently led to bankruptcy. What is referred to as the "studio era" was actually a short chapter in the history of Indian cinema.

Four important studios of this era were: Imperial Films Company in Bombay, Prabhat Film Company in Pune, New Theatres in Calcutta, and Bombay Talkies. While Imperial was significant for its efforts at technological innovation, the other three played a key role in training some of the important directors and actors of the 1950s and 1960s, thus laying the foundation for post-independence Hindi cinema.

Established by Ardeshir Irani in 1926 and functioning until 1938, Imperial Films was organized as a vertically integrated concern with its own exhibition infrastructure. Closely associated with the costumed historical genre, Imperial's (and India's) first sound feature, *Alam Ara*, was a period fantasy based on a popular Parsi Theater play about a young girl named Alam Ara who exposes an evil queen's schemes and saves a kingdom. India's top two stars from the silent era, Sulochana and Zubeida, were under contract with the studio as was a young Prithviraj Kapoor who would become one of the stars of pre-independence Hindi cinema, and literally establish an acting dynasty (see chapter 3). Many of the studio's sound films were remakes of its own silent hits. Imperial made films in at least nine languages: Hindi, Urdu, Gujarati, Marathi, Tamil, Telugu, Malay, Burmese, and Pashtu. In 1929, it became the first studio in India to shoot scenes at night using incandescent lamps, as well as producing the first indigenously processed color film, *Kisan Kanya* (Farmer's Daughter), in 1937. Imperial also produced the first Farsi language sound feature in 1933, *Dukhtar-e-Lur*, and thus an aspect of Iranian film history can be traced to Bombay.

Prabhat Film Company was established in 1929 in the south-western Maharashtrian town of Kolhapur as a partnership between five individuals, who had previously worked together in the Maharashtra Film Company. The company moved to Pune, the second largest city in Maharashtra and 170 kilometers from Bombay, in 1933 where it became western India's premier studio with a national reputation. Prabhat had many stars on its payroll, its own processing lab, well-equipped sound and editing departments, the largest stage floor in India, and an art department regarded as the country's best. Its style of filmmaking was influenced by the popular Marathi musical theater tradition known as *Sangeet Natak* and many of its early films were remakes of the Maharashtra Film repertoire. Prabhat's first major hit, *Amritmanthan* (The Churning of the Oceans; 1934), directed by V. Shantaram who became one of the most celebrated Indian directors in the 1930s, was a strongly political film about a people's revolt, but set against the backdrop of a kingdom where the conflict is between a rationalist king and a ritualistic priest. The studio pioneered new successful genres such as "saint films" – biographical films about popular poet-saints from the sixteenth and seventeenth centuries. Prabhat's success was due to good distribution arrangements and long-term contracts with exhibitors; it eventually took on distribution itself and built its own theaters in Bombay, Pune, and Madras. Prabhat lost its premier director, Shantaram, in 1942, when he broke away to set up his own studio in Bombay, and though it produced films after his departure, the studio finally closed in 1953. Its premises now form the campus of the Film and Television Institute of India.

The other regional studio with a national reputation was New Theatres, founded by B.N. Sircar in 1931. Unlike Imperial and Prabhat which produced silent films prior to their changeover to sound, New Theatres from its very inception was a sound studio. It was the most elite of Bengali studios and as such attracted significant technical and creative talent from several smaller silent studios on the brink of bankruptcy. Many of its films were based on Bengali novels and the studio aimed for the cinematic equivalent of literature. Whereas other studios usually only hired one director, New Theatres had many directors in its employ, as well as the major star of the 1930s, Kundanlal Saigal. It invested considerably in technological innovation and the technique of playback singing was first introduced by the studio in its 1935 film *Dhoop Chaon* (Sunlight-Shadow). One of the studio's most significant films was *Devdas* (see chapter 4) made in both Bengali and Hindi in 1935. Once its key director, Nitin Bose, resigned in 1941, New Theatres' success started to wane. Since the studio never established its own distribution outlets, the rise of markets in western and southern India during and immediately after World War II hastened its decline, as it was at the mercy of exorbitant commissions charged by professional distributors. New Theatres sold many of its film rights to distributors at a loss, and finally closed in 1955.

Bombay Talkies was among the largest pre-World War II sound studios in India and introduced some of the major stars and directors of post-independence Hindi cinema (Dev Anand, Raj Kapoor, Ashok Kumar, Dilip Kumar – see chapter 3). Founded by Himansu Rai after his return from Europe in 1934, it was the only major studio established as a full-fledged corporate body with a board of directors that included prominent business leaders of Bombay. It was one of the first studios with backing from major financial institutions paying a regular dividend to shareholders from its third year onwards. Rai had been involved in successful Indo-German co-productions during the silent era and much of the studio's early technical team – director, cameraman, set designer, and sound engineer – was imported from Germany. Bombay Talkies' early successes from 1936 to 1939 were directed by Franz Osten who had collaborated with Rai in Europe. These films were mainly rurally-based dramas with social reformist themes centering on the prejudices and exploitation that plagued village communities. After Rai's death in 1940, Devika Rani, his wife and the main star at the studio, took over as production controller. The studio produced one of the biggest hits of the pre-independence era, Kismet (Fate – see chapter 4), in 1943 – a crime thriller about a pickpocket being united with his long-lost family. However, Bombay Talkies was dealt a blow when some of its most successful members including the star, director, and producer of Kismet broke away from the studio in 1943–4 to form their own called Filmistan. Rani retired from film-making in 1945 and by the early 1950s, the studio went into decline.

Though its workers association tried to save it, Bombay Talkies produced its last film in 1954.

Two other noteworthy studios based in Bombay were Ranjit Movietone and Wadia Movietone. Ranjit was established in 1929 by Chandulal Shah and stayed active until the late 1960s. It was best known in its early years for mid-budget socials, satires, and stunt-derived mythologicals. The studio flourished in the early sound era with an assembly-line approach to production and was India's biggest producer of films until the 1950s. Founded in 1933 by J.B.H. and Homi Wadia, Wadia Movietone was most famous for its stunt/action films starring an Australian-born former circus performer of mixed Welsh-Greek parentage, Mary Evans, who was re-christened Fearless Nadia. The Wadias sold their studio premises to Shantaram in 1942, who converted them into his Rajkamal Kalamandir studio.

The impact of World War II and Partition

The advent of World War II had a significant impact on filmmaking in India. As a British colony, India was dragged into the war unwillingly when Britain declared war on Germany. A Film Advisory Board was set up in 1940 by the colonial government and granted a monopoly over the distribution of raw film stock. The colonial government also intensified its censorship of films which appeared to support the Indian independence movement either through words or images. By 1942, major shortages of raw stock occurred and only recognized producers received a maximum of 11,000 feet for features and 400 feet for trailers. Priority given to films supporting the war effort resulted in an overabundance of war movies. In 1943, the colonial government imposed state control over raw stock distribution which was in place until 1945. Wartime shortages in basic goods and commodities led to a thriving black market and by 1944, war profiteers increasingly laundered their illegal earnings by investing in film production. As a result, budgets skyrocketed as did stars' salaries which studios were unable to match, and gradually the studios went out of business. The influx of wartime profits is cited by Indian film historians as the single most important factor in the rapid decline of studios and the rise of the independent producer – the dominant characteristic of the Bombay film industry even today.

In addition to affecting the economic structure of filmmaking, the aftermath of World War II also had an impact on the composition of the Bombay film industry and on its audiences. The Allied Victory intensified the calls for Indian independence as nationalist leaders pointed out the hypocrisy of Britain maintaining its colonies while it waged war against Germany and Japan under the rhetoric of saving the world from tyranny and making it a haven of freedom, self-determination, and democracy. India became independent from British rule on August 15, 1947, but along with independence came the division of British India into the modern nation-states of India and Pakistan. This final legacy of British rule, referred to as "Partition" was a hurried response to the highly complicated politics of religious, regional, linguistic, and ethnic identity present in the subcontinent. The ostensible goal was to carve out a homeland for India's Muslims so that they would not be marginalized in a democratic system where they, as 25 percent of the population, were in the minority.

While the idea of a separate homeland for Indian Muslims had been discussed within the independence movement for some years, the actual logistics of dividing territories and drawing boundaries was decided in a mere month to no one's satisfaction. What was known in advance was that those areas of India with Muslim majorities would become Pakistan, which meant that Pakistan would consist of two wings, East and West, separated by over 1,400 kilometers of Indian territory. The majority of the territory in both sides of Pakistan was easily demarcated because it mainly consisted of districts with Muslim majorities,[14] but the problem lay with those regions where no one religious community was in a majority. The problem was the most severe in Punjab where many districts and communities were interspersed with Hindus, Muslims, and Sikhs.

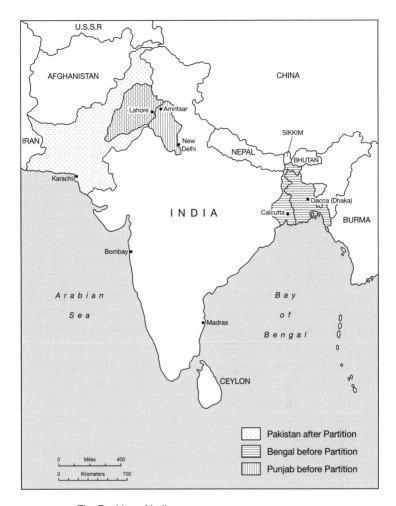

FIGURE 1.4 The Partition of India

Once the boundaries between India and Pakistan were announced, it resulted in the largest and quickest migration of people in the twentieth century. An estimated 10–15 million people literally switched sides between India and Pakistan in a period as short as two months. The majority crossed borders on foot in columns stretching for miles, some as long as 400,000 people. Nearly one million people died in the ensuing riots and clashes between Hindus, Muslims, and Sikhs, with the violence and brutality being particularly severe in the states of Punjab and Bengal, which were divided.

The most immediate impact on filmmaking was felt by those working in the Bengali film industry located in Calcutta, and the Punjabi industry in Lahore, as both industries lost personnel and audiences. The Bengali and Punjabi film markets were partitioned and the ensuing antagonistic politics between India and Pakistan resulted in very little cultural exchange or cooperation. The Bengali industry was severely affected as 40 percent of its market became East Pakistan and thus, foreign territory. Shortly after independence, Pakistan imposed taxes on imported Indian films and then in 1952, Pakistan banned the import of Indian films into its western half, with the eastern half following in 1962.

The Hindi film industry benefited from the weakening of the above industries and from the influx of people leaving Pakistan to come to cities like Bombay and Delhi. The post-independence Bombay film industry is shaped by the histories of migration and displacement set in motion by Partition. Many of the prominent actors, producers, directors, and technicians either migrated to Bombay from Pakistan or are descendants of those who did. The predominance of ethnic Punjabis in the contemporary industry is also a consequence of this history.

Another impact of Partition upon filmmaking is that the Bombay industry became one of the few sites in India where the Urdu language was kept alive. While Urdu is a language that originated and is spoken in northern India – the present-day state of Uttar Pradesh – it became the official language of Pakistan.[15] Due to the political tensions between India and Pakistan and the association of Urdu with Muslims, a process that the British initiated in the nineteenth century,[16] Urdu literature and scholarship in India suffered from official neglect as resources were poured into developing and spreading a highly Sanskritized Hindi. Hindi films however continued to be made in Hindustani and many prominent Urdu poets worked as lyricists within the Bombay film industry. It is hard to imagine film songs or dialogues without the vocabulary, metaphors, and idioms derived from Urdu language and literature. Words for love (*pyar*, *ishq*, *mohabbat*), heart (*dil*), law (*kanoon*), justice (*insaaf*), honor (*izzat*), duty (*farz*), blood (*khoon*), emotion (*jazbaat*), crime (*jurm*), and wealth (*daulat*) – all central concepts in Hindi cinema – are from Urdu's Persian and Arabic-derived vocabulary.

The final impact of Partition was that the Bombay film industry became one of the few sites in India where Muslims are not marginal, but actually enjoy some prominence and success. Much of the wealthy and middle-class Muslim population left for Pakistan, and though India as a secular country has the second largest Muslim population in the world, with the rise of Hindu nationalism, Muslims are increasingly a marginalized and beleaguered minority in contemporary India. However, some of the most popular stars of Hindi cinema, both male and female, have been Muslim, as have many of the successful directors, screenwriters, choreographers, lyricists, and composers. It is perhaps the least religiously segregated place in India today where Hindus and Muslims work together as well as intermarry. Though the Bombay film industry is not immune to the forces of Hindu chauvinism and nationalism sweeping the country, it is still primarily a place where people are judged on the basis of their achievements rather than their religious, ethnic, or linguistic identity.

HINDI FILMMAKING IN POST-INDEPENDENCE INDIA

Like other forms of cultural production such as art, literature, and music, films are a product of specific social, cultural, historical, and political contexts. While some themes and issues seem universal or timeless, others may be more specific to a particular context. In this manner, Hindi filmmaking after 1947 can be broadly categorized into three main eras which correspond to three key moments which have shaped the social and political context of life in independent India. Each era has generated certain narratives, conflicts, protagonists, and antagonists that are emblematic of the wider socio-political forces and concerns of that period. Given the prolific nature of the Bombay film industry, it is not possible in the space at hand to provide an exhaustive survey of filmmaking within each period. Instead, the following sections focus on the prominent trends and distinctive features of each era. Readers should be aware, however, that such trends do not preclude other types of films from being made.

The first era of filmmaking was shaped by the attainment of independence which set into motion the complex tasks of nation-building and economic development. It was an era heavily influenced by India's first Prime Minister Jawaharlal Nehru's approach to identifying and solving the problems facing the new country, as well as his outlook about India's position in the world. The second era of filmmaking took place against a backdrop in the early 1970s of widespread social and political unrest and growing disaffection with the government that culminated in the state of emergency put into effect by Prime Minister Indira Gandhi in 1975. Films from this era differed considerably from those of the previous one in terms of how the state, the male protagonist (commonly referred to as the hero), and villainy were represented. The third era of filmmaking has been influenced by the large-scale process of economic liberalization initiated in 1991; a period that has also witnessed the emergence of Hindu chauvinism and fanaticism into the political mainstream. Unlike the two previous eras when films had an uncontested hegemony over the media landscape because of the lack (1950s) or marginal presence of television (1970s), filmmaking since 1991 has had to adapt itself to the rivaling presence of television.

The Nehruvian era: Hindi cinema in the 1950s

While the Hindi film industry rejoiced in the end of British rule, along with the rest of the country, looking forward to a new beginning in an independent India, filmmakers were soon distressed by their treatment from the new government. The economic ideology of the newly independent nation-state constructed a hierarchy of needs where filmmaking was not perceived as an essential or important sphere of economic activity. Entertainment was not viewed as a necessity in a country that at the time of independence was 18 percent literate, had an average life expectancy of 26 years, was suffering from a food crisis, and had over a million refugees to resettle. Rapid industrialization, infrastructural development, and food self-sufficiency were the main priorities of national economic policy. A moratorium on "non-essential building" due to the shortage of cement and building materials meant that most states imposed a ban on theater construction. The repercussions of this policy are experienced till today. India has an extremely low number of movie screens – 12,900 – given the size of its annual theater-attendance which is approximately five billion.[17] In fact, despite being the world's largest film producing country, India has one of the lowest ratios of screens to population: 13 screens per one million people while the U.K. has 30 screens per million and the U.S. has 117 screens per million people (Andersen 2000).[18] Not only were colonial regulatory policies such as the entertainment tax, theater licensing, and censorship continued by the Indian government after independence, they were also intensified.

The central and regional governments viewed the various film industries, which appeared to be prospering, as a source of revenue. Whereas the entertainment tax was 12.5 percent before World War II in most provinces, with temporary wartime increases, by 1949 the rates of the entertainment tax ranged from 25–75 percent across the country with an average of 33.5 percent. Municipalities also began to levy entertainment taxes as well as duties on the transport of films from one place to another. Producers sending films to either East or West Pakistan discovered that they had to pay an exorbitant import duty to the Indian government on their own film prints in order to bring them back into the country. Additionally, there were sales taxes, other import duties, internal customs duties, income taxes, show taxes, and charges for censorship – by mid-1949, film industry organizations estimated that 60 percent of all box-office revenues were being taken by the state in the form of taxes (Barnouw and Krishnaswamy 1980: 138–9).

The other blow dealt to filmmakers was in the realm of censorship. Rather than becoming more relaxed, censorship became much stricter after independence. The censors indulged their reformist tendencies in the process of certifying films. They expressed their disapproval about most films, increasingly exercised aesthetic judgments, and ordered indiscriminate cuts in sequences. Censors began to reject both Indian and foreign films in a manner that seemed arbitrary and unfounded to filmmakers. For example, some censor rulings in 1949 simply stated:

> *Matlabi* – Hindi. Jagriti Pictures. Rejected. This is a sloppy stunt picture, not suitable for public exhibition.

> *The Madonna's Secret* – English. Republic Pictures. Prohibited as this is a crime picture without any relieving feature. Trailer is also banned.
>
> (in Barnouw and Krishnaswamy 1980: 140)

Filmmakers' initial response to the government's new policies was to patiently explain their problems and grievances. The various industry associations wrote editorials, letters, and sent delegations to meet with various authorities. However, when none of these actions produced any result, on June 30, 1949, the India Motion Picture Producers Association (IMPPA), Bengal Motion Picture Association (BMPA), and the South Indian Film Chamber of Commerce (SIFCC) joined together in an All-India Cinema Protest Day. Virtually all of the movie theaters throughout the country closed to protest heavy taxation and other related problems. Though the industry associations were pleased with the level of unity displayed by the protest, it did not lead to any concrete changes in government policies. However, later in 1949, the central government appointed a Film

Enquiry Committee comprising filmmakers and government officials to look into the problems of filmmaking and investigate issues relating to finance, distribution, exhibition, and taxation. In 1951 the Committee published its report, a comprehensive portrait of filmmaking in India at the time along with a series of recommendations, but, to the dismay of filmmakers the government ignored the report. Some of the report's recommendations were finally implemented nearly a decade later and will be discussed in the final section of this chapter.

The decade after independence was a time of nation-building and intense debate about the constitution of an "authentic Indian" culture. Film music and dance were objects of intense criticism by political leaders, bureaucrats, journalists, intellectuals, and "concerned citizens" as they represented hybrid forms and typified the "bastardization" of the classical arts (Chakravarty 1993: 64–76). Film music was regarded as overly influenced by Western music because of the use of instruments like the piano, harmonium, xylophone, and saxophone, which are unable to produce the microtones necessary to classical Indian compositions. The state's role in educating people about the "purer" traditions of Indian music began in July 1952, when All India Radio (AIR), the government-sponsored radio network, reduced its broadcasting time for film songs. The Minister of Information and Broadcasting known for his antipathy toward film music, also ended the practice of giving the song's film title, which he considered as advertising, and had only the singer's name announced. Film producers who were the copyright owners of the songs responded by revoking the performing licenses for AIR, resulting in a sudden disappearance of film songs on the radio and an abundance of classical programs – 50 percent of all broadcast music. However, AIR lost most of its audience once Radio Ceylon began broadcasting Indian film songs on its new commercial short-wave service, dominating peak listening times in India. In 1957, film producers renewed AIR's performance licenses, and it began to broadcast film music again to win back its audiences.

Though cinema in this period occupied an ambivalent cultural status and was frequently perceived by the state and middle-class society as frivolous and corrupting, from the point of view of the current Bombay film industry, the Indian media, and audiences, this era is exalted as the "Golden Age" of Hindi cinema. The present-day Bombay film industry refers to this period as a time of creativity, originality, talent, quality, genius, sincerity, and professionalism – "the good old days" which contain everything thought to be lacking in the present. While contemporary filmmakers pay lip service to Phalke and the long history of cinema in India, in terms of influences, idols, legends, and nostalgia – films and filmmakers from the 1950s and 1960s are the cinematic heritage of the contemporary Bombay film industry.

Hindi cinema in the 1950s was influenced by a variety of factors: an institution such as the Indian People's Theatre Association (IPTA), an event like the First International Film Festival of India, phenomena such as large-scale rural to urban migration, and processes such as nation-building, economic development, and social reform. IPTA was a theater movement informally affiliated to the Communist Party of India. Founded in 1943 in Bombay by a group of progressive writers, musicians, actors, artists, and activitists, IPTA's manifesto called for the "task of building a brave new world of freedom and social justice" and its motto was "workers are the salt of the earth and to be part of their destiny is the greatest adventure of our time" (in Chakravarty 1993: 92–3). Many prominent actors, composers, directors, lyricists, and writers from the Bombay film industry had been involved in this movement prior to their work in cinema. From this involvement came a concern and tendency to depict the lives and troubles of the downtrodden, marginalized segments of society, to point out the exploitative nature of capitalism, and romanticize and valorize the poor.

The International Film Festival of India held in Bombay in 1952 exposed Hindi filmmakers to a world of cinema outside of Hollywood. The large contingent from Italy with their neorealist films left a great impact as the socio-economic context represented in them appeared very similar to the Indian one. Social realism became a much celebrated and idealized, but not necessarily realized, aesthetic by the industry and the press, a trend which continues today. Films that follow the conventions of popular cinema and aim to appear more "realistic" in terms of their mise-en-scene and visual style tend to be judged as "good" films and accorded more respect, even if they do not fare well at the box-office.

After independence, migrants from rural areas poured into the cities looking for jobs. Not only did the city become synonymous with employment, wealth, and excitement, it also became a site of exploitation, crime, and danger. Some filmmakers focused on the harshness of urban life in their films and depicted the seamier side of the city by having petty thieves or other criminal elements as central characters. Even in such "crime thrillers," there was an optimism about the possibility of a better life in the future. This general sense of idealism and anticipation of a better tomorrow was the dominant attitude in films from this period. Problems facing protagonists were represented as social and economic rather than political ones. Moneylenders, *zamindars* (rural landlords), and wealthy businessman were the typical antagonist or villain in many films, while peasants, the urban working class, and middle-class professionals were the heroes. The state was represented as benevolent – as an arbiter of justice and agent of progress. In films focusing more on family dynamics and relationships, generation gaps and traditional attitudes were presented as sources of conflict.

This period also saw the proliferation of patriotic films in the wake of independence from colonial rule and subsequent wars with Pakistan and China. Akin to state discourses about "national integration," which sought to unify a vast and diverse population under the category of "Indian," films from this period emphasized the unity of the Indian nation despite its tremendous religious, linguistic, ethnic, and regional diversity. Through songs, dialogues, and characters, films continually valorized a pan-Indian identity above more specific linguistic or regional identities. While this emphasis on constructing a national identity has continued throughout subsequent decades, the representation of the state, hero, and villain has changed considerably since this period.

The crisis of the state: Hindi cinema in the 1970s

By the early 1970s, the optimism and hope of a better life in an independent India began to wane. The cost of the war with Pakistan in 1971 (leading to the creation of Bangladesh), the burden of refugee relief, acute droughts in 1972 and 1973, and the world energy crisis in 1973, led to severe economic difficulties with food shortages and spiraling inflation. The state's attempts to control food distribution and prices resulted in large-scale hoarding and a major black market in food. The deepening economic problems were accompanied by an increase in political unrest as people took to the streets in wide-scale demonstrations and protests. Universities were closed for weeks at a time due to disturbances and unions increasingly went on strike. The number of riots and incidents of violence, especially state-perpetrated, increased steadily every year and by the mid-1970s, articles about the police firing into crowds or charging into them with sticks somewhere in the country appeared almost daily in newspapers.

While elections in 1971 brought Prime Minister Indira Gandhi back to power with a commanding majority, problems soon began as she did not have a clear economic program. In the summer of 1975 when Indira Gandhi was found guilty of election-code violations regarding her 1971 election campaign and the Congress party lost badly in the state assembly elections in Gujarat, opposition parties and several national newspapers called for Gandhi's resignation as did some members of her own party. After a major rally was held in New Delhi protesting Gandhi's continued presence in office, a state of emergency was proclaimed by the President on Gandhi's behest on June 26, 1975.

During this 21-month period, the Indian government assumed extraordinary powers.[19] Civil liberties guaranteed by the Indian Constitution were suspended and over 100,000 people including intellectuals, opposition leaders, journalists, and political activists were arrested and detained without trial. Arrests were often arbitrary and people were not advised of the charges against them, nor were the police required to inform judicial authorities of the reasons for arrest. The press was rigidly censored and newspapers were barred from publishing the names of those arrested. Incidents of torture and even murder occurred in jails. In addition to political arrests, those placed under detention included "bad characters" and "antisocial" elements like smugglers, hoarders, and black marketeers. Indira Gandhi's son, Sanjay, oversaw a national population policy involving the forced sterilization of millions of mostly poor men and women. He also initiated urban "beautification" projects, which involved demolishing poor neighborhoods and clearing slums, thereby displacing thousands of people.

As increasing authority was invested in the Prime Minister during this period, Gandhi tried to justify her actions by casting herself as India's savior. During this period, she announced her 20-Point Economic Programme using the unprecedented powers of her government to promise land reform, houses for landless laborers, the abolition of bonded labor, the liquidation of rural debt, cheaper prices, higher agricultural wages, increased production and employment, the socialization of urban land, a crackdown on tax evasion, the confiscation of smuggled property, and cheaper textbooks. Gandhi presented the Emergency as the requisite "shock treatment" to get Indian democracy back on track. Since she had effectively quelled dissent, she was completely ignorant of the political climate when she optimistically called for national elections in March 1977. She and the Congress Party suffered a crushing defeat when a coalition of opposition parties won 330 of the 542 seats in Parliament. A new government was formed and the Emergency was withdrawn soon after.

Filmmaking during this period was marked by a great deal of uncertainty and insecurity. A major raw stock shortage ensued in 1973 when the government imposed a 250 percent import duty on raw stock. Imports of raw stock had already been drastically reduced in 1961 by government mandate, and the industry's trade journals between 1974 and 1975 were filled with discussions about the raw stock crisis and its affect on filmmaking, especially the uncertainty of new releases. In August 1974, the Minister of Information and Broadcasting informed leaders of the film industry that as long as Kodak did not come forward with a fair proposal for manufacturing raw stock in India, Eastman Kodak color positive would only be available for prints meant for export and not for domestic use. The following month the outright ban on Kodak positive was relaxed and the government issued a license for importing Kodak raw stock until March 1975. However, in order to receive an allotment of raw stock, producers had to apply for a permit, which due to bureaucratic red tape was difficult to obtain, thus leading to a black market in raw stock. In addition to the raw stock crisis, the film industry was also concerned about rumors that the government was going to nationalize film distribution as it had nationalized banks and other key industries. However, this never took place.

One of the most significant changes in Hindi cinema emerged in this turbulent era. In 1973, the tremendous success of *Zanjeer* (Chain), a film about a police officer (played by Amitabh Bachchan) who works outside the bounds of the law, introduced the figure of the "angry young man," which completely changed the persona of the hero in Hindi cinema. *Zanjeer's* success was particularly striking because it came at a time when the reigning superstar Rajesh Khanna (see chapter 3) had achieved his success by playing soft, vulnerable, mostly middle-class characters in musical romances devoid of violence or action. The hero popularized by Amitabh Bachchan (chapter 3) was of a disaffected, cynical, violent, urban worker/laborer. Films in this period became markedly violent and shifted their focus from the family and domestic domain to that of the state, society and the streets. The state was frequently depicted as ineffectual in solving problems like crime, unemployment, and poverty. The inability of the law to deliver justice became more pronounced in films of this period and vigilante justice was valorized. Villains in films of this era were mainly smugglers and black marketeers who frequently posed as wealthy, respectable businessmen. By the 1980s, corrupt politicians became the main source of villainy in films and frequently the only legitimate representative of the state was the police.

Another dominant narrative trend which began in the 1960s but intensified in the 1970s and continued through the 1980s was the "lost and found" genre. These films depict a nuclear family or a subset like siblings being separated ("lost") in childhood due to traumatic circumstances frequently set in motion by the villain. The family is eventually reunited ("found") after the children have become adults and defeated the people and circumstances responsible for the initial separation. This particular genre was very popular throughout the period and the traumatic separation of the family can be interpreted as an oblique reference to the traumas of Partition, experienced barely three decades earlier, where thousands of families were separated, and many not so successfully reunited. The emphasis on family and the primacy of kinship has been a significant feature of Hindi film narratives throughout the decades. Family relationships provide the basis of much of the moral dilemmas and conflicts depicted in Hindi cinema. The depiction of the family, however, changed dramatically in the 1990s.

Liberalization and the satellite "invasion": Hindi cinema since 1991

The two most significant processes and events that have shaped the context for contemporary filmmaking are the process of economic liberalization initiated by the Indian government in 1991 and the entry of satellite television in 1992. "Liberalization" refers to the relaxation of restrictions and controls around the economy.[20] Throughout the 1980s, India suffered from rising budget deficits, partly as a result of increased defense spending connected to military buildup in Kashmir and Punjab, the two regions with ongoing separatist insurgencies.[21] These deficits were also connected to government wages, salaries, and subsidies, since state-owned enterprises continually failed to generate profits and increase government savings. Economic conditions reached a low point in 1990 during the Iraqi invasion of Kuwait in August, as remittances from Indian workers in the Gulf, which formed a significant portion of India's foreign exchange earnings, decreased drastically. The invasion and ensuing war also led to a sharp increase in the price of crude oil. The reduction in remittances combined with an increase in oil prices exacerbated the problem of India's foreign currency reserves and a default on international loans and payments seemed imminent.

In 1991, the Indian government received two loans from the International Monetary Fund (IMF), which were accompanied by conditions regarding the control and reduction of the budget deficit as well as implementation of structural reforms of the economy. Radical changes were sought in the economy: devaluing the currency to make exports competitive,[22] relaxing import restrictions and import duties, reducing subsidies for certain sectors and industries, abolishing the industrial licensing system, relaxing rules for foreign investment, regarding technological collaborations as essential for economic growth, removing restrictions on large private companies, reducing the emphasis on state-owned enterprises in economic planning, and generally reducing the regulations around economic activity to make it easier to start new ventures. As the U.S. economy is held up as an ideal example by the IMF, consumption of consumer goods is encouraged as an engine of economic growth. Since 1991, state economic policy has increasingly catered to and focused on urban, middle-class consumers, to the detriment of the majority of Indian society who have no use for commodities such as automobiles, cosmetics, electronics, household appliances, and soft drinks when their basic needs of food, water, sanitation, shelter, primary education, and healthcare have not been met.

The liberalization of the economy set the stage for the entry of satellite television by reducing red tape and providing more incentives for multinational companies to set up their operations in India. Satellite broadcasting radically changed the nature of Indian television. Television did not become significant in India until the mid 1980s. The first telecast began in September 1959 as a pilot UNESCO-sponsored educational project, and the initial range of transmission was only 40 kilometers. Educational programs were broadcast for 20 minutes twice a week beginning in 1961, and throughout the 1960s, various pilot projects oriented around education were attempted, but there was no systematic program of television broadcasting. It was not until 1976 with the formation of Doordarshan, the state-owned single-channel network, that television programming was broadcast to a wider (but relatively small) audience. Color broadcasting as well as national transmission via low-power transmitters and satellite began in 1982 when India hosted the Asiad games. Commercial sponsorship of programs began in 1983 as did the first major expansion of Doordarshan's network.

Cable began unofficially in India in 1984, originally spreading through tourist hotels, then apartment blocks, and finally individual households. At first the cable networks were fed by videocassette players, linked centrally to the cable network. By May 1990, 3,450 cable TV networks existed in India mainly divided between the four major cities of Bombay, Calcutta, Delhi, and Madras. By 1991, cable networks had become equipped with satellite dishes and gained access to STAR TV, BBC, and CNN. The rapid spread of this unauthorized cable network with satellite access was one of the main reasons for the changes that occurred in the Indian television landscape in the 1990s. Rupert Murdoch's STAR TV started beaming into India in 1992 and ZEE TV, India's first private Hindi language and most successful satellite channel, was also launched in 1992. Other satellite channels followed soon after, and the experience of television for Indian viewers was transformed – from watching the single-channel state broadcasting network to having an option of 10–50 channels depending on the cable operator.

Since the entry of satellite television, Hindi filmmakers have been operating in a very different media landscape where a vast array of options, including films, is available to viewers at home. Although the Bombay film industry initially perceived the new channels as a threat, the industry has settled into a symbiotic relationship with satellite television. These channels offer filmmakers new avenues to publicize, promote, and market their films and serve as another source of revenue since they are willing to pay large sums for the telecast rights of popular films. Many of the satellite channels are hugely dependent on Hindi films, film music, film industry news, celebrity gossip, film awards shows and stage shows featuring film stars for a steady diet of programming. Even MTV, the symbol of global youth culture, is heavily reliant on Hindi film music and stars for the bulk of its programming in India. Rather than diminishing the presence of films in popular culture, satellite television is reinforcing the dominance of Hindi cinema and its stars in the Indian media landscape.

However, Hindi filmmakers acknowledge that they face competition from television as a rival outlet for films, and with the increasing popularity of certain prime-time game shows and soap operas, as an alternative source of entertainment. An attendant problem is that of cable piracy which is rampant and goes mostly unpunished, except for periodic police crackdowns on cable operators usually after a huge public protest by the film industry. Many cable channels frequently show pirated versions of newly released films at the same time that they open in theaters or sometimes even before their release date! Cable channels, unlike satellite channels, are locally-oriented, frequently serving a single locality or cluster of neighborhoods. The cable operator simply plays a videocassette or video disc of a film that is transmitted to all of the households connected to the particular cable network.

Producers assert that the pressures on the film industry are different since the advent of satellite television because audiences cannot be taken for granted. One has to work hard to entice audiences into movie theaters, as so many factors work to keep them at home. For a family of modest means, seeing a movie in a theater is less affordable than watching a movie on video or television. Additionally, producers cite the traffic congestion in large cities, and the poor conditions of theaters in smaller areas as factors that make the theater-going experience more of a chore than a pleasure for audiences. In order to entice audiences into theaters, filmmakers have been spending a great deal of money and effort to project a cinematic experience and spectacle unavailable on television. Since the mid 1990s Hindi films have vastly improved production values that include digital sound, foreign locations, extravagant song sequences, and lavish sets. Salaries have increased dramatically for stars, directors, and technicians, and distributors are willing to pay previously unheard of amounts for distribution rights. Filmmakers have also started paying much greater attention to the marketing and promotion of their films before and after their release, and since 1997, have been using the Internet as another venue to promote their films. The dramatic increase in budgets since the 1990s generates the potential for greater profits as well as the risk of greater losses, leading to the near disappearance of the average-earning film.

The changes precipitated by the liberalization of the Indian economy have also facilitated the growing internationalization of the production and distribution of Hindi films. Filmmakers are increasingly shooting a significant portion of their films in Africa, Australia, Europe, and North America. While Hindi films have been circulating internationally since the 1930s, and have been popular among African, Eastern European, Arab, and Central Asian audiences for many decades, only recently have Bombay filmmakers been able to reap revenues from the international circulation of their films. Hindi filmmakers are now consciously seeking wider audiences outside India by opening distribution offices in New York, New Jersey, and

FIGURE 1.5 Shooting for *Awara Paagal Deewana* (dir. Vikram Bhatt, 2002) in New York City's Times Square
© Tejaswini Ganti, 2001

London, creating websites to promote their films, dubbing films into English, Spanish, and French, and subtitling them in English, Hebrew, and Japanese in order to expand their markets to include areas without significant South Asian diasporic populations. Hindi films have become a visible part of the media landscape in the West as evidenced by the premieres of films in prestigious international film festivals like Cannes, Venice, and Toronto; the screenings of films in mainstream cinemas such as London's Leicester Square, New York's Times Square, and even the IMAX in Indianapolis; the nomination of *Lagaan* (see chapter 4) for an Academy Award in the Best Foreign Film category in 2001; and the release of films like Baz Luhrmann's *Moulin Rouge*, Terry Zwigoff's *Ghost World*, and Lars von Trier's *Dancer in the Dark* which explicitly reference popular Hindi cinema.

Since 1998, the international or "overseas" market has become one of the most profitable markets for Bombay filmmakers with certain Hindi films enjoying greater commercial success in Great

Britain and the U.S. than in India. While Hindi films had a theatrical presence in the U.S. in the early 1970s, with the advent of the VCR, the circulation and consumption of Hindi cinema retreated into the domestic sphere. However, the 1990s witnessed a world-wide boom for Hindi cinema with theaters springing up to screen Hindi films in places as far-flung as Singapore, Moscow, London, and Toronto. Within the United States, theaters devoted to screening first-release Hindi films were established in New York, New Jersey, Washington D.C., Chicago, Los Angeles, Houston, San Francisco, and their metropolitan areas. The box-office success of Hindi films places them regularly in the U.K.'s weekly listing of the top-10 highest grossing films and in *Variety*'s weekly listing of the 60 highest grossing films in the U.S. The success of Hindi cinema outside of India highlights the growing significance of the South Asian diaspora as a market for the Bombay film industry.[23]

The greater success of certain Hindi films outside India than within India generated debates within the Bombay film industry as to who are and who should be the target audiences for Hindi films since only certain stars and certain genres of films are successful in the overseas market. This discussion was connected to the dominance of the genre of "family entertainers" – love stories filled with songs, dances, elaborate cultural spectacles like weddings, set against the backdrop of extremely wealthy, extended, and frequently transnational, families – within the film industry from 1994–5 when the phenomenal box-office successes of *Hum Aapke Hain Koun!* (What Do I Mean to You! – chapter 4) and *Dilwale Dulhaniya Le Jayenge* (The One with a True Heart Will Win the Bride – chapter 4) solidified the trend for Hindi filmmaking in the 1990s in terms of themes, visual style, music, and marketing. While these two films and some of their subsequent clones did tremendous business both in India and globally, the continued dominance of this genre despite the eventual divergence in box-office response between Indian and overseas markets led to accusations by the Indian media and members of the film industry that films were being made specifically for South

Asians settled abroad to the neglect of domestic audiences. The Indian press castigated Bombay filmmakers for their lack of initiative and imagination and diasporic audiences for their nostalgic and narrow taste in Hindi cinema.

Films in the post-satellite era have been markedly different from their predecessors in terms of themes and content as well. The most apparent contrast between the successful films from this era and earlier Hindi films focusing on families and romance is the nearly complete erasure of class difference and the focus on wealth. All signs of poverty, economic hardship, or struggle have been eliminated from these films and rather than being working class or lower middle class as they were in earlier films, the protagonists are incredibly rich – usually the sons and daughters of millionaires. In the rare instance that a working-class protagonist is depicted, he is usually the source of tension or problem in the film. Another notable difference from earlier films is the lack of a villain and therefore the absence of the state and its representatives (police officers, judges, etc.) in films of this genre. Whereas wealthy businessmen were frequently the symbol of exploitation, injustice, and even criminality in Hindi films from the 1950s–80s, by the mid-1990s they were depicted as benign, loving, and indulgent fathers.

While in the past love stories often had class difference as the source of parental disapproval and therefore conflict, contemporary love stories feature protagonists of the same class background. With class difference removed, the source of dramatic tension and narrative conflict is internalized and centers on the conflict between individual desire and duty to one's family. The plot manifestations of this conflict either involve a love triangle or strict parents who eventually yield to their child's choice of partner. In both types of story, the character is torn between someone s/he loves and someone s/he is obliged to marry. In earlier love stories, youthful rebellion was the norm; young lovers ran away together. However, since the mid-1990s, the theme of compliant lovers willing to sacrifice their love for the sake of family honor and harmony has become dominant. The hero and heroine's passivity and obeisance to patriarchal norms of honor and notions of filial duty illustrate the essentially conservative outlook of many contemporary Hindi films, regardless of their cosmopolitan and MTV-inspired visual style. These family entertainers present a commodified Indian identity arising from a specific North Indian, Hindu cultural milieu and based on stereotypes about the "joint family."[24] Thus, the success of such films has been interpreted by the media and the state as a celebration of "family values" and an affirmation of "Indian tradition" in an increasingly globalized world.

Two other thematic trends prevalent since the late 1990s have continued trends initiated in previous eras. The first is a fascination with depicting the world of organized crime and gangsters, which has had a long history in Hindi cinema. The representations of mafia bosses and their gangs have changed from the glamorized, Westernized, and sanitized representations of earlier Hindi films to the grittier and more ethnically and regionally specific portrayals of the 1990s. Many films present a milieu specific to Bombay, notably in the use of slang and street dialect particular to the city. Earlier films went to some effort to depict how the protagonist fell into a life of crime, usually arising out of dire circumstances and sheer desperation. Contemporary films are more matter of fact and do not offer elaborate moral justifications or rationalizations. Whereas in older films, characters turned to a life of crime for basic survival when all other avenues of employment were exhausted, recent films represent organized crime as a pragmatic employment choice for poor and working-class men that enables them to participate in the luxury and consumerist lifestyle available in post-liberalization India.

The second trend is the upsurge of nationalism in films. While patriotism and displays of nationalism have been a staple of Hindi films since Indian independence, contemporary films have changed their mode of depicting intense nationalist feeling. Nationalism is a discourse of contrasts and boundaries, between insiders and outsiders, citizens and foreigners. Earlier Hindi films used stereotypes about the West as immoral, individualistic, materialistic, and lacking in culture to contrast with the moral, cultural, and spiritual superiority of India. Past villains were either Europeans or westernized Indians, but since the mid-1990s the definitive villainous figure is the terrorist. Films about terrorism which began in the late 1980s increased in the 1990s, as separatist insurgencies intensified, and bomb blasts, religious riots, high level kidnappings, and hijackings became increasingly common in contemporary India. The nation is now represented as under siege from acts of war or terrorism and its saviors are the military, paramilitary, or policemen.

A significant difference from earlier films depicting external threats to the nation is that since 1997, with the release of *Border* (dir. J.P. Dutta), filmmakers have been able to explicitly name Pakistan as the enemy and instigator of India's troubles. Prior to this film, even war films were not able to name an enemy or opponent because the censor guideline that "friendly relations with foreign States are not strained" (Ministry of Information and Broadcasting 1992) was invoked to make filmmakers excise any references to specific countries. *Border*, which is about a specific battle during the 1971 war between India and Pakistan, was the first war movie that was able to make explicit reference to Pakistan rather than the oblique references used in the past – "over there" or "the enemy". While the censor guidelines have not changed, the political climate has, with the more aggressively nationalist and hawkish (toward Pakistan) Bharatiya Janata Party (BJP) growing in power. The director's argument that his film was based on historical events and not being able to name the enemy would compromise the authenticity of his war film was accepted and paved the way for a plethora of films valorizing the military and their campaigns to protect the nation.

Therefore, nationalism is no longer depicted through a simple East–West dichotomy. The West and its materialist culture are not represented as evil or threatening and do not serve as a foil for the Indian protagonist's moral and cultural superiority. In fact since the mid-1990s, Hindi films have frequently represented Indians living abroad as more traditional and culturally authentic than their counterparts in India. While earlier Hindi films used characters of Indians living abroad for comic relief or as villains, many contemporary Hindi films have diasporic Indians as their protagonists and are set almost entirely in countries like Australia, Canada, England, or the U.S. Thus an authentic "Indian" identity – represented by religious ritual, elaborate weddings, large extended families, respect for parental authority, adherence to norms of female modesty, injunctions against premarital sex, and intense pride and love for India – is mobile and not tied to geography. One can be as "Indian" in New York, London, or Sydney as in Bombay, Calcutta, or Delhi.

THE INDIAN STATE AND ITS RELATIONSHIP TO CINEMA

Even as a British colony, India was the world's third largest producer of films. Therefore, from the point of view of the national leadership after independence, filmmaking was seen as having escaped the effects of colonialism unlike other artistic and performance traditions that had suffered greatly. In fact, the popularity of films and their music was viewed as a threat to novelists, painters, classical singers and dancers, and folk performers. A myriad of ministries, academies, and institutes were established shortly after independence to deal with the visual, performing, and literary arts, and in an effort to revive and support the "traditional arts" and "high culture," the Indian state excluded cinema from these categories and placed it under the purview of the Ministry of Information and Broadcasting rather than the Ministry of Cultural Affairs.

Unlike the U.S. government which from the early part of the twentieth century treated filmmaking as a business and helped Hollywood to distribute its films globally (Miller 1998), the Indian state did not accord filmmaking much economic significance, despite the fact that after independence, it was the second largest "industry" in India in terms of capital investment, the fifth largest in the number of people employed, and the second largest film industry in the world. Rather than thinking of the dominant mode of filmmaking as aiding the economic development of India, state policies of taxation and licensing accorded it the status of a vice.

The level of taxation on cinema is akin to those imposed on vices like gambling and horse racing. The bulk of taxation is the entertainment tax, a form of sales tax ranging from 20–75 percent, levied by individual state governments on box-office revenues, which transfers a significant portion of the industry's earnings into state exchequers. Most state governments protect their state language film industries and subject films in languages other than their official language to higher rates of entertainment tax.[25] The practice is effectively protectionist because higher tax rates translate into higher ticket prices. Since Hindi films are the only Indian films distributed nationally, they are the ones which bear the brunt of such taxation.[26] Most state governments also stipulate that cinema halls cannot be constructed near schools, colleges, places of worship, residential areas, and government offices, further emphasizing the "vice" like nature of the medium. See Table 1.1 for the various taxes levied on filmmaking.

What differentiates the Hindi film industry from film industries in other regional Indian languages is that it does not have recourse to a regional state apparatus that promotes its interests. The Hindi

TABLE 1.1 **Taxes levied on filmmaking**

	Central Govt	State Govt	Local Govt
Producer	Import Duty Excise Duty Censor-Cert. Fee		
Distributor	Excise Duty		
Exhibitor	News Reel Hire	Electricity Tariff Licence Fee Entertainment Tax Publicity Tax	Show Tax House & Water Tax

film industry is located in a state where the official language is Marathi rather than Hindi, unlike the rest of the film industries in India (Bengali, Kannada, Malayalam, Tamil, Telugu, etc.) which are located in states where the official language of the state and the language of filmmaking are the same. Other states promote film-making of their respective languages by offering incentives and subsidies whereas Hindi films are not identified with any one partic-ular state and are thus in Bombay filmmakers' terms, "motherless" and "fatherless" with respect to any regional state apparatus. This "orphan" status can be understood as one of the factors that contribute to the national character of Hindi films and the film industry.

For many years, the Hindi film industry has put forward its list of demands to the Finance Minister before the annual budget is drawn up, asking for certain concessions. These demands include the reduction or removal of import duty on raw stock since raw stock is not produced in India, and hence no domestic industry is being protected via import duties. Another longstanding demand has been the exemption of filmmakers' export earnings from income tax; currently the exemption only applies to corporations that export goods and since production companies are mostly limited partner-ships or proprietary concerns, they are not eligible for such exemptions. The most contentious issue between the film industry and the state at the regional level has been the entertainment tax, and each year filmmakers recommend to the central government that either the entertainment tax be reduced, standardized (it varies from state to state) or abolished altogether. Their arguments range from equity – that television, cable, and satellite are not subjected to entertainment tax – to the moral/philosophical – they are providing a great service to the nation by entertaining people and on what grounds can the government tax entertainment?

The roots of the Indian state's antipathy toward cinema can be found in the attitudes of nationalist leaders like M.K. Gandhi and Jawaharlal Nehru who were fighting for independence from British rule. While Phalke was explicitly nationalist in his motivation for making films – he wanted to create Indian images for Indian audiences and establish a completely indigenous or *swadeshi*[27] industry – the Indian National Congress (INC), one of the main organizations fighting against British colonial rule, did not accord the medium much importance. Most leaders viewed the cinema as "low" and "vulgar" entertainment, popular with the uneducated "masses."

One of the reasons why the INC did not regard film as an important tool in its mobilizing and organizing efforts had to do with Gandhi's antipathy toward cinema, which possibly stemmed from its being an imported rather than indigenous technology. Gandhi declared many times that he had never seen a single film and compared cinema with other "vices" such as betting, gambling, and horse racing (Das Sharma 1993: 136). When the Indian Cinematograph Committee was conducting its exhaustive study of filmmaking and film viewing in India in 1927, it sent a questionnaire to Gandhi asking him his views about the state of cinema in India.[28] Gandhi returned the questionnaire to the committee with a letter stating that he had no views about the "sinful technology." His letter dated November 12, 1927, states,

> Even if I was so minded, I should be unfit to answer your questionnaire as I have never been to a cinema. But even to an outsider the evil it has done and is doing is patent. The good if it has done at all, remains to be proved.
> (in Kaul 1998: 44)

Unlike Gandhi, Nehru was not averse to the cinema, but was critical of the kind of films being made at the time. In a message to the Indian Motion Picture Congress held in Bombay in 1939, Nehru states,

> I am far from satisfied at the quality of work that has been done. Motion pictures have become an essential part of modern life and they can be used with great advantage for educational purposes. So far greater stress

has been laid on a type of film which presumably is supposed to be entertaining, but the standard or quality of which is not high. I hope that the
industry will consider now in terms of meeting the standards and of aiming
at producing high class films which have educational and social values.
Such films should receive the help and cooperation of not only the public,
but also of the State.

(in Kaul 1998: 41)

In Nehru's view, entertainment was synonymous with poor quality
and low standards and the significance of cinema was seen in terms
of its pedagogical potential. He assessed the present as deficient and
hoped for better films in the future.

Both Gandhi's view of cinema as corrupting, and Nehru's view of
film as a tool for modernization have crucially shaped state policy
and rhetoric toward cinema in independent India. Gandhi's moral-
ism and nativism and Nehru's internationalism and modernism are
present in prohibitive policies such as censorship and taxation and in
developmental policies that established a cultural and cinematic
bureaucracy to counter the dominance of the commercially oriented
film industries.

Cinema, therefore, has played an important role in state
discourses about development, nationhood, and modernity in post-
independence India. Although television plays an important role in
these debates as the state had invested in television specifically for
pedagogical and modernization purposes, cinema has existed and
flourished in India as a mass medium for a much longer period –
over a century – and is woven into the fabric of urban life to such
an extent that it seems ubiquitous, and unlike television, is not state-
controlled. Cinema has been an object of government regulation in
India since the colonial period through censorship, taxation, alloca-
tion of raw materials, and control over exhibition through the
licensing of theaters. Cinema has also been a "problem" warranting
the attention of a number of government commissions, inquiries,
and symposia in independent India. Examples include the 1951 Film

Enquiry Committee, the Sangeet Natak Akademi Film Seminar of 1955, the Khosla Committee on Film Censorship in 1968, the Symposium on Cinema in Developing Countries in 1979, the Working Group on National Film Policy in 1980, and the National Conference on Challenges before Indian Cinema in 1998.

A striking characteristic of this state-generated discourse about cinema is the intense ambivalence – a complex mixture of pride, disdain, hope, and fear – expressed toward films and filmmaking. The dominant tone about the Bombay film industry and filmmaking in general is that most films produced in India are escapist, frivolous, formulaic; for "mere entertainment" and not "meaningful" or "artistic" enough. The statement that "Films are too important to be left to filmmakers alone," made by a former Director of the Indian Institute of Mass Communication,[29] best encapsulates official attitudes toward the medium of cinema. In this strand of discourse, the pedagogical potential of film as a medium of communication and thus as a tool for modernization and socio-economic development has not been adequately realized since filmmaking is mainly in the hands of "profiteers" rather than artists or socially conscious individuals. Elected officials and bureaucrats throughout the decades have been exhorting filmmakers to make "socially relevant" films which will "uplift" the "masses."

The Indian state's concern with "socially relevant" cinema is connected to its very simplistic, top-down understanding of media effects and influence. From the state's point of view, cinema, and audio-visual media in general, can directly influence behavior and shape attitudes. Therefore, a film is judged "good" or "bad" according to the perceived positive or negative effects its main theme may cause in viewers, and thus in society. Hence, much of the discussion about film in India communicates that it is a very powerful tool that can either be used for the greater good, or can be very dangerous in the wrong hands. It then becomes the state's responsibility to ensure the production of films that engender "positive" effects in society, i.e., those in accordance with official ideologies. This perspective provides the continued justification for film censorship. Though filmmaking in India is a private enterprise, in order to have a theatrical release, films have to be cleared and rated by the Central Board of Film Censors – a practice initiated by the British where any allusion to self-governance, the Indian nationalist movement, or Indian independence was heavily censored by the colonial authorities. Anxiety about the impact of the medium as well as distrust of filmmakers' intentions results in a continuous effort on the part of the Indian state to discipline and regulate films, filmmaking, and filmmakers.

In an attempt to foster "good" cinema and counter the dominant mode of filmmaking (as represented by the Bombay industry) the Indian state has established a vast cinematic bureaucracy. Following the recommendations of the 1951 Film Enquiry Committee, the central state expanded its relationship with cinema beyond censorship and taxation by setting up the Film Finance Corporation (FFC) in 1960 which later became the National Film Development Corporation (NFDC) in 1980. The NFDC's main task is to finance and produce low budget films of "high artistic content" (Dayal 1983:57). It is also responsible for developing distribution and exhibition facilities for films, providing loans for the construction of theaters, encouraging film cooperatives, developing subtitling facilities, importing and exporting films, and coordinating the development projects of the individual state governments and film corporations (Dayal 1983:57). While the NFDC has been relatively successful in producing films – financing 149 feature films and 57 documentaries within five years of its founding, including coproducing the Academy Award winning *Gandhi* – it has never fulfilled its promises of developing an alternative distribution and exhibition network. It built only a handful of theaters in Bombay, Delhi and Calcutta, and thus many of its films have remained unexhibited. Other government institutions set up to promote "quality" cinema are the National Film Archive, the Film and Television Institute which trains actors and technicians, the Films Division that produces both national and regional newsreels and documentaries, and the Directorate of Film Festivals which organizes film festivals, operates the Cultural Exchange Program for films, and sponsors films for international festivals.

"High artistic content" and "serious" filmmaking have been defined primarily by the rejection of the aesthetic, generic, and production conventions of Bombay cinema, and a movement began in the early 1970s known as the "New Indian" cinema. There were two widely noted influences for this group of directors: the Italian neorealist movement and the earlier "art" film directors such as Satyajit Ray, Mrinal Sen, and Ritwik Ghatak who were working in Bengali language cinema. Films falling under this category – also referred to as "parallel" or "art" cinema – were characterized by their social realist aesthetic, smaller budgets, location shooting, absence of song and dance sequences, lesser-known actors,[30] and a natural-istic style of acting as opposed to the big budgets, elaborate sets, songs, superstars, and melodramatics of mainstream Hindi cinema.

In May 1998, the Government of India finally granted filmmaking the status of an industry, thus laying to rest one of the most frequent complaints expressed by Bombay filmmakers about the state's atti-tude toward their profession. Being officially recognized by the state as an "industry" affords a variety of symbolic and concrete benefits ranging from reduced rates for electricity, which benefit exhibitors who currently pay higher rates than other industrial or commercial concerns, to making production companies eligible for bank and institutional finance. Rather than perceiving it as a vice, the Indian state, since the late 1990s, perceives commercial filmmaking as a viable, important, legitimate economic activity that should be nurtured and supported.

There are a number of reasons for the Indian state's changing atti-tude toward filmmaking. The state's most immediate reason for granting industry status has to do with trying to "rescue" the Bombay film industry from the "clutches of the underworld" or organized crime, and weaning it from its dependence on "black money" or unaccounted/untaxed cash income. Organized crime has always played a financial role in filmmaking: profits from World War II black-marketeering were invested in the Hindi film industry, and since 1997, a few high profile murders of members of the Bombay industry attributed to gang lords brought these connections into the national and international media spotlight.

The intersection of neo-liberal economic rhetoric with the rise of cultural nationalist politics signified by the Hindu nationalist and pro-business Bharatiya Janata Party (BJP) is another important factor in the state's shifting attitudes toward the Hindi film industry. It is no surprise that it was a BJP government that granted industry status since the party's support base is heavily drawn from petty traders and small businessmen who also comprise the vast distribution, exhibition, and finance apparatus for Hindi filmmaking. Since the mid-1990s Hindi films have been populated with wealthy families, Hindu rituals, and elaborate weddings – presenting a nostalgic vision of "Indian culture" and "family values" that does not challenge the BJP's own cultural rhetoric. It was also the same BJP government that conducted nuclear tests in the Rajasthan desert, confirming the world's suspicions that India possessed the ability to build nuclear weapons. Interestingly, the nuclear tests were carried out during the same week as the announcement of industry status for filmmaking (Ganti 2000).

The fact that Hindi cinema and its surrounding pop culture of music and magazines are so popular in other parts of South Asia like Pakistan and Bangladesh reinforce the Indian state's representation of itself as the regional power or hegemon in South Asia. While Pakistan and Bangladesh both ban film imports from India, there is a thriving piracy and video culture and Pakistani newspapers are filled with statements about the influence of Hindi films and Indian television. The popularity of Hindi cinema is articulated by the Indian press and the state as a manifestation of India's "soft power" within the region.

From the point of view of the English-language news-media and the Indian state, the fact that the Bombay film industry is the only other dominant, globally circulating film industry, and that Hindi films are registering equal or higher box-office grosses than Hollywood films in wealthy countries such as the U.S., Japan, and Britain has become a source of national pride and distinction. That the Australian, British, Canadian, Italian, Swiss, and other Western governments are trying to entice Hindi filmmakers to shoot in their countries, can be perceived as reversing the typical First World–Third World economic relationship which has defined India's status in the world system since independence.

In the age of globalization media has taken on new importance as a symbol of the nation and cultural identity in India. Unlike the 1950s, where debates centered on whether film could ever be an authentic, indigenous cultural form, since the late 1990s, cinema is being touted as part of India's cultural heritage. With the increased presence of Hollywood in India through dubbed films, Hindi films have suddenly taken on the mantle of cultural authenticity and Indianness vis-à-vis Hollywood films. This coupled with the increased circulation and successes of Hindi films outside India are factors that are also leading to changes in the state's attitudes about filmmaking. Though India has been exporting films from the 1950s, film exports are now seen as a potential gold mine of foreign exchange earnings. In an era dominated by the neo-liberal rhetoric of free markets and competition and the dismantling of state supports and the public sector, the Hindi film industry suddenly appears as a symbol of indigenous/native ingenuity and success (Ganti 2000).

2

THE PRODUCTION AND DISTRIBUTION OF POPULAR HINDI CINEMA

Although both Hollywood and "Bollywood" are large, commercially driven film industries, they are not organized similarly nor do they operate in the same way. The Bombay industry is highly decentralized, financed primarily by entrepreneurial capital, organized along social and kin networks, and governed mainly by oral rather than written contracts. This chapter explains the fundamentals of the structure of the Bombay film industry, its systems of financing and distribution, the basics of the production process, the practice of adapting Hollywood films, and the significance of music to Hindi cinema and the Bombay film industry. Since 2000, some changes in the financing and distribution structure have begun in response to the increasing significance of satellite television and the government's granting of industry status in 1998. These changes will be discussed briefly at the end of the chapter.

STRUCTURE OF THE BOMBAY FILM INDUSTRY

The most striking feature of the Bombay film industry is its entrepreneurial and fragmented nature in all three sectors: production, distribution, and exhibition. The industry comprises independent producers, distributors, financiers, exhibitors, and independent audio companies. All three sectors of the film industry are run by family firms, which is the dominant characteristic of business activity in India. The production sector of the industry is primarily made up of individual production companies, referred to as "banners," which were started by actors or directors who subsequently became producers. During the silent era, producers negotiated directly with exhibitors, but the coming of sound witnessed the emergence of the distributor as a mediating agent between producers and exhibitors, leading to a particular feature of Indian filmmaking – the dominance of the independent distributor and distribution system. There are hundreds of distributors throughout India and the world whose important economic role within the film industry will be discussed below.

The industry is neither vertically nor horizontally integrated in the manner of the major Hollywood studios or multinational entertainment conglomerates.[1] "Studios" within the Indian context are merely shooting spaces and not production and distribution concerns. Though there has been a move toward integration and points of convergence – some stars have ventured into production and distribution, some audio companies into production, some producers into distribution, and some distributors into exhibition, these instances are not systemic and do not preclude others from entering the business. Essentially, the "industry" is a very diffuse and chaotic place where anyone with large sums of money and the right contacts can make a film.

Although both the Western and Indian press use the metaphors of factories and assembly-line production to characterize the Bombay film industry, i.e., "Bombay's dream factories churn out hundreds of films a year," in reality the industry is extremely decentralized and flexible and a more apt comparison would be to a start-up company financed with venture capital. Each Hindi film is made by a team of people who operate as independent contractors or freelancers and work together on a particular project rather than being permanent employees of a particular production company. Films are often financed simply on the basis of a star-cast, the germ of a story idea, and a director's reputation. The lack of a well-defined division of labor among the principle players means that most people play multiple roles, so the industry is filled with people who are both producers and directors, writers and directors, editors and directors, actors and producers, actors and writers, or even a combination of actor-director-producer. Power resides in the stars, directors, and producers. The industry contains very few non-value-added people such as executives, lawyers, agents, professional managers, i.e., the "suits," who do not contribute to the actual filmmaking process. There are also no intermediaries such as casting agents, talent scouts, or agencies like ICA and William Morris.

While the Hindi film industry is very diverse in terms of the linguistic, regional, religious, and caste origins and identities of its members, what is striking is the intensification of kinship networks within the contemporary industry. These networks provide a source of personnel, a site for training, and a form of organization for the film industry. Though many of the producers, directors, and stars, age 40 or older, within the contemporary industry had no family connections when they first started their careers, their children, nephews, and nieces are taking up the family business with a passion. While there are other means of trying to enter the industry – through professional training institutions such as the National School of Drama or the Film and Television Institute of India (FTII), the latter provides a pool of technical skill for the industry, in the realm of acting (and increasingly directing), the dominant method is through kin and social networks. With most film people marrying other film people and with their children entering the industry, the Bombay film industry appears to be literally reproducing itself.

The extremely personalized nature of the film industry obviously creates barriers for those individuals who have no kin or social connections within the industry. For outsiders, the absence of any defined method or system to gain access to the industry makes the already idiosyncratic and contingent process of trying to "get a break," that much more haphazard and accidental. This reliance on chance can render both men and women even more vulnerable to exploitation in what is already an exploitative world. More significantly, the excessive reliance on chance means that when outsiders do manage to get a break and succeed, their stories, which are aberrations, are touted as the norm and become a way for the industry to present itself as a place where anyone with talent will always succeed.

Systems of finance and distribution

The finance capital for filmmaking in India is connected to the vast unofficial or "black" economy which some scholars estimate is nearly half the size of the official economy. One of the results of the high rates of taxation in India is the creation of a parallel economy with high amounts of unregulated economic activity – mainly cash transactions – and large sums of unreported and thus untaxed income, commonly referred to as "black money." The Bombay film industry is one of the main places to invest unreported income in India. As most financial institutions such as banks have shied away from financing filmmaking due to the high-risk nature of the enterprise, finance is raised in alternative finance/capital markets. There is an established network of financiers for filmmaking, and their numbers ebb and flow depending on current economic conditions. They have made money in a variety of other fields such as construction, jewelry, diamond trading, real estate, manufacturing, as well as organized crime. Producers borrow money at monthly rates of interest of 3–4 percent, which works out to an extortionary 36–48 percent per year. The nature of finance means that the majority of financial transactions and business dealings in the film industry are in cash where the accounting is highly secretive and most contracts are oral. Though most films fail at the box-office and the Bombay industry constantly represents itself as being in a state of financial crisis, it is sustained by new infusions of capital from people within India and abroad who are drawn by the glamour and potential for colossal profit – if a film is successful, it can double, triple, even quadruple one's investment.

Budgets for Hindi films presently range from 15 million rupees for low-budget ventures to 650 million rupees for glitzy, star-studded action extravaganzas or song and dance spectacles.[2] An average big-budget Hindi film costs between 150–200 million rupees, out of which the leading actor's salary is the single highest expense. Top male stars in the Bombay film industry currently earn between 10–30 million rupees per film, while the leading female stars earn between 8–15 million. Thus the salaries of the male and female leads in the film could easily amount to 20–25 percent of a film's budget. Table 2.1 lists the breakdown of a Hindi film with a budget of 150 million rupees. In order to gain a perspective on how wealthy film stars are and how much money goes into filmmaking, one must bear in mind that the per capita income in India in 2002 was 23,781 rupees (World Bank 2003).

As mentioned earlier, production and distribution are not integrated in the Bombay film industry, and Hindi films are distributed throughout India and the world by a decentralized network of independent distributors. For the purposes of Hindi film distribution, India is divided into five major territories: Bombay; Delhi/U.P.(Uttar Pradesh)/East Punjab; C.P. (Central Province)/C.I. (Central India)/Rajasthan; Eastern; and South (see Figure 2.1).

TABLE 2.1 Cost structure of big budget Hindi film

Salaries of cast & crew	45%
Production costs	35%
Post production costs	10%
Publicity costs	10%

Source: Ganapati 2002

A sixth territory, known as the "overseas territory," previously used to be undifferentiated from the point of view of distributors in India, but is now subdivided into North America, United Kingdom, Gulf States, South Africa, etc. The five territories in India are divided into 14 sub-territories, which may be further divided.[3] These subdivisions have become more important as a single distributor is unable to bear the cost of an entire major territory. With the exception of the Rajshri Group which distributes Hindi films throughout India, all other distribution concerns are specific to a territory or a sub-territory.

Hindi film producers finance their films primarily through the sale of theatrical distribution rights to their films. Producers start trying to sell the distribution rights of their film from the moment it is "launched" or its particulars announced at a ritual known as the *mahurat*.[4] The ritual role of *mahurats* in the production process will be described in the following section. Distributors bid for and buy the rights to distribute a film for 5–10 years in their particular territory, usually while the film is under production. Distributors also raise money through the alternative capital markets mentioned above, as well as by subdividing their territories and selling off rights, and by receiving advances from exhibitors.

There are three main types of distribution arrangements: outright sale, commission basis, and minimum guarantee. When distributors buy a film on an outright basis, they pay the producer for the right to distribute a film for a certain amount of time. All expenses incurred in the distribution of the film as well as all income earned are solely the distributors'. Not a very common practice in India, outright sale was the most common arrangement for overseas distribution until the late 1990s. When a film is distributed on a commission basis, distributors bear the least amount of risk because the most they may invest in a film are in its publicity and print costs. Distributors deduct a certain percentage (25–50 percent) of box-office receipts as a commission and remit the rest to the producer.

The most common distribution arrangement in the film industry is the minimum guarantee or "MG" system where the distributor

FIGURE 2.1 Indian film distribution territories

guarantees the producer a specific sum which is disbursed in install-
ments from the onset of production. Distributors normally pay
30–40 percent of the contracted amount during the production
phase and the remainder on delivery of prints. Even if a film's rights
have been sold for all of the territories, a producer will still need

finance to bridge the gap between the advance and the final payment. When a film is released, distributors pay for the print and publicity costs as well as theater rental. After distributors cover their costs – rights, prints, publicity, theater rental – and take their 25 percent commission, any remaining box-office collections are shared equally with the producer.

In such a system, distributors bear the majority of the risk since the producer is guaranteed a certain price for the rights. Producers with clout price their films in order to make a profit, as there is such high uncertainty about the box-office success of any film. Even though the minimum guarantee system ostensibly accrues profits for producers once there is an overflow – the term used for the remainder of box-office revenues after distributors cover their cost and earn their commission – the chance of one's film generating an overflow is only between 10–15 percent. The other factor in producers' pricing decisions is that they cannot trust distributors to share the overflow since distributors frequently use the revenues from successful films to cover their losses from unsuccessful films. Such a scenario is a consequence of the absence of a transparent system of data collection, especially when distributors are based far from Bombay.

In addition to dividing India into territories and sub-territories, the distribution network also subdivides each territory by revenue-earning potential into "A-, B-, and C-class centers." A-class centers are generally more populated – cities and large towns – with more cinemas and thus generate the largest revenues for the distributor. Another defining feature of an A-class center is the ability to fully collect revenues, for producers and distributors frequently comment that once their films are in B- or C-class centers, which include touring cinemas, they have no means of accurately tracking a film's earnings. In practice, such a division means that films are first released in A-class centers to garner their full commercial potential after which they slowly make their way to B- and C-class centers.

Before the advent of video and its concomitant, piracy, Hindi films were not released in all of the major cities simultaneously.

Films would first be released in Bombay and then open a few weeks later in other cities like Calcutta or Delhi. The simultaneous release of films in A-class centers is to thwart the problems of video and cable piracy in the higher revenue centers. Piracy is an even greater problem for distributors in smaller centers since there is a time lag between when a film is released in an A-class center and its screening in a B- or C-class center by which time a pirated print of the film may have been aired extensively on the local cable channel.

Since the number of prints released per Hindi film in India is anywhere between 200–500 prints for a big-budget, much anticipated film, the simultaneity of the film-viewing experience in a movie theater is limited to audiences in A-class centers, which also include overseas audiences in cities such as New York, Toronto, London, and Dubai. The small number of prints in comparison to Hollywood is misleading because the seating capacities of movie theaters in India are much larger than the U.S. Seating capacities range anywhere between 600–2,500 for a single screen, and "mini-theaters" are

FIGURE 2.2 **Eros Cinema, near Churchgate station, is one of Bombay's main movie theaters**
© Tejaswini Ganti, 2000

those which seat 150–300. The simultaneous release of films in India and abroad is a measure to counter piracy, but is also related to expected audience numbers. Areas with large South Asian populations, such as much of North America, the U.K., South and East Africa, and the Gulf countries in the Middle East would have Hindi films being released on the same day as they are in India. However, in areas with unexpected audiences – ones that distributors in India are unaware of – like parts of Africa without South Asian communities, contemporary films may make their way slowly.

CLASSIFYING AUDIENCES AND COMMERCIAL SUCCESS

While the driving force within the Bombay industry is commercial success, it is a difficult goal achieved by few and pursued by many, as the reported success rate of Hindi films at the box-office ranges only from 15–20 percent every year. The trade evaluates commercial success from the distributor's point of view; a film is categorized as a hit only when distributors earn a profit. Since nearly all of the revenues from a first-run film are from its domestic theatrical release, enticing audiences into movie theaters is seen by the industry as a gargantuan task.[5]

Although filmmakers frequently claim that they have no idea how audiences judge a film before its release and decide to see it or not, they do mobilize certain assumptions about audience taste and expectations while conceiving and making films. Rather than emerging from any formal pre-release market research, these assumptions are based mainly on observations of the commercial outcome of films. "Hits" and "flops" are the primary way that Hindi filmmakers relate to their audiences. Commercial success or failure is interpreted by filmmakers as an accurate barometer of social attitudes, norms, and sensibilities, thus providing the basis for their knowledge about audiences (Ganti 2000).

Commercial outcome carries such heavy significance because the ratio of hits to flops is very low and filmmakers acknowledge that the majority of their audiences possess very limited disposable income and cannot afford to see each and every film in the cinema hall. While film-viewing is represented as entertainment, the decision to see a particular film is not viewed as frivolous. Since going to see a film in a theater involves an investment of time and money, the act of choosing a film is accorded tremendous symbolic significance by filmmakers (Ganti 2000).

As the finance for Hindi films is generated from all over India and all over the world, everyone involved in the production, distribution, and exhibition of Hindi films strives to reach the widest possible audience. While Hindi filmmakers aim for mass rather than niche appeal, with audiences spread throughout India and the globe, members of the Bombay film industry do not perceive their audiences as an undifferentiated whole, but classify them in various ways with accompanying tastes. One of the main ways of classifying audiences is regionally, along the geography of the distribution network so that taste is related to place, thereby implicitly mapping film-viewing preferences onto ethnic and linguistic markers of identity. Audiences are also classified in terms of age, residence (city, town, small town, etc.), gender, and class. These categories however, are not the highly differentiated, excessively demographic categories of American market research. The categories of "ladies audience, youth or youngsters, and family audience" are broadly encompassing and highly imprecise as are the two other ways of classifying audiences: the binaries of "classes and masses" and "cities and interiors."

These binary classifications of audiences are based upon perceptions of how education, occupation, and residence shape people's personalities and tastes. These perceptions are also grounded in long-standing government discourses in India which designate the vast majority of the population as "backward" and in need of "upliftment" or "improvement" (Ganti 2000). The city-interior binary maps onto the division of distribution territories into A-B-C class centers with B- and C-class centers comprising the "interiors." Each territory and sub-territory has its interiors, but there are entire sub-territories in central and northern India that are regarded as the "interiors" from the perspective of industry members in a cosmopolitan city like Bombay. Interior audiences are perceived by filmmakers to be less educated and sophisticated then city audiences.

The "classes-masses" binary is the dominant mode of representing audiences. The "masses" are vaguely defined in terms of occupation – such as domestic workers, manual laborers, rickshaw drivers, factory workers – and characterized as either illiterate or having had very little formal education. Other terms for the masses are "laboring classes" or "the common man" in English or "*janta*"(people) in Hindi. Filmmakers claim that for the masses the main criterion for seeing a film is entertainment, which allows them a few hours of escape from their harsh lives, and that they are entertained by spectacle, action, slap-stick humor, bombastic dialogues, titillation, and a fast narrative pace. Another characteristic of the masses discernible from filmmakers' statements is that they seem to be entirely men and do not have the means to watch films other than in cinema halls. The "classes" are defined as the exact opposite of the masses: educated men and women, usually English-speaking, sophisticated, preferring realism, able to handle a slower-paced film, open to innovation in subject matter, and more likely to view films in the comfort of their homes. The Bombay film industry's attitude toward its audiences especially those it classifies as the "masses" is overwhelmingly patronizing and reveals the vast social distance between the industry and the majority of its audiences.

The division of the viewing audience is also integrally connected to the spatial hierarchies present inside the cinema hall. Film exhibition practices in India are akin to theatrical or concert performance practices in the U.S. with advance reservations,[6] assigned seating, and differential rates of admission connected to seat location. Cinemas have assigned seating ranging from two (stalls and balcony) to four classes of ticket prices in ascending order: lower stalls, upper stalls, dress circle, and balcony. The "masses" are those who sit in the cheaper seats located in the stalls, while the "classes" occupy the balcony. The balcony with its more expensive tickets is also associated with women and family audiences. A more specific category known as the "front-bencher," used to describe those viewers who sit in the cheapest seats in the very front, has become a shorthand reference by the press and some members of the film industry for poor or working-class male viewers whose tastes in cinema are perceived and represented as the most prurient and distasteful to other segments of the viewing audience, specifically the classes, women, and families.

The goal of Hindi filmmakers is to make a "super hit" or a "universal hit" film which appeals to everyone. Since a film has to appeal widely, these audience categories operate more as boundaries, rather than niches for whom specific kinds of films are made. What is continually stressed in the Bombay film industry is that filmmakers need to transcend these categories or discover what appeals to all of these categories to achieve true success. Members of the film industry frequently feel a need to negotiate the extremes of taste and find a middle path which would increase the potential audience for any film.

Since 2000, certain changes in exhibition conditions have introduced a new audience category into the Bombay film industry's vocabulary. With the emergence of multiplexes in major metropolitan areas such as Bombay and Delhi, a subset of the "city" or "class" audience referred to as the "multiplex audience" has become a niche audience for Hindi filmmakers. Smaller budget, off-beat films focusing on elite, urban lifestyles produced for limited release are now becoming economically viable due to the smaller sizes of theaters within multiplexes, since filling a 200 seat theater is much easier than filling a 2,000 seat one.

THE PRODUCTION PROCESS

This section will briefly describe distinctive features of all three phases of making a film: pre-production, production, and post-production. The production of music is treated separately in the following section. The dominant misrepresentation circulated by the Indian media, audiences, as well as Hindi filmmakers, is that the Bombay film industry works in a lackadaisical and impromptu fashion. The most enduring stereotype perpetuated by industry members themselves is that scripts are rarely written and hardly followed. Members of the industry constantly bemoan the lack of professionalism, organization, and discipline within the Bombay industry. This has been a remarkably consistent narrative throughout the decades, from the 1930s to the present. These characterizations of the film industry by industry members offer a way for particular members to assert their "difference" from a fictitious norm. Nearly everyone in the industry presents themselves as more organized, more professional, and more quality-conscious than the "typical" Hindi filmmaker.

The actual process of making a Hindi film is marked by a high degree of flexibility and variation from one production company to the next. Due to the diffuse structure of the film industry, rather than one set process, there are multiple ways that a film can be initiated. Story ideas can be generated by a variety of people – writers, actors, directors, producers, assistants, but how an idea for a film manages to become a film reveals the sites of power within the industry. Producers and directors are not the only people with the power to give a film the go-ahead. Male stars frequently initiate projects or are the first ones consulted about a project. If aspiring writers, producers, or directors – individuals who have not yet made a mark for themselves in the industry – can persuade a male star about their story idea or script, the chances of it turning into a film are very high since casting a leading male star is usually the first step in putting together a Hindi film. A star's willingness to participate signals to producers, financiers, or directors the viability of a project. While producer/directors with standing and power in the industry initiate their own film projects, these projects are conceived with a particular star or set of stars in mind. Some producers regard themselves as star-makers and try to bypass stars, but often their introduction of new actors is balanced by the presence of established ones.

Though crucial to the process, screenwriters have much less power and status in the Bombay film industry as compared to other creative personnel such as actors, directors, composers, and choreographers. The most common complaint within the film industry is about the lack of talented writers and good writing, but screenwriters point out that the level of remuneration and respect for writers is not commensurate with the rhetoric and concern espoused in the industry about writing quality. Although everyone harps on about the importance of the script, writers maintain that the industry is not willing to invest time and money in developing quality scripts. Part of the Bombay screenwriters' dilemma is that screenwriting is not generally regarded by members of the industry as a specialized craft that requires training or specific skills. Many directors write their own scripts, and assistants or technicians nursing a desire to become a director are usually working on their own scripts. Most Bombay screenwriters work on scripts commissioned by a producer, director, or a star, and do not have the time or influence to write an independent script and have it made into a film. In order for writers to get an independently written script produced as a film, they need to get a star on board or convince a producer that a particular star would be perfect in the film.

An important characteristic of the Hindi filmmaking process is its emphasis on face-to-face interaction. Films, deals, and commitments are made on the basis of interaction and discussion between key players, rather than intermediaries or written materials. For example, if producers want a particular star for their film, they will communicate directly with the star rather than go through his or her agent. In fact, in the Bombay film industry, agents do not exist in the same sense as they do in the Western entertainment industries. Hindi film stars have people known as "secretaries" who primarily keep track of and manage a star's work schedule. While a few secretaries in the industry have reached some positions of power, using their connections with stars to become producers, most secretaries are marginal to the negotiations between a producer and a star. Secretaries can serve as gatekeepers when dealing with the public, the press, and people of lesser power, but a producer or a director would regard having to negotiate or consult with a star's secretary as an insult and a sign of disrespect. Producers meet with the star directly and the location of their meeting is an indication of relative status and power. If producers meet stars in their homes, it signals that the star is more powerful. When stars are summoned by producers to their office or home, it indicates that the producer has the upper hand. Due to these complex politics of status and respect, producers will frequently meet stars when they are shooting a film, as the set – but not the makeup room – is perceived as a neutral space. This emphasis on personal interaction results in a highly orally oriented work culture where verbal commitments become the equivalent of contracts. If a producer discusses a film project with a star, the assumption is that unless the star states otherwise, he or she is in the film. Therefore, producers approach stars one at a time, rather than several at once to avoid any confusion or misunderstanding.

Another example of the importance of personal interaction and oral working-style is that the key cast and crew in a film are usually told or "narrated" the script. It is very common to hear members of the industry state in television interviews that they decided to do a particular film after "hearing the script." Rather than reading a script, key members of the production team gather together to hear the writer or director relay the film's story. These sessions are known as "narrations" within the industry, and are undertaken throughout the pre-production process as a way of bringing cast and crew on board a particular film. Narrations can last anywhere from half an hour to several hours depending upon the completeness of the script.

Narrating a film is in itself considered a skill and certain directors and writers are renowned in the industry for their narrating prowess. The significance of narrations has to do with the fact that the script is often incomplete prior to casting. Even if a script is finished, writers usually read it aloud to small groups of cast and crew.

While the narration of a script is in Hindi or "Hinglish" – a mix of Hindi and English prevalent among urban elites, many contemporary screenwriters first write their scripts in English and then translate the dialogues themselves into Hindi or work with a dialogue writer who is more proficient in the language. The specifics of a screenplay such as location, time of day, scene descriptions, and camera movement are always in English. The presence of English as a language of production may surprise readers, but is testament to the cosmopolitan nature of the Bombay film industry where people come from every linguistic region of India, and are not necessarily native Hindi speakers. Due to the incredible linguistic diversity within India, English frequently serves as a lingua-franca among urban, middle-class Indians living in major cities like Bombay because of having been educated in schools where English is the medium of instruction. As a consequence, although the language of the films may be Hindi, the language of production is multi-lingual, encompassing all of the major Indian languages, of which English has become one. This reliance on English by screenwriters is a recent phenomenon and also signals a shift in their background. In the earlier decades of Hindi cinema, screenwriters were often Hindi or Urdu poets, playwrights, or novelists who supported their literary endeavors by working in the film industry. Today, the majority of screenwriters are not from such literary backgrounds, but come from a wide range of professional as well as film industry backgrounds. As mentioned above, writing is also the least specialized aspect of the division of labor during film production, so that a variety of people contribute to or try their hand at script writing.

Once producers finalize the basic cast and crew such as the director, lead actors, music director, and writer, they usually announce the film to the industry and press by way of a *mahurat*. *Mahurat* refers to a specific date and time deemed auspicious by astrological calculations with which to start any new venture.[7] These rituals take place, sometimes months in advance, before any actual shooting of the film begins and can range from simple ceremonies in studios or other production sites to elaborate, ostentatious affairs in luxury hotels. One of the central features of a *mahurat* is the enactment of the filming process where the principal actors in the film perform a brief scene for the camera and the spectators present. The customary nature of the event is emphasized by the fact that the scene is written especially for the occasion and the shot footage is never incorporated into the final film. The goal is to impart the essence of the film since at this stage the film is usually a germ of an idea – a script has not even begun to be written. Other aspects of the event that highlight its ritualized nature is the frequent incorporation of features from Hindu ritual worship such as the breaking of a coconut before the "Roll Camera!" command or even the performance of an *arati* – the rotational display of an oil lamp or a camphor flame – to the film camera. Another common ritual while a film is under production is the daily breaking of a coconut and the distribution of its pieces after the first shot of the day is taken. This quasi-devotional relationship with the instruments of cultural production is commonplace in India; it can be witnessed between classical musicians and their instruments, dancers and their ankle bells, painters and brushes, actors and the stage, etc.

The *mahurat* primarily serves as a form of publicity for producers, especially in their efforts to raise finance for their project, of which selling the distribution rights is a very significant component. From the time of the *mahurat* producers start selling their film – or more accurately "the package" which at the bare minimum includes the director, the male star, and the music director who have been hired for the project – to distributors. Because of their past record as well as the marketability of the key personnel involved, some producers are able to declare "all territories sold" on the day of the *mahurat* itself.

The mahurat, although reported about in newspapers, film magazines, and television shows, is not a significant form of publicity for the viewing audience. While it can generate some expectations, the amount of time that usually elapses between the mahurat of a film and when it actually reaches the theaters is a couple of years, and in some cases many more. It is also a common feature of Hindi filmmaking that many films – and in certain cases, some highly publicized ones – never progress beyond the mahurat stage.

The pre-production process is a very collaborative one. Whether writing the script or composing music, individuals rarely work alone, but in teams of two or more and the director is deeply involved with the film in every aspect. Much of the time is occupied by brainstorming or discussion sessions between the director and key members of the production team where the script and music are finalized. These sessions are referred to as "story sittings" or "music sittings" in industry parlance. The main details that are worked upon during this phase are the screenplay and dialogues in terms of the script, the melodies and lyrics in terms of the music, and locations, sets, props, and costumes in terms of production details. The remainder of the casting is usually decided upon and finalized during this phase. Since Hindi filmmakers rarely work with story boards, decisions about lighting, blocking, and camera placement and movement are not made until the sets are constructed and shooting commences. While directors do not story board their films, they discuss the film in visual terms, mentioning on-screen action in relation to camera angles and movement. Directors frequently assert they have the film "running in their heads" and can mentally visualize every scene.

A characteristic feature of the production phase of a Hindi film is that films are not completed in a continuous schedule but are usually shot in discontinuous segments over a length of time. Frequently, producers do not have all of the finance required for their film at the outset, so rather than being shot from start to finish over several weeks or a couple of months, most Hindi films are shot in a series of "schedules" ranging from two days to two weeks over the span of months or even years, as producers try to raise finance throughout the production process.[8] Therefore, the elapsed time from the commencement of production (shooting) to theatrical release can take several years. Within the Bombay industry, completing a film within a year is regarded as swift and efficient, and most contemporary big-budget films are finished in approximately 15–20 months.

Due to the discontinuous and fragmented nature of production, actors do not rehearse beforehand and everything is learned on the set. A great deal of time is spent on lighting so actors have the time to read and memorize their dialogues which they usually receive on the set itself. If a song sequence is being shot, actors learn their dance steps on the set, and after having heard the song over and over again, are able to lip-synch to the lyrics without memorizing the song beforehand. Rehearsals prior to a shoot are rare and may occur for elaborate musical production numbers, but for the chorus dancers rather than the stars. A typical eight-hour shift is marked by a great deal of rehearsing so that the performances can be approved in a minimum number of takes. As raw film stock is imported and expensive, comprising about 10 percent of a film's budget, Bombay filmmakers do not want to waste it with a lot of re-takes, re-shooting, or extra shooting.

A distinctive feature of the production process is that films are not shot with synchronous sound. Filmmakers use older cameras which do not record sound simultaneously. Due to camera noise, actors' speech is recorded separately on the sets only for reference and editing purposes, and all of the sound in a Hindi film from dialogues to music to sound effects is added in the post-production phase. Actors dub their own speech after a film has been shot and edited in special dubbing studios where they watch their performance and repeat the dialogues to match their lip movements on-screen. They re-enact the film without the interaction of co-stars as dubbing is done individually rather than in groups. Instead of working from a script, actors use their aural and memory skills; they listen to the lines that they had uttered and repeat them verbatim. One of the assistant directors is usually responsible for overseeing the process and making sure that the pronunciation, grammar, and syntax are correct. The amount of time that dubbing takes depends on the actor's experience and the length of their role; an experienced lead actor can finish dubbing for a film in a few days.

One advantage of dubbing is that Bombay filmmakers can cast actors who do not speak Hindi and have a professional dubbing artist or a well-known Hindi-speaking actor dub for them; the reverse is true with Hindi film actors who act in films made in other Indian languages. Of course, during the shooting, actors still have to be able to make the correct lip movements so that the dubbed speech is synchronous. There are also instances where directors and producers have literally "taken away" the voice of actors by having someone else dub in their place, but this is interpreted as an affront or insult. The practices of playback singing and dubbing mean that in popular Indian films, the speaking voice, singing voice, and actor's on-screen body can be three different entities. Since 2000, a few popular Hindi films have been shot with synchronous sound and the actors who have worked on these projects proclaim their preference for this method as they feel that it is difficult to recreate the dramatic impact and spontaneity of their performance in exactly the same way while dubbing. However, synchronous sound remains an impractical proposition for most filmmakers. This is partly due to the advantages of dubbing as outlined above and because sound-proof shooting conditions currently do not exist, hence using synchronous sound would require a great deal of re-shooting and consumption of raw stock.

Though Hindi films exhibit high production values and are frequently elaborate visual spectacles, the production conditions are surprisingly simple and use minimal technology. With the exception of certain elaborate action or song sequences, Hindi films are shot with a single camera unit. Filmmakers did not start working with video-assist technology, where a video camera records the

FIGURE 2.3 **A façade of a mansion in Film City, a large open air production facility in suburban Bombay**
© Tejaswini Ganti, 1996

scene simultaneously so that it can be viewed on a monitor, until 1998–9, and many still do not use the technology. Equipment such as cranes and dollies are manually operated. Clapboards are not electronic, but handwritten with chalk. Ordinary sheets of black paper and white styrofoam boards serve as lighting equipment. Films started being edited digitally on computerized editing systems only in 1998–9. While the means of visual production are relatively simple, sound is another matter. Filmmakers use state-of-the-art sound recording and mixing technologies and most Hindi films are presented in Dolby Digital sound.

Bombay filmmakers are also remarkably efficient in working with limited resources. For example, wood for constructing a set is rented and can therefore be re-used rather than discarded after one use. Sometimes entire sets are also re-used. When a scene requires a smoky atmosphere, rather than using a dry ice machine, smoke is created by throwing water on hot coals in a shallow metal basket and having a crew member walk through the set carrying the basket. When shooting on location, Hindi filmmakers tend to work with the surroundings rather than trying to shape the surroundings to their shooting needs. Generally, the working style of Bombay filmmakers counters the stereotypes held in the West of feature filmmaking invariably involving large, intrusive, disruptive and troublesome film crews.

REMAKES AND ADAPTATIONS

The Bombay film industry is frequently derided by the English language media in India for producing "cheap copies" of Hollywood films. Television shows as well as film magazines regularly "expose" the industry by detailing which Hindi films are copies of American films. Often the accusations are exaggerated so that a Hindi film is labeled as a "copy" when it has a similar type of scene. For example, Yash Chopra's *Darr* (Fear; 1993) is consistently described as a "copy" of *Cape Fear* despite the vast differences in plot, characterization, and theme, because it portrays a dramatic fight sequence on a storm-swept boat.

Although the print and broadcast media see themselves as divulging secrets, Hindi filmmakers are quite open about their sources of inspiration. The origins of story ideas have never been that important, since the first feature films in India were mythologicals based on stories from Hindu myths which have been part of oral and performance traditions that predate cinema. Thus the first narratives depicted on film were not sui-generis. Within the Bombay industry, it is common to encounter statements such as "Every film is based on the *Ramayan* or *Mahabharat* (the Hindu epics)" or "How many stories are there in the world?" Descriptions of contemporary films are usually articulated in terms of older films. Much of the discussion within the industry is about how most stories are not unique, but that the presentation and treatment of the story should be novel and "fresh."

Many filmmakers believe that once something is in the public domain, it is fair game and think nothing wrong of being "inspired" by a particular film. The idea of the public domain is much more expansive in India than it is in the U.S. The Copyright Act in India – introduced in 1957 and amended in 1984, 1994, and 1999 – protects the original expression of an idea but not the idea itself. Since many people can have the same idea, the concept of originality refers to how an idea is expressed. The underlying rationale is if ideas rather than their expression are protected, that would in effect restrict the freedom to think. Therefore, the idea behind an expression is considered to be in the public domain, and an individual can copy another's idea and not violate copyright as long as the idea is expressed in a different manner. Such an interpretation of copyright is in accordance with international copyright laws. Only when a writer copies an entire story or a substantial number of plots word for word from another work is copyright violated (Gopakumar and Unni 2003). Hence, when Bombay filmmakers take or "copy" plot ideas from Hollywood films, they are not breaking any copyright laws since the finished product is substantially altered or "Indianized" according to industry parlance, to fit into the conventions of Hindi cinema. In the context of filmmaking, copyright laws in India are called upon primarily to protect the distribution and circulation of films and music from piracy.

Hollywood films as well as films in other Indian languages have been a source of plot ideas for decades, and the reverse also holds true, as Hindi films have been remade in other languages. Neither a universally condoned nor condemned practice within the industry, adaptations of Hollywood, Telugu, Tamil[9] and older Hindi films are one of the strategies employed by Bombay filmmakers in their continuous quest for novelty and desire to reduce the chances of box-office failure. Bombay filmmakers regard box-office successes or "hits" in other Indian languages as attractive remake material, because having already succeeded with one set of audiences, such films are perceived as having a higher probability of succeeding with Hindi film audiences as well. Hollywood films, however, are not selected on the basis of box-office outcome, but chosen for plots which seem novel and amenable to adaptation. Adapting Hollywood films is by no means a universal practice in the Bombay film industry. Many condemn the practice and view it as a symptom of the decline in the quality of writers in the industry and a sign of excessive commercialism which leads to short cuts in the creative process. That some of the biggest box-office successes of Hindi cinema have not been adaptations of Hollywood films is regarded as a vindication of the "originality" and hard work by those critical of the practice.

While remakes from other Indian languages resemble the original screenplay, adaptations of Hollywood films barely do as they have been transformed, or "Indianized." The three main elements of "Indianization" are adding "emotions," expanding the narrative, and inserting songs. Hindi filmmakers frequently describe Hollywood films as "dry" or "lacking in emotion," and claim that in order to Indianize a film, one has to "add emotions." For Hindi filmmakers, emotions are not about individuals but about their relationships with others. Rather than referring to internal states, filmmakers are referring to social life in their discussions about emotion. Therefore, "adding emotions" to a film involves adding family members and placing characters in a web of social relations of which kin are the most significant and common in Hindi films (Ganti 2002).

The inclusion of "emotions" also leads to greater narrative complexity since close family relationships provide moving stories of their own, according to writers. Hollywood films are frequently described as "single-track" and Hindi filmmakers express their amazement and envy at how films can be made on "one line" – a phrase denoting a story's simplicity as it can be relayed in a sentence. However, such films are considered inadequate for audiences in

India and adapting a Hollywood film involves enhancing the narrative in a variety of ways. Writers characterize a Hindi film as comprising four acts while a Hollywood film comprises three, and therefore, sub-plots or the inclusion of parallel "tracks" – romantic, comedy, dramatic – are seen as necessary additions. The most obvious way that a Hindi adaptation is different from its Hollywood "original" is through the inclusion of songs and the next section discusses in greater detail the production of film music and its social, narrative, and economic significance.

THE SIGNIFICANCE OF FILM MUSIC

Popular film and popular music are inextricably linked in India, as music has played an integral role in Indian cinema since the onset of sound in 1931. The centrality of music has its roots in older performance traditions which influenced cinema. Classical Sanskrit drama, folk theater, and Parsi theater all tightly integrated music, song, and dance, with each element being essential to the entire performance. Perhaps the most defining and distinctive feature of popular cinema in India is the presence of music in the form of songs sung by characters in nearly every film. Until the early 1980s, these film songs were the only form of popular music in India that was produced, distributed, and consumed on a mass scale, and even today film music accounts for the majority – nearly 80 percent – of music sales in India.[10] Entering a music store in India, one is faced with a staggering selection of film music: categorized and packaged by films, music directors, singers, actors, actresses, directors, decades, and themes, as well as the more recent phenomenon of remixes.

Any visitor to India is struck by the ubiquity of film music in towns and cities. Film songs are part of wedding processions, election rallies, and religious festivals; they blare from cassette players in tea stalls and from speakers in taxis and auto-rickshaws. A good chunk of radio programming is film music from the hit parades counting down the latest songs to programs of "classics" familiarizing new generations of listeners with songs from earlier eras. As well as having an aural presence, film music has a visual presence through television which has been packed with film-based programming, predominantly oriented around film music since the onset of satellite television in 1992. Dozens of shows air the song sequences from Hindi films in a weekly top-10 countdown format. Advertisements for upcoming films feature slickly edited montages of song sequences. Game shows that test contestants' skills at recognizing and remembering film songs, and talent searches where singers are judged on their renditions of film songs are the more participatory instances of film music on television. Film songs have also generated national controversies, reaching the chambers of Parliament. In 1993, the hit song *Choli ke peeche kya hai?* ("What is behind my blouse?") from *Khalnayak* (Villain; chapter 4) triggered such a storm of protests over its "vulgar" lyrics that members of Parliament debated banning the song, which not surprisingly made the song and its associated film even more successful. During election campaigns political parties also produce and circulate audio-cassettes of their political slogans set to the melodies of popular film songs.

Music is central to categorizing cinema in India. The presence or absence of songs operates as a method of generic differentiation, and is the main basis by which films are labeled: "art" films usually do not have songs; "middle cinema" – refers to an art film with songs; and "commercial" cinema to films which unquestionably have songs. Songs are perceived as the quintessential "commercial" element in a film. Filmmakers working outside the mainstream treat songs as a way of reaching larger audiences, and this gets characterized by the press as either accommodating or pandering to popular tastes. The omission of songs is interpreted as an oppositional stance; a way of making a statement against the dominant form of cinema as well as circumscribing one's audience. Song sequences are also iconic of "bad cinema" and seen as an impediment to "good cinema" according to state and intellectual discourses.

To those unfamiliar with popular Hindi cinema, song sequences seem to be ruptures in continuity and verisimilitude. However, rather than being an extraneous feature, music and song in popular cinema define and propel plot development. Many films would lose their narrative coherence if the songs were removed. Some scholars have described the popular film as operatic where the dramatic moments "are often those where all action stops and the song takes over, expressing every shade of emotional reverberation and doing it far more effectively than the spoken word or the studied gesture" (Prakash 1983: 115). Hindi filmmakers spend a great deal of time and energy crafting the song sequences which have a wide variety of functions within a film's narrative as well as provide the main element of cinematic spectacle.

Songs are produced in a very collaborative and informal manner. The first step is at the "story sitting" where the screenplay is worked out with the "song situations" – the points in the screenplay where songs will appear. These moments are created by the screenwriter in concert with the director who then narrates the "situation" to the music director and the lyricist. The skill of a writer and/or director is demonstrated by how well the song situations are integrated into the screenplay. While there are plenty of examples of Hindi films where the songs seem either very loosely connected to the narrative or simply pop out of nowhere, such a lack of integration is considered "sloppy," "lazy," or simply bad filmmaking.

One of the main functions of songs within a screenplay is to display emotion, and in the case of Hindi cinema this is overwhelmingly related to love. The general belief in the film industry is that love and romance are best expressed musically. In films where a love story is not the main focus of the plot, a "romantic track" is developed primarily through songs between the male and female leads. Even a love story focuses on the overcoming of obstacles to marriage rather than the process of falling in love, so songs provide a more efficient way to depict the romance developing between two characters than many scenes of dialogue. For example, the entire process of falling in love – from initial attraction to the realization of being soul mates – can be established over the course of four or five songs, or about 30 minutes of screen time.

Songs are also used as the primary vehicles to represent fantasy, desire, and passion. A common scenario that has become a cliché is one with characters singing and dancing in the rain. Rain has always been invested with erotic and sensual significance in Indian mythology, classical music, and literature, as it is associated with fertility and rebirth. Indian classical music has many songs where the anticipation of the monsoon rains is likened to the anticipation of one's lover. Utilized in many films over the years, these often highly erotic sequences – with wet clothes clinging to bodies – are part of an elaborate system of allusions to, rather than explicit portrayals of, sexuality and physical intimacy as filmmakers navigate the perceived moral conservatism of their audiences, as well as the representational boundaries set by the Indian state through its censorship codes.

In addition to expressing intense emotion and signifying physical intimacy, songs are frequently used to facilitate the passage of time as well as evoke memories: children can become adults over the course of a song, or a song can take a character back to an earlier time. Songs can aid in characterization when they are used to introduce the leading actors in a film. Songs are also a mode of indirect address whereby characters can articulate thoughts and desires which may be inappropriate to state directly. For example, a man can sing of his lover's betrayal in front of her and her husband at a social gathering without the husband suspecting anything. Once the song situations have been determined, the director then collaborates with the music director (as composers are referred to within the industry) and lyricist on the actual songs.

In the past, the prevalent practice was for the lyricist to write the words of the song, expressing the necessary sentiments and moods demanded by the screenplay. The music director would then set the words to music, finding a melody that accommodated the mood and meter of the song. Nowadays, the basic melody is often composed before the lyrics have been written and the lyricist has to find the words to convey the situation and fit them into the prescribed melodic structure created by the music director. After the melody and lyrics are finalized, a task accomplished in a series of meetings known as "music sittings" between the music director, director, producer, and their assistants, the music director then works with an arranger to determine the musical interludes between stanzas, the instrumentation, and other details before recording the music. However, even as songs are being recorded, a great deal of flexibility is maintained in the process. Changes are frequently made during song recordings, based on input from the director and others who are present. The whole process is also very oral: the music director does not write down any music, but composes it orally with his harmonium; after listening to the melody, the arranger translates the music from Indian notes and chords into sheet music with Western notation for the orchestra.

Once the songs are recorded, the director works in conjunction with the dance director (as choreographers are known) to conceptualize and choreograph, and with the cinematographer, to stage and shoot the sequence. This process which is referred to as "picturization" can take from three days to three weeks to shoot. The amount of time is determined by how many dancers are involved; how intricate and complicated the choreography and cinematography is; and how often sets, locations, and costumes are changed.

The most common way the Indian press describes the choreographed song sequences in Hindi films is with snide references to "running around the trees." This phrase is used incessantly to refer to the love songs in films where the leading couple bursts into song, mostly in picturesque locales such as gardens, meadows, and forests, far removed from the actual setting of the film, often with multiple costume changes, and sometimes with scores of dancers in the back-

FIGURE 2.4 **Shooting a song sequence for *Kuch Na Kaho* (dir. Rohan Sippy, 2003) in Mehboob Studios, Bombay**
© Tejaswini Ganti, 2000

ground. This penchant for sylvan, pastoral landscapes, so commented upon and ridiculed has very functional origins: in the early talkie era, before the techniques of playback singing and dubbing, when sound was recorded directly on the set, the simplest way to hide musicians and microphones was to use bushes and trees as camouflage.

Songs are the main reason why popular Indian films are much longer than their Western counterparts. Hindi films are two and a half to three hours long, of which at least 40 minutes of screen time are occupied by song sequences. Every film contains an intermission that divides the film into two halves. The first half of a film establishes the characters and their context, and usually contains more songs than the second half. Most songs are composed of three to four stanzas with a refrain, in six- or eight-beat cycles, with musical interludes in between the stanzas. The instrumentation varies from the use of a few instruments to 100-piece orchestras. The length of a song ranges from 3–12 minutes, with the longer songs tending to be performances or other elaborate spectacles within the film.

As nearly all popular Indian films contain songs, the presence of music in and of itself is not the defining feature of a genre, but the genre of a film governs the use and style of music within it. Most Indian films defy Western descriptions of genres such as the "musical," "comedy," "drama," "action," and "love story," since each film may contain all of these elements and more (see chapter 4). The genre of a film depends upon which element is foregrounded as the driving force of the plot and other narrative and stylistic conventions. In the mid-1970s, when films emphasizing action and revenge were the dominant trend, the number of songs dwindled to just three or four per film, a sharp contrast to films from earlier decades which contained anywhere between seven to ten songs. Since the late 1980s with the success of romantic films, the average number of songs in a film has increased to six or seven. One of the factors determining the number of songs in a film today is pressure from audio companies who want at least five songs, preferably six, for the purposes of audio-cassette production so that cassettes can be produced with three songs on each side. In some instances, songs which are on the audio-cassette never make it into the film.

Songs are absolutely essential to the marketing of a popular Hindi film. There have been very few examples of popular Hindi films without songs. Not having songs communicates that a film is outside the mainstream of the Bombay film industry, possibly even an "art film", and to most people in the industry this means death at the box office. To anyone working within the dominant system of financing, distribution, and exhibition, songs are an indispensable element in films. There are plenty of rumors and stories within the industry about producers, distributors, and financiers pressuring filmmakers to add songs to films to increase their prospects at the box office.

Since the beginning of the 1990s, when new entrants into audio production challenged the music company HMV's[11] monopoly, film music has played an increasingly important economic function within the Bombay film industry. The sale of music rights has become another source of finance for filmmaking as audio companies vying for the top production companies in the industry are willing to pay sums that may amount to as much as 25 percent of a film's budget. Audio companies are willing to pay such prices since albums from successful Hindi films sell in the millions. Companies such as Venus and Tips, flush with success in the marketing and sales of film music, have also entered the realm of film production, where they understandably pour resources into the song sequences.

Songs have become the most significant form of a film's publicity on television. Songs are recorded before a film is shot and a few song sequences are shot early on in the production phase so that they can be used to sell a film to distributors. The release of a film's music is a carefully orchestrated event by the producer and audio company. Even before a film has completed production, sometimes months in advance, its song sequences start airing on the numerous film-based programs on television, or appear as commercials in between other programs. A film's music is released into the market at least two months prior to its opening. This action is preceded by an "audio release" function in Bombay organized by the producer and audio company to which the entire glitterati of the film industry is invited as well as distributors, exhibitors, music wholesalers, and journalists. Clips of the song sequences are screened, and a prominent member of the industry, invited as the chief guest for the evening officially "releases" the audio-cassettes – unwraps a package of cassettes and hands them out – to the cast and key members of the crew, while photographers and television cameras capture every moment. Although this event is ostensibly for the industry and the trade, it also promotes the film to the general public, given the heavy media coverage, especially when famous film stars are present. In an environment where market research is rarely done, music sales are also the only early indicator a producer has of audience interest in a film – 30–40 percent of the sales are made prior to a film's release (Chaya 1996: 42).

With the proliferation of film-song-based programs on television by the late 1990s, producers, distributors, and exhibitors see songs as the main way of enticing audiences into theaters, and producers have been spending inordinate amounts of money on the visualization of songs. Regardless of their theme and plot many films have an elaborate production number with lavish sets, spectacular costumes, hundreds of extras and dancers, and special effects, costing millions of rupees. These sequences, referred to as "item" numbers, add to a film's "repeat value." Members of the film industry assert that for a film to strike gold at the box-office, it must possess a quality that makes people want to see a film not just once, but multiple times at the theater. The most successful films of Hindi cinema have been marked by the phenomenon of repeat audiences – people seeing a particular film 10, 20, 50, even a 100 times. Renowned contemporary painter M.F. Husain made news with reports that he had seen the 1994 box-office success *Hum Aapke Hain Koun!* – commonly referred to as "HAHK" by the press and by viewers – which had 14 songs, 85 times! Songs are probably the critical element in a film's repeat value. Soon after the release of *Khalnayak*, there were reports in the press about how often people were seeing the film, but only until the main item number of the film – *Choli ke peeche kya hai?*

Part of the quest for repeat value is to shoot songs in "exotic" locations such as Europe, North America, and Australia. Switzerland, with its meadows, valleys, and mountains has been a long-time favorite of Hindi filmmakers. Nevertheless, filmmakers are constantly in search of new locations that have not been shown on the Indian screen and in the recent past, song sequences have been shot in sites as varied as Hungary, Mexico, New Zealand, Norway, Scotland, and South Africa. Although some songs are set in foreign settings ostensibly because the characters are visiting that area, most foreign locations have no relevance to the plot and function as pure spectacle and novelty. Producer-director Yash Chopra (see chapter 3) went to Holland just to shoot two love songs amidst vast fields of tulips for his 1981 film, *Silsila* (Affair). The producers of the 1998 film *Jeans* boasted how theirs was the first film to have a song which featured all "Seven Wonders of the World." The song where the two leads sing of their love for each other at the Great Wall in China, the Pyramids in Egypt, the Taj Mahal in India, the Eiffel Tower in Paris, the Empire State Building in New York, the Leaning Tower of Pisa, and the Coliseum in Rome, became the main marketing point of the film. Thus, songs also operate as virtual tourism as filmmakers have shot sequences all over the world. Since Hindi films circulate globally from Japan to Israel, from Peru to Britain, many governments view such sequences as a way to promote tourism and offer a variety of incentives to attract Bombay filmmakers to shoot in their respective countries. In fact, as filmmakers increasingly scout out new locations because Switzerland is perceived as passé and overexposed, the Swiss government has been aggressively trying to woo Hindi filmmakers back to their country.

FIGURE 2.5 Rehearsing dance steps before shooting a song on the *Intrepid* aircraft carrier, New York City
© Tejaswini Ganti, 2001

Though shooting in foreign locales would appear expensive, Bombay filmmakers can be more efficient when filming abroad because they take along a minimal cast and crew, very little equipment, and maximize each shooting day. Filmmakers tend to go to Europe and North America in the summer in order to take advantage of the temperate climate and long days. By using natural rather than artificial light, and landmarks, cities, or natural landscapes rather than sets, filmmakers can cut the time it takes to shoot a song sequence in half. Another reason filmmakers like to go abroad is that they are more assured of having their actors' complete attention, unlike in Bombay where shooting is regularly disturbed by a continuous stream of visitors, journalists, and fans. Finally, producers can curb some star-related costs abroad that they would be unable to in India. For example, when shooting on location in India, producers frequently have to foot the bills of stars' retinues which could include their family members, make-up artist, hair-dresser, driver, personal assistant, and/or friends. Producers do not follow this practice when shooting in foreign locations and are able to insist that stars travel alone or with a reduced entourage. While star status in India necessitates that they be housed in five-star luxury hotels, when abroad, the producer can afford to be more budget-conscious and stars have to make do with more modest accommodation. Thus, despite the significant amount of money involved in foreign shoots, for both aesthetic and economic reasons, Hindi filmmakers continue to find foreign location shooting an attractive option.

THE IMPACT OF SATELLITE TELEVISION AND INDUSTRY STATUS

Since 2000, certain changes have been introduced in the financing and distribution sectors of the Bombay film industry as a result of industry status and the growing influence of satellite television. Industry status has paved the way for greater variety in financing within the industry. Both the banking and corporate sectors have begun to invest in filmmaking either by providing loans or by creating production companies. Some of the largest Indian industrial houses and corporations have created media subsidiaries which are entering into television and film production. Another source of finance is the stock market and some film production companies have become public limited companies and their stock listed and traded on the Bombay Stock Exchange. Industry members hail these developments as positive steps to bringing about greater discipline, efficiency, and financial transparency into filmmaking. "Corporatization" is the favorite term bandied about by Hindi film-makers and the Indian press to describe the efforts of the Bombay film industry to become more organized and less dependent on dubious sources of finance. As older systems of finance are still dominant, it is still too early to determine the overall impact of corporate and institutional financing on the Bombay film industry. However, with more consistent financing, films can be produced in a shorter amount of time. This reduces costs significantly, and increases the chances of a film's commercial success.

In a bid to win audiences, satellite channels have been competing aggressively to buy the telecast rights for Hindi films and their will-ingness to pay substantial sums has made satellite rights a significant source of revenue for producers. When a film does not do well at the box office, satellite rights offer producers a chance of recovering some revenue. The sale of telecast rights, however, has resulted in conflicts between distributors who have traditionally obtained the rights to exploit a film for at least five years, and producers who have been selling the broadcast rights for films, months after their release. Distributors protest that producers are denying them their right to recover their investment when films are broadcast on television before distributors have had a chance to exploit the film theatrically in their areas. With the legitimate film print being broadcast on satel-lite channels just months after its theatrical release, distributors and exhibitors whose business is based in B- and C-class centers complain of significant losses due to the drop in theater attendance in these areas for the particular films. Though producers and distributors came to an agreement in June 2000 that producers should wait one year before their new films are broadcast on television, the fierce bidding wars between satellite channels for broadcast rights has made it difficult for many producers to honor the agreement. Producers and distributors came to a stand-off in April 2003 when producers decided to withhold all new releases as a protest against distributors' demands that they wait at least six months before releasing their films on television. The boycott lasted for about four weeks and no new Hindi films were released, throwing off exhibition and release schedules. The tensions between producers and distributors continue and are indicative of an industry where power is diffuse and distributed between many players with competing interests.

3

KEY FIGURES IN THE BOMBAY FILM INDUSTRY

Although by no means an exhaustive or comprehensive list of significant members of the Bombay film industry – due to space constraints – the lists below are meant to introduce readers unfamiliar with Hindi cinema to some of the important and noteworthy directors, composers, and actors in the industry.[1] The following individuals have been chosen for the popularity of their films, their power within the industry, and their impact on the style and substance of Hindi cinema. Films listed in bold indicate those that will be described in greater detail in the following chapter. Sources for this chapter include the *Encyclopaedia of Indian Cinema* (Rajadhyaksha and Willemen 1999) and *The Hundred Luminaries of Hindi Cinema* (Raheja and Kothari 1996).

A note about film titles

The titles in the filmographies have been translated for the sake of readers unfamiliar with Hindi. These are the author's translations rather than official international titles. Film titles that are not translated are names of a character, usually the male or female lead, or a place in the film. Regardless of where they circulate, Hindi films are known by and referred to by their original Hindi titles, or in the case of films with long titles, by abbreviations coined by journalists. The practice of abbreviating a film's title in the English alphabet based on a transliterated title (Hindi written in Roman characters) – *Hum Aapke Hain Koun!* becomes HAHK – is a phenomenon that began in the late 1980s.

Readers will notice that birth places are mentioned for most of the individuals listed. This is to indicate the cosmopolitanism of the Bombay film industry, which comprises people from every ethnic and linguistic region in India as well as beyond. Readers will also notice that many of the older generation of directors and stars were from areas that are in present-day Pakistan – a consequence of large-scale migrations that took place as a result of the Partition of British India. In addition to the regional, ethnic, and linguistic diversity, the Bombay film industry is marked by a high level of religious diversity. Every major religious group in India – Hindu, Muslim, Sikh, Christian, Jain, Jew, and Zoroastrian – is represented. What is distinctive about the film industry as compared to the rest of Indian society is the high rate of inter-marriage across religious, ethnic, regional, linguistic, and caste lines, and frequently within the industry itself. The film industry becomes the primary social identity and community for most people, so that rather than being seen as belonging to a particular ethnic or religious group, an actor or director is identified more as a "film-*wallah*" or film person.

Rather than one set path, there are a variety of ways that people become involved in the Hindi film industry. Some members of the industry have been trained at prestigious professional institutions such as the National School of Drama or the Film and Television Institute of India. Others have worked in advertising, theater, or television before making a foray into films. However, the most common practice especially for directors and composers, has been to work as assistants within the film industry. The majority of Bombay filmmakers have learned their craft in this hands-on manner rather than through formal film school training. In terms of acting, the paths are even more varied and do not necessarily involve any formal training or experience. Actors in leading roles tend to start their careers as leading men and women rather than gaining experience in supporting roles or bit parts. Many actors are "discovered," but what has become the most common way to break into acting is to be the son or daughter of an actor, director, producer, etc. Given the multiple avenues for entering the film industry, members of the industry come from a wide range of educational backgrounds – from obtaining Master's degrees to not even finishing high school. While there is no educational norm, higher education is definitely valorized and respected within the industry and those who have college degrees tend to make known this aspect of their background.

Despite being a selection of only the most popular or defining films, the filmography lists a high number of films per individual. What perhaps differentiates Indian filmmakers and actors most readily from their Western counterparts is that they commonly work on multiple films simultaneously and therefore have huge bodies of work. This style of working is a consequence of the financial scenario that emerged after the breakdown of the studio system in the late 1940s. Due to the lack of steady finance, Hindi films are shot in a series of schedules (see chapter 2). Rather than being out of work while a particular film is not being shot, actors take on multiple assignments so they are assured a steady stream of work and earnings. Of course, this system has bred its own vicious cycle where even if a producer has the requisite finance for a film, the actors may not be available for one continuous production schedule as they have other film commitments. It is only within the last decade or so that some actors, directors, and composers have begun to cut down on the number of projects they undertake, and are attempting to space them out. While many A-list directors in the current Bombay industry work on one film at a time, actors still work on multiple projects, but the numbers are much less than before – 3–5 rather than 10–15, although new entrants into the industry frequently take on a rash of assignments. However, most actors publicly proclaim their desire to work on only one film at a time as that is perceived as a mark of quality and commitment to better cinema. Producers and directors with clout and respect can demand "block" dates from their actors and try to finish their shooting in one or two continuous schedules.

Except for the list of actresses under the category of stars, there are no other women represented. The Bombay film industry is primarily a male-dominated one where the most prominent women in the past have been actresses and playback singers. In the contemporary industry, women have made their mark as choreographers, costume designers, editors, screenwriters, and art directors, but their male counterparts still outnumber them in each category. There has been no female cinematographer or stunt/action coordinator to date, and there are very few women who are composers or lyricists. Currently there is a handful of women directors, but they have not achieved the type of commercial success which accords power in the industry. In the history of the Bombay film industry thus far, the most commercially successful, cinematically influential, and powerful directors, producers, and composers have been men.

The reasons for the marginal presence of women have to do with the disreputable image of the Bombay film industry within Indian society and the nature of its work culture. The industry has long been viewed as an unsavory place for women due to its historical connections to courtesan culture (see chapter 1), organized crime, and stereotypes about the "casting couch." Assistants who normally begin in their teenage years work long hours, frequently into the night and are at the beck and call of their bosses. Such a working scenario is perceived by many families as having the potential for sexual harassment or exploitation. The fact that formal education is not necessary for success differentiates the film world even further from the norms of Indian middle-class respectability. Women from middle-class or more elite backgrounds are simply not encouraged or are even actively discouraged by their families from trying to pursue commercial filmmaking as a profession. Women, however, have a much stronger presence in documentary filmmaking, small-budget/art house filmmaking, and television. Since the late 1990s, the image of the film industry has been improving from the point of view of the Indian media and the middle classes due to the increased global success and circulation of Hindi cinema, the state's recognition of filmmaking as an industry, and the increased numbers of upper middle-class men and women entering the industry. More women are working as assistants to directors, producers, and art directors within the Bombay film industry, gaining the necessary experience, so that in the future, more women will be in positions of creative and financial decision-making power in the industry.

DIRECTORS

Too often, standard treatments of popular Hindi cinema have described the Bombay film industry in mechanistic and homogenous terms and ignored individual directors and their styles. If popular directors have been written about or described in any detail, they have tended to be those from the earlier era of Hindi cinema such as the 1940s and 1950s. This list, however, describes 14 directors spanning over six decades of Hindi cinema and encompassing many different approaches to filmmaking.[2]

Mehboob Khan (1906–64)

Mehboob Khan is regarded as one of the most important influences on post-1950s Hindi cinema. Born as Ramjan Khan in Bilimoria, Gujarat, he ran away to Bombay to join the film industry and started as an extra in Imperial Studios where he met his future cameraman and screenwriter. He acted as one of the thieves in Imperial's *Alibaba and the Forty Thieves* in 1927. Khan acted in 16 more films before he made his directorial debut at Sagar Movietone in 1935 with *Judgment of Allah*, a period film set in the Ottoman Empire. He then moved to National Studios in 1940, but left in 1942 to start his own production company. The logo for Mehboob Productions was a hammer and sickle even though Khan was not formally associated with the Communist Party. Khan's films were marked by their focus on political themes and social critique, but always within the conventions of popular cinema. Focusing on the evils of capitalism, feudalism, and imperialism, and the clash between pre-capitalist rural values and those of a modernizing, industrializing state, Khan's films were successful on an international scale and were distributed in Africa and Europe. His *Andaz*, a triangular love story and statement about the role of women in a modernizing nation, is regarded by scholars as the first Indian film set in "modern times" among an affluent middle class, exerting an enormous influence on later films such as those by Raj Kapoor. Khan's *Mother India* about the trials and tribulations of a peasant woman is reportedly India's most successful film ever and was the first Hindi film to be nominated for an Academy Award for Best Foreign Film.

Select filmography

Aurat (Woman; 1940), *Roti* (Bread; 1942), *Humayun* (1945), *Anmol Ghadi* (Priceless Moment; 1946), *Andaz* (Style; 1949), *Aan* (Honor; 1952), *Amar* (Eternal; 1954), Mother India (1957)

Bimal Roy (1909–66)

Bimal Roy was one of the most awarded and respected directors of his era, winning six Filmfare Awards for Best Director in a span of 10 years.[3] He was regarded as the master of social realism in the Bombay film industry. Born in Dhaka (now Bangladesh) into a landholding family, Roy studied in Calcutta and was hired as a camera assistant for New Theatres, and then became a cameraman in the 1930s. Roy made his directorial debut with a Bengali film in 1944, *Udayar Pathe*, which was about an author's fight against exploitation, and proved to be quite successful. When this film was released in Hindi as *Hamrahi*, Roy was actively courted by the Bombay industry.

He left New Theatres in 1950 and moved to Bombay where he worked briefly for Bombay Talkies and then set up Bimal Roy Productions in 1952, making 11 films in 13 years. Influenced by the neorealist style of the Italian filmmaker Vittorio De Sica (*Bicycle Thieves*), Roy introduced a new era of post World War II romantic-realist melodrama focusing on the oppressive nature of social conventions and the exploitative character of capitalism. His *Do Bigha Zameen*, about a dispossessed peasant who moves to Calcutta and pulls a rikshaw to pay off a loan in order to save his small plot of land, won critical accolades for the realistic depiction of its characters, setting, and narrative outcome. Many of Roy's films had women either as the central protagonist or crucial to the narrative (*Parineeta*, *Madhumati*, *Sujata*, *Bandini*) His 1958 reincarnation saga, *Madhumati*, was one of the biggest hits of the 1950s. Roy supported younger Bengali filmmakers who followed him to Bombay. His filmmaking team contained many talents who went on to become major filmmakers themselves such as Hrishikesh Mukherjee.

Select filmography

Do Bigha Zamin (Two Plots of Land; 1953), *Parineeta* (Married Woman; 1953), *Naukri* (Job; 1954), *Biraj Bahu* (Eldest Daughter-in-Law; 1954), *Devdas* (1955), Madhumati (1958), *Sujata* (1959), *Bandini* (Female Prisoner; 1963)

Hrishikesh Mukherjee (b. 1922)

Born in Calcutta, Hrishikesh Mukherjee studied science at Calcutta University and then worked as a teacher and a freelance artist at All India Radio. He joined Calcutta's leading studio, New Theatres, in 1945 as a laboratory assistant. He worked as an assistant director and editor for Bimal Roy. Mukherjee was renowned as an editor, earning the reputation of being able to rescue films that went out of control during shooting. He introduced editing conventions basic to Hindi cinema such as the insertion of a close-up as a link between incompatible shots. Mukherjee's *Anand* featuring reigning superstar Rajesh

Khanna and a pre-superstar Amitabh Bachchan introduced a new genre in Hindi cinema – "cancer films," which were a very popular type of melodrama featuring terminally ill characters. His films in the 1970s were mainly low-budget family stories dealing with the dilemmas – frequently comical – of middle-class families in urban settings. Mukherjee's directorial career spanned from 1957 to 1988. He was the chairman of the Central Board of Film Certification (Censor Board) in the early 1980s and was also the president of the National Film Development Corporation (NFDC). Mukherjee emerged from retirement in the late 1990s to make *Jhoot Bole Kauva Kaate* (If You Lie, the Crow Will Bite) which released in 1998, but unfortunately did not fare too well at the box office. In 1999, he received the Dadasaheb Phalke Award from the Indian government for his lifetime contribution to Indian cinema.[4] In 2001, Mukherjee received the country's second highest civilian honor, the *Padma Vibhushan*.[5]

Select filmography

Anari (Naïve; 1959), Anand (1970), *Guddi* (Doll; 1971), *Bawarchi* (Cook; 1972), *Abhimaan* (Pride; 1973), *Namak Haram* (Traitor; 1973), *Chupke Chupke* (Quietly; 1975), *Mili* (1975), *Golmaal* (Fraud; 1979), *Khubsoorat* (Beautiful; 1980)

Raj Kapoor (1924–88)

Raj Kapoor was a hugely popular and successful actor, producer, and director who was frequently referred to by the press and the film industry as "the showman" of Hindi cinema. Kapoor was born in Peshawar (now Pakistan) and was the son of a famous stage and screen actor, Prithviraj Kapoor, who had migrated to Bombay in the late 1920s. Raj Kapoor worked with his father as a stage actor, production manager, and art director. His first film role was at the age of 11. He worked as an assistant director at Bombay Talkies and at Ranjit Studios before setting up his own production company, R.K. films, in 1948, to produce his first directorial venture, *Aag* (Fire). His 1951 film, *Awara* became a huge success not just in India but also in the Middle East, the Soviet Union, and China. Kapoor and his leading lady in many films, Nargis, became a vaunted international star pair – visiting the U.S., the Soviet Union, the U.K., and other parts of the world to promote their films. Kapoor's most memorable screen persona as an actor is that of a lovable tramp similar to Charlie Chaplin. Kapoor's films displayed two main concerns: social critique and love that transcended social barriers. While his earlier films focused on the former – frequently with Kapoor playing a poor everyman who points out the exploitative nature of capitalism and urban life, his later films dealt with the obstacles to the realization of true love. Kapoor was known for his highly sexualized portrayal of women in his films – frequently inciting controversy (*Satyam Shivam Sundaram*).

Kapoor and his family are often regarded as the "first family" of Hindi cinema. Kapoor's two younger brothers – Shammi and Shashi – were also popular stars of Hindi cinema in the 1960s and 1970s. His three sons followed in his footsteps by acting in Hindi films and then subsequently turning to production and direction. Two of his daughters-in-law were popular actresses of their generation. Kapoor's granddaughters, Karisma and Kareena, are currently among the top actresses in the Bombay industry – representing the fourth generation of the Kapoor family in the industry. Kapoor was a recipient of the Dadasaheb Phalke award in 1987.

Select filmography

Kapoor acted in many of the films that he directed. The ones with an * indicate films that he only acted in, and ** indicate films that he only directed.

Barsaat (Rain; 1949), Awara (Vagabond; 1951), *Shree 420* (Mr. 420; 1955), *Chori Chori* (Secretly; 1956), *Jis Desh Mein Ganga Behti Hai* (The Land in Which the Ganga Flows; 1960), *Sangam* (Union; 1964), *Mera Naam Joker* (My Name Is Clown; 1970), **Bobby (1973), **Satyam Shivam Sundaram* (Truth, God, Beauty; 1978), **Prem Rog* (Afflicted by Love; 1982), **Ram Teri Ganga Maili* (Ram, Your Ganga Is Defiled; 1985)

Guru Dutt (1925–64)

Guru Dutt is one of the most revered and highly regarded directors from the 1950s – by scholars, filmmakers, and the popular press alike. Born in Bangalore as Gurudatta Padukone, Dutt was educated in Calcutta, and then studied dance at Uday Shankar's India Cultural Centre from 1942–4. He worked as a telephone operator in Calcutta before joining Prabhat Studios in 1944 as an actor, subsequently working also as a choreographer and assistant director. It was at Prabhat that Dutt met actor Dev Anand and became part of an informal group of ex-IPTA members associated with Anand's production company, Navketan, which produced Dutt's first film, *Baazi* in 1951. Dutt set up his own production house in 1953 with *Baaz* (Falcon), a period film set in the sixteenth century about a group of revolutionaries fighting Portugese rule in India. His films frequently addressed exploitation and were laced with social critique, but worked within the conventions of popular cinema. Dutt's films are notable for their outstanding cinematography and innovatively staged song sequences. Though Dutt made a variety of genres – adventure films, comedies, love stories, and crime thrillers, he is best remembered for his films *Pyaasa* and *Kaagaz Ke Phool* which examined the plight of the artist – his alienation and disillusionment – in contemporary society. *Kaagaz Ke Phool*, a flop at the box office, was India's first Cinemascope film. After the film's commercial failure, Dutt refused to direct films but continued as an actor and producer. He committed suicide in 1964 at the age of 39 – an act foreshadowed in the autobiographical *Kaagaz ke Phool*.

Select filmography

Guru Dutt acted in many of the films he directed. The films which he directed but did not act in are indicated with an *, while those which he did not direct are marked with **.

Baazi (Wager; 1951), *Jaal* (Trap; 1952), *Aar Paar* (Across; 1954), *Mr & Mrs. '55* (1955), Pyaasa (Thirsty One; 1957), *Kaagaz ke Phool* (Paper Flowers; 1959), **Chaudvin ka Chand* (Full Moon; 1960), **Sahib Bibi Aur Ghulam* (Master, Wife, and Slave; 1962)

Yash Chopra (b. 1932)

Yash Chopra is currently one of the most successful producer/directors in the contemporary Hindi film industry with a career spanning over 40 years and at least one hit in each decade starting from the late 1950s. Born in Jullunder, Punjab, Chopra started his career as an assistant to director I.S. Johar and then to elder brother B.R. Chopra – also a producer/director. Chopra made several films for his brother's production company, B.R. Films, the first in 1959. He started his own production company, Yashraj Films, in 1973, but directed for other producers throughout the 1970s. While his films have spanned many genres and themes, including some of Amitabh Bachchan's best known "angry young man" films (*Deewar*, *Trishul*, *Kaala Patthar*), Chopra is most identified with lavishly produced, upper-class love-stories centering around love triangles, extra-marital affairs, or conflicts between individual desire and family duty. His two sons have become involved in filmmaking as well. His elder son, Aditya who started assisting him in 1991, turned director in 1995 with *Dilwale Dulhaniya Le Jayenge* (DDLJ), which Chopra produced. His younger son, Uday, made his acting debut in *Mohabbatein* (Loves; 2000), directed by Aditya and produced by Yash. Chopra's production company has now diversified into both domestic and overseas film distribution and has offices in London and New York. Chopra received the prestigious Dadasaheb Phalke Award for 2001.

Select filmography

Waqt (Time; 1965), *Ittefaq* (Chance; 1969), Deewar (Wall; 1975), *Kabhi Kabhie* (Sometimes; 1976), *Trishul* (Trident; 1978), *Kaala Patthar* (Black Stone; 1979), *Silsila* (Affair; 1981), *Chandni* (1989), *Lamhe* (Moments; 1991), *Darr* (Fear; 1993), *Dil to Pagal Hai* (The Heart Is Crazy; 1997)

Vijay Anand (1935–2004)

Vijay Anand is an actor, producer, writer, editor, and director who had a significant impact on the visual and musical style of Hindi cinema in the 1960s. Born in Gurdaspur, Punjab, Anand received a B.A. from the University of Bombay. Some of Anand's best known and successful films were made for Navketan Films, a production company started by his two older brothers Dev, one of the top stars of Hindi cinema, and Chetan – an influential director, writer, and actor of 1950s and 1960s cinema. He wrote the script of *Taxi-Driver* which starred Dev, was directed by Chetan, and proved to be an important film in their respective careers. Anand had his directorial debut in 1957 with *Nau Do Gyarah* starring his brother. His directorial ventures for Navketan played a crucial role in shaping his brother Dev's screen personality as a clever, streetwise man-of-the-world. Anand also made the critically acclaimed *Guide*, based on R.K. Narayan's novel, which was the first Indo-American co-production. Anand's films are known for their outstanding musical sequences which frequently derived from his innovative use of locations and narrative placement. He put music to creative use in genres like murder mysteries (*Teesri Manzil*) and crime thrillers (*Jewel Thief*, *Johnny Mera Naam*). Although he was regarded by the film industry as the director who could blend critical acclaim with commercial success, Anand became disillusioned with filmmaking and virtually stopped directing from the mid-1970s onwards, only making films sporadically. He continued to act in a small number of films in the 1970s, but had more or less left the film world by the next decade. Anand reappeared briefly on Indian television playing a detective in the television series, *Tahqiqat* (Investigation) in 1994.

Select filmography

The films which Anand both acted in and directed are marked with an *.
    Nau Do Gyarah (To Run Away; 1957), *Kala Bazaar* (Black Market; 1960), *Tere Ghar Ke Saamne* (In Front of Your House; 1963), Guide (1965), *Teesri Manzil* (Third Floor; 1966), *Jewel Thief* (1967), *Johnny Mera Naam* (My Name Is Johnny; 1970)

Manmohan Desai (1936–94)

Manmohan Desai was one of the defining producer/directors of 1970s and 1980s Hindi cinema. Born in Bombay, he was the son of Kikubhai Desai, the founder of Paramount Studio which later housed Filmalaya Studios (est. 1958). Desai started as an assistant director in the late 1950s. His first directorial venture was *Chhalia* in 1960, a film about a family separated during Partition, starring Raj Kapoor. Desai turned independent producer with his blockbuster, *Amar Akbar Anthony*. In the mid-1970s, the nation-wide state of emergency delayed the release of some of his films so that in 1977, four of his hits – *Dharam Veer*, *Chacha Bhatija*, *Parvarish*, and *Amar Akbar Anthony*, were running simultaneously in theaters. His most successful films were with Amitabh Bachchan who starred in 8 of the 20 films that Desai directed during his career. Desai's trademarks were multi-starrers centering around mistaken identity, lost and found siblings, and highly improbable feats. It is his style of film-making which provides the basis for the stereotypes about "Bollywood" as escapist, unconcerned with logic or characterization, and lacking genres. His last film, *Ganga Jamuna Saraswati* also starring Bachchan was a commercial disaster. Plagued by ill health and depression, Desai, committed suicide in 1994 at the age of 58. His son, Ketan is currently a producer in the Bombay industry.

Select filmography

Chhalia (Trickster; 1960), Amar Akbar Anthony (1977), *Dharam Veer* (Righteous Warrior; 1977), *Parvarish* (Upbringing; 1977), *Suhaag* (Matrimony; 1979), *Naseeb* (Destiny; 1981), *Coolie* (1983)

Subhash Ghai (b. 1943)

Subhash Ghai is one of the most influential and commercially successful producer/directors of the contemporary Bombay film industry. Born in Nagpur, Maharashtra, Ghai graduated as an actor from the Film and Television Institute of India in 1968. He first worked as an actor and a writer before he turned to directing. Ghai started his own production company, Mukta Arts in 1978. His films in the 1980s and early 1990s tended to be big-budget, multi-star cast, lavishly produced epics focusing on family feuds, terrorist threats, and the quest for justice. Since 1997, Ghai has turned his attention to films featuring the South Asian diaspora in upscale urban settings who are frequently torn between desire and duty in the domain of romantic relationships. His 1999 film, *Taal* was the first Hindi film to debut as the twentieth highest grossing film in the U.S. for the week that it opened. Ghai is the first Bombay producer to take his company public and list it on the Bombay Stock Exchange. He is currently involved with establishing a film and television institute, which can provide a steady pool of talent and skills for the Bombay film industry.

Select filmography

Karz (Debt; 1980), *Meri Jung* (My Battle; 1982), *Vidhaata* (God; 1982), *Hero* (1983), *Karma* (Action; 1986), *Ram Lakhan* (1989), *Saudagar* (Merchant; 1991), Khalnayak (Villain; 1993), *Pardes* (Foreign Land; 1997), *Taal* (Rhythm; 1999)

Ramesh Sippy (b. 1947)

Ramesh Sippy is the director of one of the biggest hits of Indian cinema – *Sholay* (1975), a film that has influenced contemporary Bombay filmmakers immensely and set new standards in Hindi filmmaking in terms of cinematography, editing, stunt sequences, and the depiction of violence. Born in Karachi (now Pakistan), Sippy graduated from Bombay University. He made most of his films for the production company started by his father, G.P. Sippy. Sippy's debut film in 1971, *Andaz*,[6] was an unconventional love story between a widow and a widower. Sippy's films have ranged from a comic love story involving a pair of identical twin sisters (*Seeta aur Geeta*), to a Bond-like thriller (*Shaan*), a love triangle (*Saagar*), and a drama involving father and son on opposite sides of the law (*Shakti*). Sippy was also one of the first filmmakers to get involved with television and he made the first major television series in India, *Buniyaad*

(Foundation, 1987–8) which detailed the life and times of a family from Partition to contemporary India. Sippy broke off from his father's production company and started his own, R.S. Enterprises in the mid-1990s which produced his son, Rohan's directorial debut, *Kuch Na Kaho* (Don't Say Anything; 2003), starring Amitabh Bachchan's son, Abhishek.

Select filmography
Andaz (Style; 1971), *Seeta aur Geeta* (Seeta and Geeta; 1972), Sholay (Flames; 1975), *Shaan* (Pride; 1980), *Shakti* (Power; 1982), *Saagar* (Sea; 1985)

Mahesh Bhatt (b. 1949)
Born and educated in Bombay, Mahesh Bhatt is best known for films that focus on troubled personal relationships. His films about illegitimacy and extramarital affairs were frequently drawn from his personal experience. After assisting director Raj Khosla in the early 1970s, Bhatt made his first film *Manzilein Aur Bhi Hain* (There Are Aspirations Other Than (Love)) in 1973. This film, which depicted a woman living with two men, was banned for 14 months by the censors for allegedly mocking the "sacred institution of marriage." Bhatt has always attracted a fair share of controversy with his outspoken and blunt statements in the press about censorship, filmmaking, and Indian social norms. Many of his successful films in the 1990s were love stories starring his daughter Pooja. Bhatt is himself the son of a director, Nanabhai Bhatt, who made costume dramas in the 1950s and 1960s. Bhatt's two brothers are involved in the film industry as well – one is a producer and the other is a writer. Though he retired from directing in 1998, Bhatt continues to be involved in filmmaking by writing screenplays and producing films.

Select filmography
Arth (Meaning; 1982), *Saaransh* (Summary; 1984), *Naam* (Name; 1986), *Daddy* (1989), *Aashiqui* (Romance; 1990), *Dil Hai Ke Maanta*

Nahin (The Heart Is Such, It Doesn't Agree; 1991), *Sadak* (Street; 1991), *Sir* (1993), *Hum Hain Rahi Pyar Ke* (We Are Love's Wayfarers; 1993), *Tamanna* (Aspiration; 1997), *Zakhm* (Wound; 1998)

David Dhawan (b. 1954)

David Dhawan is one of the most prolific and commercially successful directors in the contemporary Bombay film industry. Between 1989 and 2003, he directed 32 films. A graduate of the Film and Television Institute of India, Dhawan began his career in the industry as an editor in the early 1980s. He started directing in 1989, but did not taste commercial success until 1992 with his films, *Bol Radha Bol* (Speak Radha Speak) and *Shola aur Shabnam* (Fire and Dew). His film *Aankhen* broke all previous box-office records and is one of the 10 biggest blockbusters of Hindi cinema. However, it was only after Dhawan delivered a consecutive string of hits between 1993–8, that he garnered respect and was categorized as an A-list director within the industry. However, unlike the other directors in this list, Dhawan has not been the subject of any scholarly or journalistic analysis. He formed a successful team with the actor Govinda and together they carved a niche for themselves with their particular brand of comedy – zany, slapstick, low-brow and replete with coin-cidences, mistaken identities, and lookalikes. The immediate precursor to Dhawan's style of filmmaking is Manmohan Desai. While the 1990s were mainly populated with upper middle-class or wealthy protagonists, Dhawan's films starring Govinda frequently had working-class protagonists. However, rather than being the "angry young man," which was the popular depiction of the working-class male in the 1970s, Dhawan's working-class hero was a comical, fast-talking, wise guy.

Select filmography

Aankhen (Eyes; 1993), *Raja Babu* (King; 1994), *Coolie No. 1* (1995), *Saajan Chale Sasural* (Husband Goes to His In-Laws; 1996), *Hero No. 1* (1997), *Deewana Mastana* (Crazy and Funny; 1997), *Bade*

Miyan Chote Miyan (Big Guy-Little Guy; 1998), *Biwi No. 1* (Number One Wife; 1999), *Haseena Maan Jayegi* (The Beauty Will Come Around; 1999), *Jodi No. 1* (Number One Pair; 2001)

Ram Gopal Varma (b. 1961)

Ram Gopal Varma is a director and producer who first worked in Telugu cinema before he became involved with Hindi cinema. His first film in Hindi, *Rangeela*, which is about the dreams and aspirations of a chorus dancer in Bollywood and the local ticket scalper who loves her, was one of the box-office successes of 1995. Originally a civil engineer by profession, Varma had no formal training or experience in filmmaking before he made his first film, *Shiva*, in 1990. A keen film buff who owned a video rental shop in Hyderabad, Varma's knowledge of filmmaking stemmed from his avid film-viewing. What stands out about Varma is his willingness to take risks within the conventions of popular cinema and make films in a variety of genres. His films have ranged from a songless horror film (*Bhoot*), a chase caper (*Daud*), and gritty gangster films (*Satya, Company*) to a love story between a movie star and her ardent fan (*Mast*). His penchant for producing films by debutante directors and introducing new actors, has led the Indian press to nickname Varma as the unofficial talent scout for the Hindi film industry.

Select filmography

Rangeela (Colorful; 1995), *Daud* (Run; 1997), *Satya* (Truthful; 1998), *Mast* (Fun-loving; 1999), *Kaun* (Who; 1999), *Jungle* (2000), *Company* (2002), *Bhoot* (Ghost; 2003)

Sooraj Barjatya (b. 1965)

Sooraj Barjatya redefined Hindi cinema in the mid-1990s with his second film, *Hum Aapke Hain Koun!* (1994) which broke all previous box-office records and went on to become the biggest hit of Indian cinema. Even his first film *Maine Pyar Kiya* released in 1989 is counted among the 10 most successful films of Hindi cinema. Barjatya is the third generation of his family to be involved in the film industry. His grandfather, Tarachand Barjatya, started the first nation-wide distribution concern, Rajshri Pictures, in 1947, which then expanded into film production in 1962, focusing on small-budget, family-oriented melodramas. Barjatya assisted filmmakers Mahesh Bhatt and N. Chandra in the mid-1980s before embarking on his own directorial venture. His films celebrate and valorize the Hindu joint family and frequently focus on the conflict between desire and duty. While the themes may appear traditional, the milieu and lifestyle represented in Barjatya's films emphasize and support the sort of modern consumerism that is a significant aspect of elite identity in contemporary India since the advent of economic liberalization in the mid-1980s.

Select filmography

Maine Pyar Kiya (I Have Loved; 1989), Hum Aapke Hain Koun! (What Do I Mean to You? 1994), *Hum Saath Saath Hain* (We Are in This Together; 1999), *Main Prem ki Diwani Hoon* (I Am Crazy for Love; 2003)

MUSIC DIRECTORS

The composers for Hindi films are referred to as music directors within the Bombay industry. With music being an integral part of filmmaking, an entire song-writing and music-composing industry came into existence after the advent of sound in 1931. Most music directors are musicians schooled in the tradition of North Indian classical music. Although drawing from Indian classical and folk repertoires, they have fashioned a distinct musical genre by incorporating an eclectic range of instruments, rhythms, and musical elements. Each music director develops a characteristic style, recognizable to listeners, and gains nation-wide fame and recognition as film songs take on a life of their own and circulate far beyond the context of the film.

Sachin Dev Burman (1906–75)

S.D. Burman was one of the most successful music directors of the 1950s and 1960s. Born into the royal family of Tripura, he first trained in classical North Indian music under his father who was a sitar player and then subsequently trained with other classical musicians. He initially worked in radio and made a reputation in the 1930s in Bengal as a singer of folk and semi-classical music. Burman's entry into the world of film was first as a singer and then as an actor, both in 1935. He worked as a music director in Calcutta from 1939 until 1944 when he moved to Bombay and worked at Filmistan Studios. Some of Burman's most popular and memorable soundtracks were from his collaboration with Guru Dutt and Navketan Films. He remained Dev Anand's main composer for many years. He also scored films for Bimal Roy. Burman's soundtrack for *Aradhana* (1969) contributed to the super success of the film and still has a presence today as the songs from the film are a favorite with re-mix artists. Unlike his contemporaries Naushad and Shankar-Jaikishen who at the time were partial to heavy orchestration, Burman preferred to compose music that only relied on a few Indian musical instruments. Burman's compositions were influenced by the folk melodies from his native northeastern India. As a singer, his thin but powerful voice was often used in background songs which served as a commentary within the film. Between 1944 and 1975, Burman composed music for 105 films.

Select filmography

Baazi (Wager; 1951), *Taxi Driver* (1954), *Munimji* (Clerk; 1955), *Paying Guest* (1957), Pyaasa (Thirsty One; 1957), *Chalti Ka Naam Gaadi* (Life Goes On; 1958), *Kala Paani* (Black Water; 1958), *Sujata* (1959), *Kala Bazaar* (Black Market; 1960), *Tere Ghar ke Samne* (In Front of Your House; 1963), Guide (1965), *Jewel Thief* (1967), Aradhana (Worship; 1969), *Prem Pujari* (Worshipper of Love; 1970), *Abhimaan* (Pride; 1973)

Naushad (b. 1919)

Naushad was a defining composer of 1940s and 1950s film music. He was one of the first composers to introduce sound mixing and the separate recording of voice and music tracks in playback singing. He was also known for using large orchestras with over 100 musicians. Since early childhood, he was an avid listener of the live orchestras accompanying silent films. Born in Lucknow, Uttar Pradesh, Naushad studied classical North Indian music under a number of teachers. Before moving to Bombay in 1937, he composed music for amateur theatricals. In Bombay, he worked as a pianist in a music director's orchestra, and then later assisted prominent music director Khemchand Prakash at Ranjit Studio. He scored his first film in 1940 and then became the in-house composer at Kardar Studio in 1942. He became an independent music director from 1946 and scored a number of films for Mehboob Khan. Naushad's signature style was the incorporation of North Indian classical forms into film music – persuading some prominent North Indian classical singers to sing for his film scores. He scored the music for 66 films between 1940 and 1995. He won the Dadasaheb Phalke Award in 1981. Though he does not compose anymore, Naushad is still involved in the world of music. In 1998, he inaugurated the Naushad Academy of Hindustani Sangeet, established to preserve and popularize North Indian classical music.

Select filmography

Rattan (Jewel; 1944); *Anmol Ghadi* (Priceless Moment; 1946), *Andaz* (Style; 1949), *Babul* (Father; 1950), *Baiju Bawra* (1952), *Amar* (Eternal; 1954), *Udan Khatola* (Magic Carpet; 1955), Mother India (1957), Mughal-e-azam (The Age of Mughals; 1960), Ganga Jumna (1961), *Mere Mehboob* (My Love; 1963), Pakeezah (The Pure One; 1971)

Shankar-Jaikishen (b. unknown – 1987) and (1929–71)

Shankarsinh Raghuwanshi and Jaikishen Dayabhai Panchal, more commonly referred to as Shankar-Jaikishen, were the most commercially in demand as music composers for most of the 1950s and 1960s. They started as orchestra musicians in Prithviraj Kapoor's Prithvi Theatres where they first met Raj Kapoor. They assisted the composer Ram Ganguly in Kapoor's debut production, *Aag* and then received their first break with Kapoor's *Barsaat*. After the tremendous success of *Barsaat*'s soundtrack, the duo started their long-term association with Raj Kapoor and scored the soundtracks for most of his films, including the very successful *Awara* and *Shree 420*. Their title track for *Awara*, "*Awara Hoon*" (I'm a vagabond) was immensely popular world-wide, leading to local versions of the song in Greece, the Middle East, the Soviet Union, and China. By the early 1960s, they had become the highest-paid music directors in the industry with an unbroken string of successes. Around this time they changed their style to incorporate more Western style rock and pop elements into their music. After Jaikishen's death in 1971, Shankar continued composing until 1986 using their joint names, but could not recreate the success that they had enjoyed during the heydays of their partnership. Together they composed for over 100 films from 1949 to 1971.

Select filmography

Barsaat (Rain; 1949), Awara (Vagabond; 1951), *Shree 420* (Mr. 420; 1955), *Chori Chori* (Secretly; 1956), *Anari* (Naïve; 1959), *Jis Desh Mein Ganga Behti Hai* (The Land in Which the Ganga Flows; 1960), *Jab Pyar Kisise Hota Hai* (When One Falls in Love with Someone; 1961), *Junglee* (Wild; 1961), *Sangam* (Union; 1964), *An Evening in Paris* (1967), *Brahmachari* (Bachelor; 1968), *Mera Naam Joker* (My Name Is Clown; 1970)

Rahul Dev Burman (1939–94)

R.D. Burman was the defining music director of the 1970s who influenced a whole generation of younger music directors. He began his career as an assistant to his father, S.D. Burman, often playing the harmonica in his father's orchestras. He trained under the renowned classical sarod player, Ali Akbar Khan. Burman's independent career coincided with the wave of early Rajesh Khanna love stories. He brought Hindi film music into the era of electronic rock with a series of enormously popular youth movies. Burman worked mostly with the singers Asha Bhonsle (whom he later married) and Kishore Kumar, providing much of the music that defines their reputations. He also produced independent albums including one with the British pop star, Boy George. His compositions have also provided the fuel for the vast amount of re-mix albums by South Asian DJ's in the U.K. and North America, the most famous being Bally Sagoo's *Bollywood Flashback*. Burman composed for hundreds of films between 1961 and 1994 and occasionally sang his own songs in a unique style.

Select filmography

Teesri Manzil (Third Floor; 1966), *Kati Patang* (Torn Kite; 1970), *Amar Prem* (Eternal Love; 1971), *Hare Rama Hare Krishna* (Praise the Lord; 1971), *Jawani Diwani* (Youth is Crazy; 1972), *Yaadon ki Baraat* (Procession of Memories; 1973), *Aandhi* (Storm; 1975), Deewar (Wall; 1975), Sholay (Flames; 1975), *Hum Kisise Kam Nahin* (We're No Less Than Anyone Else; 1977), *Satte Pe Satta* (Seven on Seven; 1981), *Sagar* (Sea; 1985), *1942 A Love Story* (1994)

A.R. Rehman (b. 1966)

Rehman is an innovative and phenomenally successful contemporary Tamil and Hindi composer whose style transformed film music in the 1990s. He is a former member of the Madras-based rock group, Nemesis Avenue. Rehman became a major star with his music in *Roja* followed by hit scores for Mani Rathnam's and Shankar's films in Tamil. The music in all of these films proved equally successful in dubbed Hindi versions as did his formal debut in Hindi, *Rangeela*. His electronics-derived music, often scored on computer, is seen as belonging to the tradition of R.D. Burman. He is considered a musical genius by the Bombay film industry and, in terms of how much autonomy and control he is allowed over his compositions and working style, he holds tremendous power over film producers and directors. Currently, Rehman is the most sought after music director and is very selective about his assignments. He also released a very successful non-film music album, *Vande Mataram* (Hail to the Motherland) in 1997 to coincide with the fiftieth anniversary of India's independence. Rehman's talent has been noticed by Western music personalities such as Michael Jackson who appeared in concert with him in Germany, and Sir Andrew Lloyd Webber (*Cats*, *Sunset Boulevard*, etc.) with whom he collaborated on a West End/Broadway musical titled, *Bombay Dreams*, which is set against the backdrop of the Bombay film industry. Rehman has been honored by the Indian government several times – receiving the *Padma Shri*, the fourth highest civilian honor, in 2000, and four National awards. He recently expanded the scope of his film assignments by composing for the Chinese film, *Warriors of Heaven and Earth*, directed by He Ping.

Select filmography

Roja (1992), *Gentleman* (1993), *Thiruda Thiruda* (Thief, Thief; 1993), *Kadhalan* (Lover; 1994), *Bombay* (1995), *Rangeela* (Colorful; 1995), *Hindustani* (India; 1996), *Dil Se* (From the Heart; 1998), *Taal* (Rhythm; 1999), *Pukar* (Call; 2000), Lagaan (Land Tax; 2001), *Saathiya* (Companion; 2002)

STARS

The Bombay film industry is primarily defined by and identified with its stars. Hindi film stars are men and women in leading roles who not only have tremendous drawing power at the box office, but are global icons epitomizing a variety of attributes such as power, strength, sophistication, desirability, beauty, masculinity, and femininity. Ever since the decline of the studio system in the aftermath of World War II, the Hindi film industry is a star-oriented, star-driven, and many would complain, star-controlled industry. Producers frequently raise finance for their films on the strength of the star cast rather than the script. Scripts are usually written with specific male stars in mind and stars possess the power to promote or destroy projects. As a result of such power, stars frequently turn to production and sometimes direction, after having spent a number of years in the industry.

Like Hollywood, male stars wield a great deal more power in the Bombay industry than their female counterparts. Male stars are perceived as having greater box-office drawing power and thus are paid more and hired first. The prevailing attitude among distributors and producers is that "heroines" – the common term used for actresses in leading roles – do not "open" a film, that is, they do not pull in the crowds and generate the sold-out shows that guarantee a successful first weekend at the box office. Therefore, it is difficult to market a film that is characterized as a "heroine-oriented" one within the industry, as top male stars tend not to act in projects where they play a supporting role.

As in Hollywood, actors have much longer careers as leading men in the Hindi film industry than do women, who are sidelined into supporting roles soon after they turn 30. Actresses begin their careers when they are teenagers, while actors start in their twenties, so even if an actress has spent a decade in the industry, she is not necessarily advanced in actual years, but the press, industry, and audiences tend to dismiss her as "mature." Filmmakers are constantly on the lookout for "fresh, new faces." Men continue to act with women much younger than themselves, but the reverse is much less common. When it does occur, reviewers and the press frequently comment upon the inappropriate pairing between a younger man and older woman. Often, even when the two are of the same age, women are more apt to be criticized for having lost their youthful charm and looking older than the actor. There have been instances where actresses who have played the romantic lead opposite a particular actor, end up playing the actor's mother a year or two later![7]

There is also an expectation among the press, industry, and audiences that once a woman marries, she will retire from acting as she will take on other responsibilities such as raising a family. Even though there have been a number of married actresses within the Hindi film industry, some who continued to act in leading roles even after having children, the immediate conclusion that producers, journalists, and audience members jump to when hearing of an actress's decision to marry is that she is in effect, announcing her retirement. Such assumptions lead many women to delay marriage or in some cases even hide their marriages. Recently, some actresses have turned to production and direction, which is a sign of their increasing power within the industry,[8] but the fact that their identity as women is constantly commented upon by the media and the industry reveals the essentially patriarchal norms of the Bombay film industry.

ACTORS

Ashok Kumar (1911–2001)

Ashok Kumar was one of the first stars of Hindi cinema. Born in Bhagalpur, Bihar, Kumar's given name was Kumudlal Kunjilal Ganguly. The son of a lawyer and deputy magistrate, Kumar briefly studied law in Calcutta and then joined mentor and future brother-in-law, S. Mukherji, at Bombay Talkies, initially as a lab assistant. He got his first break by being cast opposite Devika Rani, the leading star and later, head of Bombay Talkies, in *Jeevan Naiya* (New Life) and *Achhut Kanya*. Kumar had a trio of successes with *Kangan*, *Bandhan*, and *Jhoola*. His most famous role was in the crime thriller *Kismet*, which changed his image from a clean-cut, romantic ideal type to a cocky, chain-smoking, morally ambiguous anti-hero. Kumar's way of holding a cigarette in *Kismet* became a trademark. He left Bombay Talkies to set up a rival studio, Filmistan, with S. Mukherjee, but later returned as production chief and even directed some of their films, though he never took official credit. Kumar acted with his younger brothers, Kishore and Anoop, in some classic comedies of the 1950s like *Chalti Ka Naam Gaadi*. From the 1960s, Kumar started acting in character roles, frequently playing the sympathetic parent or avuncular neighbor. He anchored the television serial, *Hum Log* (We the People) and appeared in many others. Acting in hundreds of films in a career that spanned over six decades, Ashok Kumar was the first to bring a more natural and less theatrical style of acting to the screen, one incorporating an everyday manner of speaking and behaving. In 1988, he received the Dadasaheb Phalke Award for his contribution to Indian cinema, and in 1999, he received the *Padma Bhushan* – the country's third highest civilian honor.

Select filmography

Acchut Kanya (Untouchable Girl; 1936), *Kangan* (Bracelet; 1939), *Bandhan* (Bonds; 1940), *Jhoola* (Swing; 1941), Kismet (Fate; 1943), *Mahal* (Palace; 1949), *Parineeta* (Married Woman; 1953), *Chalti Ka Naam Gaadi* (Life Goes On; 1958), *Howrah Bridge* (1958), *Kanoon* (Law; 1960), *Bandini* (Female Prisoner; 1963), *Jewel Thief* (1967), Pakeezah (The Pure One; 1971), *Chhotisi Baat* (A Little Matter; 1975)

Dilip Kumar (b. 1922)

Dilip Kumar was one of the three top stars of the 1950s and 1960s and is currently one of the most respected seniors in the Hindi film industry. Born in Peshawar (now Pakistan) as Yusuf Khan to a family of 12 children, Kumar emerged from humble origins. While one account states that his family moved to Maharashtra as fruit merchants (Rajadhyaksha and Willemen 1999), another states that Kumar ran away from his family to Pune and eventually set up a fruit stall (Raheja and Kothari 1996). What is known for certain is that Kumar worked in a British army canteen in Bombay in 1940. Devika Rani is said to have discovered him and recruited him for Bombay Talkies. Noted Hindi novelist, Bhagwati Charan Varma renamed him Dilip Kumar. He attained stardom with *Jugnu* and super stardom with Mehboob Khan's *Andaz*, co-starring Raj Kapoor and Nargis. Kumar achieved a lasting reputation for naturalistic, underplayed acting. He frequently depicted characters who were innocent loners caught in and destroyed by conflicting social pressures. Kumar's first block of successful films (*Mela*, *Andaz*, *Babul*, *Jogan*, *Deedar*) depicted him as a tragic lover. By the time he portrayed the doomed lover in *Devdas*, where he drinks himself to death, Kumar apparently had to seek psychiatric counseling as the surfeit of tragic roles took their toll on his mental health. He was advised to move away from tragedy and changed to a more masculine, heroic image (*Aan*, *Azad*, *Kohinoor*, *Gunga Jumna*), although he maintained his romantic image as well (*Mughal-e-azam*, *Madhumati*). Though nicknamed the 'Tragedy King' by the Indian press, Dilip Kumar also appeared in comic roles (*Gopi*, *Ram aur Shyam*). After taking a break from acting for about eight years, he made a comeback with *Kranti* (1981) and *Shakti* (1982). In the latter he starred as Amitabh Bachchan's unyielding, morally upright police-officer father. His legendary star status was further confirmed by his series of films with Subhash Ghai (*Vidhaata*, *Karma*, *Saudagar*). Although he virtually directed some of his films (*Gunga Jumna*), his first official directorial credit is for *Kalinga*, which was held up in production and was never released. Kumar was a recipient of the Dadasaheb Phalke Award in 1994.

Select filmography

Jugnu (Firefly; 1947), *Mela* (Fair; 1948), *Andaz* (Style; 1949), *Babul* (Father; 1950), *Jogan* (Female Ascetic; 1950), *Deedar* (Sight; 1951), *Aan* (Honor; 1952), *Azad* (Free; 1955), *Devdas* (1955), Madhumati (1958), *Kohinoor* (1960), Mughal-e-azam (Age of Mughals; 1960), Gunga Jumna (1961), *Ram aur Shyam* (Ram and Shyam; 1967), *Gopi* (1970), *Kranti* (Revolution; 1981), *Shakti* (Power; 1982), *Vidhaata* (God; 1982), *Karma* (Action; 1986), *Saudagar* (Merchant; 1991)

Dev Anand (b. 1923)

Along with Raj Kapoor and Dilip Kumar, Dev Anand completes the trio of the top male stars from the 1950s and 1960s who established the dominant acting style of post-independence Hindi cinema. Born in Gurdaspur, Punjab, as Devdutt Pishorimal Anand, to a well-off family (his father was a lawyer) Anand received a B.A. with honors in English Literature from Government College, Lahore (now Pakistan) and then went to Bombay to join elder brother Chetan in the Indian People's Theatre Association (IPTA). He began his acting career at Prabhat Studios in *Hum Ek Hain* (We're All One), and even did a film for Bombay Talkies, *Ziddi* (Stubborn), but his first big hit was *Baazi* produced by Navketan Films, the production company Anand started with his brother Chetan in 1949, and directed by Guru Dutt whom he had met at Prabhat. Unlike the tragic romantic persona of Dilip Kumar or the Chaplinesque naïf of Raj Kapoor, Anand's dominant screen persona was of a suave, worldly, smooth-talking man about town. Many of his successful roles were morally ambiguous characters living on the margins of respectable society: the cardsharp in *Baazi*, the smuggler in *Jaal*, the pickpocket in *House Number 44*, the black-marketeer in *Kala Bazaar*, and the convict in *Bambai ka Babu*. His more mannered acting deviated from the celebrated and lauded naturalist style of Ashok and Dilip Kumar, and therefore his acting abilities were challenged on occasion by Indian critics who accused him of being a star more than an actor. With his hairstyle and clothes, Anand was a dominant style icon of the 1950s and 1960s with many young men imitating his trademark puff and buttoned-up shirts. Anand turned director in 1970 with *Prem Pujari* (Love's Worshipper), and his *Hare Rame Hare Krishna* about hippies and drug culture in South Asia introduced Zeenat Aman who transformed the image of the heroine in Indian cinema. Anand has been dubbed the "Evergreen Hero" by the press and the film industry as he continues to produce and direct films starring himself along with young men and women making their acting debuts. While these films are not the commercial successes that he once enjoyed, Anand always manages to find financing due to the goodwill that he enjoys in the film industry and his status as a cultural icon. In 2001, Anand received the honor of *Padma Bhushan* from the Indian government.

Select filmography

Films that Dev Anand also directed are marked with an *.

Baazi (Wager; 1951), *Jaal* (Trap; 1952), *Taxi Driver* (1954), *House Number 44* (1955), *Munimji* (Clerk; 1955), CID (1956), *Nau Do Gyarah* (To Run Away; 1957), *Paying Guest* (1957), *Kala Paani* (Black Water; 1958), *Bambai ka Babu* (Gentleman from Bombay; 1960), *Kala Bazaar* (Black Market; 1960), *Hum Dono* (The Two of Us; 1961), *Jab Pyar Kisise Hota Hai* (When One Falls in Love with Someone; 1961), *Tere Ghar Ke Saamne* (In Front of Your House; 1963), Guide (1965), *Jewel Thief* (1967), *Johnny Mera Naam* (My Name Is Johnny; 1970), *Hare Rama Hare Krishna* (Praise the Lord; 1971), *Heera Panna* (1973)

Rajesh Khanna (b. 1942)

Rajesh Khanna enjoyed stardom unparalleled until the arrival of Amitabh Bachchan. He became a national sensation with two popular love stories that were released simultaneously within a month of each other in 1969 and shaped his screen image significantly – *Aradhana* and *Do Raaste*. In the first, he essayed the double role of a father and son, both of whom are dashing Air Force officers and in the latter, he played a devoted son and younger brother whose romance is carried out against the backdrop of family conflict. Khanna had 11 more hits between 1970 and 1972 and is usually hailed as the first superstar of Indian cinema by the press. He had a tremendous female fan-following and rumors abound about how women wrote him letters in their own blood. Originally named Jatin Khanna, he acted in theater prior to his acting in films. He got his first break after being chosen in the United Producers' Talent Contest. Though his first four films were box-office failures, Khanna had already landed 14 films prior to his breakthrough, *Aradhana*. Khanna's image in many of his films was of a vulnerable, wounded, romantic needing the love of a good woman. His most memorable roles were of terminally ill characters (*Anand*, *Safar*) who bravely faced their impending death with humor and good cheer, brightening the lives of those around them. Khanna's stardom went into decline as quickly as it had emerged, when he suffered eight consecutive flops at the box office in 1972. Though he did manage a few successes through the rest of the 1970s, they were no match for the type of hits generated by Amitabh Bachchan from 1973 onwards. Khanna continued to act through the 1980s, but in the early 1990s, he retired from acting and entered national politics, and was elected Member of Parliament in 1992 from New Delhi. While he is currently no longer an MP, Khanna is still actively involved in the Congress Party.

Select filmography

Aradhana (Worship; 1969), *Bandhan* (Bonds; 1969), *Do Raaste* (Two Paths; 1969), *Ittefaq* (Chance; 1969), *Khamoshi* (Silence; 1969), Anand (1970), *Kati Patang* (Torn Kite; 1970), *Safar* (Journey; 1970), *Amar Prem* (Eternal Love; 1971), *Dushman* (Enemy; 1971), *Haathi Mere Saathi* (My Elephant Companion; 1971), *Bawarchi* (Cook; 1972), *Daag* (Stain; 1973), *Namak Haraam* (Traitor; 1973), *Prem Nagar* (City of Love; 1974), *Avtaar* (Incarnation; 1983), *Souten* (Mistress; 1983)

Amitabh Bachchan (b. 1942)

Amitabh Bachchan is Hindi cinema's and India's biggest superstar. Born in Allahabad, Uttar Pradesh, Bachchan is the son of the noted Hindi poet, Harivanshrai Bachchan. Before his career in cinema, he worked as a radio announcer and as a freight company executive in Calcutta. Although he initially had difficulties being accepted as an actor due to his height, long legs, lanky frame, and unconventional looks, and his first 12 films did not fare well at the box office, eventually Bachchan's films determined the health of the entire Bombay industry. His breakthrough film *Zanjeer* about a police officer who avenges his parents' murder outside the bounds of the law introduced the "angry young man" to Indian cinema in 1973.[9] Although he achieved his fame from playing brooding, working-class characters who fight against an exploitative and unjust state and society,

Bachchan solidified his stardom by adding romantic and comic dimensions to his screen image as well. Bachchan was frequently referred to as the "One-Man Industry" and the "Number One" star by the press and the film industry as he reigned supreme over the box office for two decades. When he suffered a near-fatal accident in 1982 while shooting for the film, *Coolie*, the press, radio, and television issued daily bulletins on his health. Close family friend Prime Minister Indira Gandhi even cut short her trip to the U.S. to return to India. His stardom provided the model for the protagonist featured in Salman Rushdie's novel, *Satanic Verses*. Bachchan was elected as a Member of Parliament for the Congress Party in 1984, but soon abandoned politics following a military kickbacks scandal involving his younger brother. He officially retired from acting in 1992, and then re-emerged as the head of his own entertainment company, Amitabh Bachchan Corporation Limited (ABCL), which produced his "comeback" film, *Mrityudaata* (Angel of Death; 1997). Unfortunately, it was a disaster at the box office and Bachchan became the butt of a great deal of media criticism. However, since 2000, Bachchan's career has been revived by his hosting of the Indian version of "Who Wants to be a Millionaire?" – *Kaun Banega Crorepati*? on television. He has also been in a number of box-office successes playing the stern, but loving patriarch. A testament to the power he still holds in the Bombay industry is that filmmakers are designing projects keeping him in mind specifically, so that the 62-year-old Bachchan is playing a much greater variety of roles than would normally be available to an actor his age. Bachchan has a huge fan following among non-South Asians throughout Africa, the Caribbean, the Middle East, and West Asia.[10] His global popularity was confirmed when he was voted as the "Star of the Millenium" on a BBC-online poll, beating actors like Lawrence Olivier, Marlon Brando and Humphrey Bogart. Responding to popular demand, a statue of Bachchan was installed in Madame Tussaud's Wax Museum in London in 2000. Bachchan's wife, Jaya Bhaduri, was a popular actress in the 1970s and has recently resumed her acting career. Bachchan's son, Abhishek started his acting career in 2000. Bachchan was a recipient of the *Padma Bhushan* in 2001.

Select filmography

Anand (1970), *Abhimaan* (Pride; 1973), *Namak Haraam* (Traitor; 1973), *Zanjeer* (Chain; 1973), *Chupke Chupke* (Quietly; 1975), Deewar (Wall; 1975), Sholay (Flames; 1975), *Kabhi Kabhie* (Sometimes; 1976), Amar Akbar Anthony (1977), *Don* (1978), *Muqaddar ka Sikander* (Conqueror of Destiny; 1978), *Trishul* (Trident; 1978), *Laawaris* (Bastard; 1981), *Naseeb* (Destiny; 1981), *Satte Pe Satta* (Seven on Seven; 1981), *Silsila* (Affair; 1981), *Namak Halaal* (Loyal; 1982), *Shakti* (Power; 1982), *Coolie* (1983), *Agneepath* (Path of Fire; 1990), *Hum* (Us; 1991), *Mohabbatein* (Loves; 2000), *Aks* (Reflection; 2001), *Kabhie Khushi Kabhi Gham* (Sometimes There's Happines, Sometimes There's Sorrow; 2001), *Aankhen* (Eyes; 2002), *Armaan* (Cherished Desire; 2003), *Boom* (2003)

Aamir Khan (b. 1965)

Aamir Khan is one of the most popular and highly regarded actors of contemporary Hindi cinema. Khan comes from a family involved with filmmaking: his father, Tahir Hussain, produced films in the 1970s and 1980s, his uncle, Nasir Hussain, was a successful producer-director from the late 1950s to the late 1970s, and his cousin Mansoor Khan is a respected director in the Bombay film industry. After finishing high school in 1983, Khan assisted his uncle Nasir Hussain for three years, before he appeared in his first leading role in *Qayamat se Qayamat tak* (QSQT) directed by his cousin, Mansoor, in 1988. This Romeo-Juliet like story about lovers from feuding families was an enormous success and catapulted Khan to stardom. Though the press portrayed Khan as a clean-cut, wholesome boy-next-door, he did not allow himself to be trapped by this image professionally and has managed to essay a variety of roles: an avenging boyfriend in *Raakh*; a smart aleck and opportunistic reporter in *Dil Hai ke Manta Nahin*; a sensitive single father in *Akele Hum Akele Tum*; a wisecracking and carefree ticket scalper in *Rangeela*; a good-hearted but hot-headed taxi driver in *Raja*

Hindustani, a brave and dedicated police officer in *Sarfarosh*; and a determined and spirited peasant in *Lagaan*. While his films immediately after QSQT were not successful, since *Dil* in 1990, Khan has had a box-office hit nearly every year. Within the industry and by audiences he is regarded as a consummate actor and perfectionist who devotes himself entirely to a film. His attention to detail and concern about the quality of his performance has led Khan to significantly reduce the number of films he works on, and he is one of the few actors in the industry who is closest to the goal of working on one film at a time. Khan started his own production company, Aamir Khan Productions in 1999, whose maiden venture, *Lagaan*, was a huge commercial and critical success in 2001, winning awards in European film festivals and earning an Oscar nomination for Best Foreign Film. In recognition of his achievements in helping to expand the audiences for Hindi cinema, Khan was awarded the *Padma Shri* by the Indian government in 2003.

Select filmography

Qayamat se Qayamat tak (From Catastrophe to Catastrophe; 1988), *Raakh* (Ashes; 1989), *Dil* (Heart; 1990), *Dil Hai ke Manta Nahin* (The Heart Is Such, It Doesn't Agree; 1991), *Jo Jeeta Wohi Sikander* (Those Who Win Are Triumphant; 1992), *Hum Hain Rahi Pyar Ke* (We Are Love's Wayfarers; 1993), *Andaz Apna Apna* (We Have a Style of Our Own; 1994), *Rangeela* (Colorful; 1995), *Raja Hindustani* (1996), *Ishq* (Love; 1997), *Earth* (1998), *Ghulam* (Slave; 1998), *Sarfarosh* (Willing to sacrifice one's life for others; 1999), Lagaan (Land Tax; 2001), *Dil Chahta Hai* (The Heart Desires; 2001)

Shahrukh Khan (b. 1965)

Shahrukh Khan has been the top star of Hindi cinema since the mid-1990s, with some of the biggest blockbusters of the decade to his credit. He managed to gain a foothold in the Bombay industry without any family or social connections. During his schooling and college years in New Delhi, he was actively involved in theater. Khan made his debut on television in the late 1980s in the serial *Circus* and then gained fame with his portrayal of a young army officer in the serial, *Fauji* (Soldier). He was the first television actor to achieve such success in films. Khan's first screen role was in avant garde filmmaker, Mani Kaul's version of Dostoevsky's *Idiot* in 1991. His first leading role in a Hindi film was in *Raju Ban Gaya Gentleman* where he plays a small-towner who arrives in Bombay to achieve his dreams of being a rich and successful engineer. Khan's stardom came about from his extremely unconventional "negative" roles in *Baazigar* and *Darr* both released in 1993. In the former he plays a killer on the prowl seeking vengeance for his family's misfortune, and in the latter he plays a psychotic obsessed with another man's wife. After playing the villain in three films, Khan had a complete change of image in 1995 with the blockbuster *Dilwale Dulhaniya Le Jayenge* where he plays a lovable and romantic hero from England who goes to great lengths to win over his love's family. While Khan has played working-class characters (*Koyla*) and bumbling, comical ones (*Baadshah*, *Duplicate*), his major successes have been from his wealthy, sophisticated, cosmopolitan roles (*Dil to Pagal Hai*, *Kuch Kuch Hota Hai*, *Kabhie Khushi Kabhi Gham*). Khan started his own production company in 1999 – Dreamz Unlimited – with the actress Juhi Chawla, his co-star in many films, and the director Aziz Mirza. The trio produced three films between 1999 and 2003, of which, *Chalte Chalte*, starring Khan and directed by Mirza, became one of the biggest box-office hits of 2003. Though Khan has reduced his workload considerably and newer entrants into the industry are touted by the media as challenging his stardom and audience appeal, his films still make a significant impact at the box office and command the media spotlight. The 2002 remake of *Devdas* starring Khan – a film that has been made a number of times throughout the decades – was the most expensive Indian film made to date, the biggest box-office success of the year, and the first popular Indian film to premiere at the Cannes Film Festival.

Select filmography

Raju Ban Gaya Gentleman (Raju Has Become a Gentleman; 1992), *Baazigar* (Gambler; 1993), *Darr* (Fear; 1993), *Kabhi Haan Kabhi Na* (Sometimes Yes, Sometimes No; 1993), Dilwale Dulhaniya Le Jayenge (The One with a True Heart Will Win the Bride; 1995), *Karan Arjun* (1995), *Yes Boss* (1997), *Koyla* (Coal; 1997), *Pardes* (Foreign Land; 1997), *Dil to Pagal Hai* (The Heart Is Crazy; 1997), *Kuch Kuch Hota Hai* (Something Happens; 1998), *Duplicate* (1998), *Baadshah* (1999), *Mohabbatein* (Loves; 2000), *Phir Bhi Dil Hai Hindustani* (Yet the Heart Is Still Indian; 2000), *Kabhie Khushi Kabhi Gham* (Sometimes There's Happiness, Sometimes There's Sorrow; 2001), *Asoka* (2001), *Devdas* (2002), *Chalte Chalte* (Step by Step; 2003)

ACTRESSES

Note: Many actresses become known simply by their first names and are listed as such on-screen, as well as referred to in this manner by the film industry, the media, and audiences.

Nargis (1929–81)

Born in Allahabad, Uttar Pradesh, as Fatima A. Rashid, Nargis was introduced to films at the age of five by her mother – actress, singer, and filmmaker Jaddanbai. Nargis acted in five films as "Baby Rani," and then starred in her first leading role at the age of 14 in Mehboob Khan's *Taqdeer* (Luck). Although her first success came from her role as the ultra modern, Westernized woman in Mehboob Khan's *Andaz*, Nargis is best known for being Raj Kapoor's romantic lead in some of the most popular films of the late 1940s and 1950s. Kapoor used an image of Nargis swooning in his arms from *Barsaat* as the logo for his R.K. Films. After *Awara*, Nargis worked exclusively with Raj Kapoor and they acted in 15 films together until 1956. Their on-screen chemistry was said to be fueled by their off-screen romance, which has since become part of the legends and lore of the Bombay film industry.[11] The pinnacle of Nargis's career was her role in *Mother*

India where she plays the role of a strong-willed peasant woman who undergoes many physical, emotional, and financial hardships, but emerges with her dignity and honor intact. After her marriage in 1958 to actor Sunil Dutt who played her son in *Mother India*, Nargis retired from acting but remained an important public figure doing charity work with disabled children and becoming an appointed Member of Parliament (in the *Rajya Sabha* or Upper House). She was the recipient of many honors by the Indian as well as Soviet governments. She was the first film personality to receive a *Padma Shri*, a national honor bestowed by the Indian government on individuals for their achievements in a variety of fields. Shortly after seeing her son, Sanjay Dutt, make his screen debut in *Rocky* (1981), Nargis died of pancreatic cancer in 1981. In her memory, husband Sunil Dutt established the Nargis Dutt Memorial Foundation in New York City to help patients suffering from cancer in India be able to afford the necessary treatment. The public respect and regard for Nargis is apparent from the fact that a street is named after her in Bombay, and that in 1984 the Indian government, renamed their award for the Best Feature Film on National Integration – given to films which are perceived as bridging gaps between communities and helping in the process of nation building – the Nargis Dutt Award.

Select filmography

Aag (Fire; 1948), *Andaz* (Style; 1949), *Barsaat* (Rain; 1949), *Babul* (Father; 1950), *Jogan* (Female Ascetic; 1950), Awara (Vagabond; 1951), *Deedar* (Sight; 1951), *Anhonee* (Impossible Event; 1952), *Aah* (Sigh; 1953), *Shree 420* (Mr. 420; 1955), *Chori Chori* (Secretly; 1956), Mother India (1957), *Lajwanti* (1958), *Raat aur Din* (Night and Day; 1967)

Meena Kumari (1932–72)

Born in Bombay to performer parents – her father was a Parsi theater actor, singer, and music teacher, her mother a dancer – who fell upon hard times, Meena Kumari was introduced to films at the age of six in order to help support her family. Originally named Mahajabeen, she was renamed Baby Meena and cast in Vijay Bhatt's *Leatherface* (1939). She became the main earning member of her family and starred in a number of mythologicals in the late 1940s and early 1950s. Her first big hit was Bhatt's *Baiju Bawra* in 1952, where she was renamed Meena Kumari. During the 1950s, Kumari acted in both comedies (*Azad, Ilzaam, Miss Mary*) and dramas (*Daera, Parineeta, Ek hi Raasta*), but from 1960 onwards most of her roles were of a melancholic and despondent nature, earning her the nickname, "Tragedy Queen." Her main screen persona was shaped by films where she was unlucky in love (*Daera, Yahudi, Sahib Bibi aur Ghulam*) culminating in her most famous film, *Pakeezah*, in which she played a courtesan yearning for true love and a place in respectable society. Kumari's off-screen life extended her image as the lovelorn woman who drowns her sorrows in alcohol. Though her troubled marriage with filmmaker husband Kamaal Amrohi broke apart in 1964, the couple eventually completed *Pakeezah*, which they had jointly conceived and took 15 years to make. Within weeks of *Pakeezah*'s release, Kumari died of cirrhosis of the liver on March 31, 1972. Audiences flocked to see the film – her death confirming the martyr-like image that had become such a dominant feature of her reputation in her later years. She also wrote poems in Urdu under the pen-name Naaz.

Select filmography

Baiju Bawra (1952), *Daera* (Circle; 1953), *Parineeta* (Married Woman; 1953), *Azad* (Free; 1955), *Ek Hi Raasta* (Only One Path; 1956), *Sharda* (1957), *Miss Mary* (1957), *Yahudi* (Jew; 1958), *Dil Apna Preet Parayi* (The Heart Is Mine, but My Love Is Not; 1960), *Sahib Bibi aur Ghulam* (Master, Wife, and Slave; 1962), *Dil Ek Mandir* (The Heart Is a Temple; 1963), *Phool Aur Patthar* (Flower and Stone; 1966), *Mere Apne* (My Own; 1971), Pakeezah (The Pure One; 1971)

Waheeda Rehman (b. 1938)

Introduced to Hindi cinema by Guru Dutt, Waheeda Rehman is considered by the media and the contemporary film industry to be one of the most accomplished actresses and classic beauties from 1950s and 1960s Hindi cinema. Born in the southern city of Hyderabad, Rehman studied the classical dance form, *Bharatnatyam* and made her screen debut in a Telugu film in 1955. Her second Telugu film, *Rojulu Marayi*, released in the same year was a colossal hit, bringing her to Guru Dutt's attention. He cast her as a vamp in his production *CID*, which also launched the directorial career of his assistant, Raj Khosla. Rehman's skillful performance in the film led Dutt to give her one of the leading roles, that of the sympathetic, sensitive prostitute, in *Pyaasa*. The commercial success of *Pyaasa* resulted in many film offers for Rehman, and though she had an exclusive contract with Dutt, he allowed her to work in films by other producers. Dutt and Rehman's romance is another legendary love story within the film industry. However, they co-starred in only four more films (*Twelve O' Clock*, *Kaagaz ke Phool*, *Chaudhvin ka Chand*, *Sahib Bibi aur Ghulam*) as her successes elsewhere and his already being married led to the end of their professional and personal partnership. Ironically, their break-up was foreshadowed in *Kaagaz ke Phool* where Dutt plays a director and Rehman his discovery whose success leads to their estrangement. Rehman's other successful pairing was with Dev Anand – they starred in seven films together. She managed to combine both critical and commercial success throughout the 1960s, balancing conventional romantic roles with more somber ones. Although she appeared in many tearful dramas, Rehman's understated acting style steered her clear of melodramatic excess. Her most significant role was as Rosie in *Guide*, the dancer who walks out on her domineering and impotent husband to pursue her passion for dance and her love for a tour guide. The film also showcased her dancing abilities. After a series of critical successes and commercial failures, Rehman got married in 1974 to a businessman who had co-starred with her in *Shagun* (Blessing; 1964). She settled in Bangalore, raising a family as well as successfully marketing her own brand of breakfast cereal. Rehman continued to act selectively in Hindi films through the 1970s and 1980s, primarily with Amitabh Bachchan and for Yash Chopra.

Select filmography

CID (1956), Pyaasa (Thirsty One; 1957), *Kaagaz ke Phool* (Paper Flowers; 1959), *Chaudhvin ka Chand* (Full Moon; 1960), *Kala Bazaar* (Black Market; 1960), *Bees Saal Baad* (20 Years Later; 1962), *Sahib Bibi aur Ghulam* (Master, Wife and Slave; 1962), *Mujhe Jeene Do* (Let Me Live; 1963), Guide (1965), *Teesri Kasam* (Third Vow; 1966), *Ram aur Shyam* (Ram and Shyam; 1967), *Khamoshi* (Silence; 1969), *Reshma aur Shera* (Reshma and Shera; 1971), *Kabhi Kabhie* (Sometimes; 1976), *Trishul* (Trident; 1978), *Lamhe* (Moments; 1991)

Hema-Malini (b. 1948)

Born in Madras and trained in *Bharatnatyam*, Hema-Malini was the third major South Indian actress to achieve success in Hindi cinema.[12] She was regarded by the press and the film industry as the most popular actress of the 1970s due to her tremendous fan following and steady stream of box-office hits. After being ejected from a Tamil film in 1964, for apparently having no star appeal, Hema-Malini made her Hindi film debut in 1968 with Raj Kapoor in *Sapnon Ka Saudagar*. The sentence from the publicity posters for the film – "Watch the Dreamgirl seduce Raj Kapoor" – anticipated her success in the Bombay film industry where she became known as the "Dreamgirl," which also became the title of one of her films in 1977. That she received top billing in 1972 for her dual role in *Seeta aur Geeta* is evidence of her rapid rise to stardom and dominance within the film industry merely four years after her debut. The film where she played the roles of twin sisters separated at birth possessing diametrically opposite personalities – one meek and submissive, the other rambunctious and assertive – went on to become one of the biggest hits of the year. Although not considered a great actress by film critics, Hema-Malini is noteworthy for taking risks early in her career by playing a deglamorized widow in *Andaz* and a vengeful mistress in *Lal Patthar*. In a decade dominated by male-driven action/revenge stories, Hema-Malini acted in women-centered, small-budget dramas (*Kinara*, *Khushboo*, *Meera*) where she played deglamorized characters. She even produced the art-house film, *Swami*, directed by Basu Chatterjee in 1977. What is notable is that most of Hema-Malini's early commercial successes were not starring opposite either of the two superstars of the time, Rajesh Khanna or Amitabh Bachchan.[13] Her most successful pairing was with the actor, Dharmendra, with whom she made an astonishing 28 films – mostly crime thrillers and love stories, as well as the mega-hit, *Sholay*. Given her conservative, middle-class, South Indian upbringing, and a mother who never left her side on the sets, Hema-Malini surprised the film industry and the public when she disregarded social convention and became Dharmendra's second wife in 1980. That she faced no public outrage or scandal and continued to act after her marriage and motherhood is testament to how Hema-Malini has been able to control and manage her career and image quite successfully. By the late 1980s and early 1990s, she concentrated on character roles, frequently with feminist under-tones. She directed the film *Dil Aashna Hai* (The Heart Is the World) in 1991, but its failure at the box office led her to concentrate on directing television serials, editing a Hindi women's magazine, and renewing her dance career. She began to tour internationally in the 1990s with her dance troupe, staging elaborate *Bharatnatyam* dance dramas. In 2000, she received the *Padma Shri* from the Indian government and was also appointed the chair of the National Film Development Corporation. In addition to her NFDC duties, Hema-Malini is also busy assisting her daughter, Esha Deol's fledgling acting career, and has chosen to return to film acting – appearing opposite Amitabh Bachchan in 2003, after a gap of 19 years.

Select filmography

Sapnon ka Saudagar (Dream Merchant; 1968), *Johnny Mera Naam* (My Name Is Johnny; 1970), *Andaz* (Style; 1971), *Lal Patthar* (Red Stone; 1971), *Seeta aur Geeta* (Seeta and Geeta; 1972), *Amir Garib* (Rich-Poor; 1974), *Prem Nagar* (City of Love; 1974), *Khushboo* (Fragrance; 1975), Sholay (Flames; 1975), *Dream Girl* (1977), *Kinara* (Shore; 1977), *Swami* (Master; 1977), *Meera* (1979), *Naseeb* (Destiny; 1981), *Satte pe Satta* (Seven on Seven; 1981), *Razia Sultan* (1983), *Rihaee* (Release; 1988), *Lekin* (But; 1991), *Baghbaan* (Gardener; 2003)

Zeenat Aman (b. 1951)

Zeenat Aman is a former model and beauty queen who redefined the image of the heroine in Hindi cinema from a demure, virginal, ideal type to a bold, unabashed sex symbol. Born in Germany, and educated at a Catholic boarding school in Panchgani – a hill resort about 170 miles from Bombay – where she excelled academically, Aman won a scholarship when she was 17 to study in Los Angeles for a year. After her return, rather than finishing her college education, Aman started modelling. She entered beauty pageants and won the Miss Asia title before she landed a bit part in the film, *Hulchul* (Commotion; 1971). Although her father was a screenwriter, he did not play a part in her film career as her parents divorced when she was only one and her father died when she was 12 years old. Her first major role was in Dev Anand's *Hare Rama Hare Krishna* where she played the marijuana-smoking, commune-living, "hippie" sister of Anand, introducing the look of the Westernized, "liberated" young woman in Hindi cinema. Aman did not shy away from capitalizing on her sex appeal or from playing unconventional and potentially unsympathetic characters – a happy-go-lucky prostitute (*Manoranjan*), an adulteress who is trying to get rid of her husband (*Dhund*), an ambitious career woman wanting an abortion (*Ajnabee*), an opportunistic girlfriend who abandons her unemployed boyfriend for a millionaire (*Roti, Kapda aur Makaan*), a karate/kung-fu practicing gangster's moll (*Don*), and a courageous rape victim (*Insaaf ka Tarazu*). Despite roles which would have relegated her to the category of actresses playing vamps in earlier Hindi cinema, Aman became a major star and played the romantic lead opposite the top male stars of the 1970s and 1980s. Even in more typical love stories, she was able to challenge the moral codes that attempt to control female sexuality. Aman gained further notoriety with Raj Kapoor's *Satyam Shivam Sundaram* (1978) where she played the role of a partially disfigured village girl who falls in love with an engineer overseeing the construction of a dam in her area. The film attracted a great deal of press attention and public controversy due to Aman's scant clothing and kissing scenes. By the mid-1980s her career was faltering, and Aman retired from acting by the late 1980s to focus on her family. However, Aman has re-emerged in the media spotlight since 1999 by acting in select films, hosting a show on Indian television, and making her stage debut in a Hindi play in 2002.

Select filmography

Hare Rama Hare Krishna (Praise the Lord; 1971), *Dhund* (Fog; 1973), *Heera Panna* (1973), *Yaadon ki Baraat* (Procession of Memories; 1973), *Manoranjan* (Entertainment; 1974), *Ajnabee* (Stranger; 1974), *Roti Kapda aur Makaan* (Food, Clothing, Shelter; 1974), *Dharam Veer* (Righteous Warrior; 1977), *Don* (1978), *Satyam Shivam Sundaram* (Truth, God, Beauty; 1978), *Shalimar* (1979), *Dostana* (Friendship; 1980), *Insaaf ka Tarazu* (Scales of Justice; 1980), *Qurbani* (Sacrifice; 1980), *Lawaaris* (Bastard; 1981), *Bhopal Express* (1999), *Boom* (2003)

Rekha (b. 1954)

Rekha has the distinction of acting in more films as a heroine – over 100 films – than any other Hindi film actress. The daughter of South Indian film stars, Gemini Ganesan and Pushpavalli, Rekha began her film career as "Baby Bhanurekha" in a Telugu film in 1966 and debuted as the lead role in another Telugu film in 1970. After failing to make an impact with this film, Rekha moved to Bombay. Her family's troubled financial situation compelled her to quit school, and take a role in the Hindi film, *Anjana Safar* (Unknown Journey). On her very first day of shooting for the film, she was made to kiss the star. Though the shot was censored, it made it to the cover of *Life* magazine that year. Her first Hindi film released, however, was *Saawon Bhadon* in 1970, which was an enormous success and made Rekha an instant star. The industry was surprised by her success as her dark complexion, plump figure, and garish clothing contradicted the norms of beauty prevalent in the film industry and in society. Rekha continued to have hits throughout the 1970s, many of them starring opposite Amitabh Bachchan with whom she made nine films. By the late 1970s, Rekha, along with Zeenat Aman and Hema-Malini, was one of the actresses most sought after in the industry. She also began her physical transformation at this time – losing weight and focusing on her make-up, hair, and clothing – a transformation so complete that she became the epitome of beauty, glamour, and sophistication. She became a fitness and beauty guru similar to Jane Fonda, dispensing advice about diet, exercise, and cosmetics. Till today the media and younger actresses indulge in hyperbole and cliches – "the ugly duckling turned into a swan" – about Rekha's beauty and allure. Along with her physical makeover, Rekha transformed herself as an actress, taking on more challenging and substantive roles. While she played the typical romantic heroine whose world revolves around the hero in many of her earlier films, from 1978 onwards Rekha's roles became more diverse. She played a traumatised rape victim in *Ghar*, the spunky, chatterbox younger sister in *Khubsoorat*, the elegant other woman in *Silsila*, and an avenging wife in *Khoon Bhari Maang*. Her performance as the tragic courtesan in the period film set in the nineteenth century, *Umrao Jaan*, won her the National Award for Best Actress in 1981. Though newer actresses emerged on the scene from the late 1980s and early 1990s, Rekha continued to act, and was one of the few actresses to have a successful career into her late thirties. Since the mid-1990s she has moved into character and supporting roles which are often more substantial than the norm – a sign of the respect and adulation she commands in the film industry. The most well-known directors of the current Bombay film industry are working with Rekha, and her presence in a project generates a great deal of media attention. Rekha is frequently described by the press as Hindi cinema's ultimate diva.

Select filmography

Saawan Bhadon (Monsoon; 1970), *Namak Haram* (Traitor; 1973), *Do Anjaane* (Two Strangers; 1976), *Ghar* (Home; 1978), *Muqaddar ka Sikander* (Conqueror of Destiny; 1978), *Mr. Natwarlal* (1979), *Judaii* (Separation; 1980), *Khubsoorat* (Beautiful; 1980), *Kalyug* (Age of Sin; 1981), *Umrao Jaan* (1981), *Silsila* (Affair; 1981), *Utsav* (Festival; 1984), *Khoon Bhari Maang* (Blood-Filled Hair-parting; 1988), *Phool Bane Angaarey* (Flowers Become Embers; 1991), *Khiladiyon ka Khiladi* (Player Among Players; 1996), *Kama Sutra: A Tale of Love* (1996), *Aastha* (Faith; 1997), *Zubeidaa* (2001), *Lajja* (Modesty; 2001), *Bhoot* (Ghost; 2003), *Koi Mil Gaya* (Found Someone; 2003)

Madhuri Dixit (b. 1967)

Madhuri Dixit was the leading female star of the 1990s. Born in Ratnagiri, Maharashtra, into a middle-class family – her father is an engineer and her siblings are professionals settled in the U.S. – Dixit was studying biology at Parle college, when she was offered the chance to act in the Hindi film, *Abodh* (Innocent; 1984). Though the film failed commercially, Dixit received other film offers, and tasted success in 1988 with N. Chandra's *Tezaab* where she played the role of a dancer. The song she performed in the film, '*ek, do, teen*' (1-2-3), became a nation-wide hit. One of the keys to Dixit's initial success was her combination of middle-class, girl-next-door persona and a sensuality, expressed through her dances, which in the past had been relegated to the vamp in Hindi cinema. Her reputation culminated with the controversial song "*Choli ke peeche*" in Subhash Ghai's

Khalnayak. Although many of Dixit's early roles were those of a conventional romantic lead, she infused them with substance and character, thus making her presence felt in a film. While her dancing abilities could have easily relegated her to roles where she appeared in song sequences and not much else, her versatility as an actress – including roles from the comic to the dramatic, the rustic village belle to the urban sophisticate, and everything in between – led Dixit to receive more substantial roles than her peers. After the success of *Hum Aapke Hain Koun!*, Dixit was catapulted to mega-stardom and was regarded as the foremost female star by the media and became the highest-paid actress in the film industry. Even prior to her success in HAHK!, Dixit played strong characters such as the defiant daughter-in-law in *Beta*, a determined police woman in *Khalnayak*, and an avenging widow in *Anjaam*. Afterwards, her roles became even more central (*Raja*, *Prem Granth*, *Mrityudand*) and films were being conceptualized with her in mind – a privilege usually enjoyed by the male stars in the industry. Her popularity in South Asia is such that a popular joke circulating in India claims that Pakistanis have said "*Madhuri de do, Kashmir le lo*" (Give us Madhuri, and you can take Kashmir) alluding to the decades-long conflict between both countries over the region of Kashmir. Renowned contemporary Indian painter, M.F. Husain, is rumored to have seen HAHK 85 times and was inspired to do a whole series of paintings, as well as make a film, *Gaja Gamini*, about the essence of "Indian womanhood" featuring Dixit. Although Dixit married an Indian doctor living in the U.S. in 1999, she divided her time between Los Angeles and Bombay and continued to act in select Hindi films and even briefly hosted a television show in India in 2002. In 2003, Dixit gave birth to a son and moved to Colorado.

Select filmography

Tezaab (Acid; 1988), Parinda (Bird; 1989), *Ram Lakhan* (1989), *Dil* (Heart; 1990), *Kishan Kanhaiya* (1990), *Saajan* (Lover; 1991), *Beta* (Son; 1992), *Sangeeth* (Music; 1992), *Khel* (Game; 1992), Khalnayak (Villain; 1993), *Anjaam* (Consequence; 1994), Hum

Aapke Hain Koun (What Do I Mean to You? 1994), *Raja* (1995), *Prem Granth* (Book of Love; 1996), *Koyla* (Coal; 1997), *Dil to Pagal Hai* (The Heart is Crazy; 1997), *Mrityudand* (Death Sentence; 1997), *Gaja Gamini* (Gait as Graceful as an Elephant; 2000), *Pukar* (Call; 2000), *Lajja* (Modesty; 2001), *Devdas* (2002)

4

KEY FILMS OF POST-INDEPENDENCE HINDI CINEMA

As mentioned in chapter 1, popular Hindi cinema owes a great deal to Parsi theater in terms of its narrative structure, language, generic form, and visual style. Just as Parsi theater was an amalgam of dramatic forms, Hindi cinema is also a hybrid form, absorbing influences from mythology, folklore, literature, other Indian-language films, European cinema, and Hollywood. Before launching into a description of some of the significant films of post-independence Hindi cinema, this chapter will first introduce some of the key features of the narrative structure, generic form, and visual style of popular Hindi films so that readers can watch these films in a more informed and receptive manner.

NARRATIVE

Most popular Hindi films are melodramas[1] – a narrative form characterized by the sharp delineation of good and evil, the use of coincidence, an excess of emotion, and the privileging of moral conflicts over psychological ones. The leading characters in a film, as well as the actors who play them, are popularly referred to as the "hero," "heroine," and "villain." Hindi films present a moral universe, the disruption of which initiates the narrative action. The disruption can have taken place in a previous generation or be very subtle and communicated briefly, but restoring order or resolving the disruption is usually the goal of the narrative (Vasudevan 1989). Suspense is not key to keeping viewer interest. How or why something happens is more important than what or when (Vasudevan 1989). Hindi cinema's world is ruled primarily by the logic of kinship relations and plots are frequently driven by family conflicts (Vasudevan 1995).

The word "story" holds some very specific meanings within the Bombay film industry. According to screenwriters, a story has to do with narrative movement with high points and low points and most importantly, should take the characters out of their ordinary routine. Films chronicling a slice of life, or a day in the life of a character, would not be considered as having a story. Examples of what writers think are "good" stories are films which deal with multiple generations, family relationships, consequences of past actions, moral conflicts, and sacrifice – leading many films to have an epic quality. The mark of a good story is that it should completely involve the audience for the two and a half to three hours that comprise the average running time of a Hindi film (Ganti 2000).

Viewers new to Hindi films often comment upon their length – films usually have a running time of 165 minutes. Hindi films tend to be much longer than their Western counterparts because of the fragmented nature of the narrative and the inclusion of song sequences, comic episodes, and sub-plots. The films are presented in two halves, with an intermission referred to as the "interval" placed at a point of suspense or at a dramatic turn in the narrative. The absence of a straightforward linear narrative is a result of the myriad dramatic influences on Hindi cinema and its roots in older Indian theatrical and performance traditions.

Lalitha Gopalan (2002) characterizes popular Indian cinema as a "cinema of interruptions" where elements such as song sequences and the interval interrupt the narrative. Rather than thinking of these elements as extraneous, Gopalan argues that such "interruptions" are crucial in shaping the narrative structure and viewing pleasure associated with Hindi cinema. For example, the song sequences serve to distract the viewer and work as a device to delay the development of the plot. The interval is a crucial punctuating device, producing two opening and closing sequences and structuring narrative expectation, development, and resolution. Therefore, one of the distinctive features of popular Indian cinema is that it is structured around and celebrates spatial and temporal discontinuities (Gopalan 2002).

GENRE

A common term used by the film industry, the Indian media, and audiences to describe many popular Hindi films is "*masala*." A Hindi word meaning a blend of spices, *masala*, when applied to films, refers to those that contain a potpourri of elements – music, romance, action, comedy, and drama – designed to appeal to the broadest range of audiences. However, not all Hindi films are *masala* films. Though it is a term used for a specific kind of film, it has become the basis for the most common stereotype held by Western commentators and viewers unfamiliar with the form: that Hindi cinema lacks genres or that multiple genres are combined within a single film. These perceptions reveal a misunderstanding of the concept of genre and are founded upon notions that genre categories specific to American or European cinema are somehow universal, timeless, and absolute. Genres, however, result from a combination of film industry marketing strategies, audience expectations, film criticism, and academic analysis.

At its most basic level, genre refers to the systems of expectation and hypothesis that viewers have while watching a film. Stephen Neale, one of the foremost theorists of genre, explains,

> These systems provide spectators with means of recognition and under-
> standing. They help render films and the elements within them, intelligible,
> and therefore explicable. They offer a way of working out the significance
> of what is happening on the screen: a way of working out why particular
> events and actions are taking place, why the characters are dressed the
> way they are, why they look, speak and behave the way they do, and so on.
> ... These systems also offer grounds for further anticipation.... These
> systems involve a knowledge of various regimes of verisimilitude, various
> systems of plausibility, motivation, justification and belief.
>
> (Neale 1990: 46)

Hence, viewers who are unfamiliar with popular Indian cinema are frequently confused, perplexed, or frustrated by Hindi films mainly because they disrupt their systems of expectation and anticipation that have been developed from watching other sorts of films. Therefore, to someone who has never seen a Hindi film, a tough, street-wise hoodlum fighting violently in one scene and singing a love song in another may appear jarring and nonsensical, but to acculturated viewers, this is an expected feature of popular Hindi cinema. In fact, viewers would be surprised if the leading characters did not break out into song.

Thus genre is basically a way of categorizing and creating differences based on the expectation of the repetition of certain features. It is a relational rather than an absolute concept. For example, "Bollywood" can be regarded as a separate genre vis-à-vis Hollywood (or Indian "art cinema") since viewers expect certain aesthetic and narrative features to be present in the former that are not in the latter, and vice versa. However, within popular Hindi cinema, viewers will categorize films based on plots, themes, and narrative emphasis. They will differentiate between family films, gangster films, comedies, teenage love stories, lost and found stories, revenge dramas, etc. Stars and directors can also operate as genres in the sense that audiences expect different types of films from different directors and stars. Genre categories are also generated by filmmakers in their efforts to market films to distributors, the media, and audiences.

Genre, therefore, is a dynamic concept that accounts for historical and cultural specificity. Different filmmaking cultures and different historical periods will generate their own specific genres. Indian cinema has its own particular genres such as the mythological, devotional, reincarnation, dacoit, lost and found, as well as its own renditions of global genres like the action film, gangster film, and romantic comedy. Though nearly all popular Indian films contain songs, the category of "musical" is only used by Bombay filmmakers to refer to films that are specifically about music, musicians, or musical performance. From the perspective of Hindi film audiences, "musical" is an irrelevant genre category as it does not meaningfully differentiate between films.

VISUAL STYLE

Popular Indian cinema is very open and comfortable with the artifice that is at the heart of feature filmmaking. The visual style of popular Hindi films departs from continuity editing, naturalistic lighting, and realist mise-en-scene conventions typical of Hollywood. Hindi filmmakers are not overly concerned with realism even though a realist aesthetic is prized and valued as a higher form of filmmaking by the state, media, and many filmmakers. Unlike Hollywood films which go to a great deal of effort through their production design, editing, lighting, and camera practices to hide the fact that they are films, a Hindi film does not pretend that it is presenting an unmediated view of reality. Bombay filmmakers do not go to the same lengths as their Hollywood counterparts to hide the process of filmmaking. An example of how the two industries approach shooting on location should convey this difference. When an American film is shot in New York City on the street, spectators are shooed away or herded behind barricades completely out of the camera's field of vision because the goal is to show a "typical" street scene where people are walking along and not standing and watching a film being made. When a Hindi film is shot in a similar public situation, spectators are frequently incorporated into the background as long as they are not disturbing the production process. It is very common when watching a Hindi film to see curious bystanders onscreen watching the same action – a reminder that the scene was filmed in front of people. If the scene is shot in India, it is not uncommon to see a huge crowd in the background of the frame observing the sequence; sometimes during a song sequence, the spectators onscreen form a large circle around the actors.

The editing, lighting, art direction, and cinematography in popular Hindi films highlight the constructed, artificial nature of filmmaking. Hollywood films primarily follow the system of continuity editing, which is a pattern of cutting that strives for continuous and clear narrative action. It relies upon matching screen direction, screen position, and temporal relations from shot to shot. Continuity editing focuses on maintaining the 180-degree axis of action, which dictates that the camera should stay on one side of the action to ensure consistent spatial relations between objects to the right and left of the frame (Bordwell and Thompson 1993).[2] The central philosophy underlying continuity editing is that films should be edited in a manner that makes them appear seamless and unedited. Viewers should not notice the editing as the process should not call attention to itself.

Popular Hindi films follow the rules of continuity editing unsystematically and often combine them with other visual modes. Editing practices are most notable in song and action sequences, but dialogue scenes are not immune from changes in screen direction and camera placement that break the rules of continuity editing. Maintaining the 180-degree axis of action is not a major concern. Song sequences frequently display an utter disregard for rules of time and space. Many songs just begin with the characters instantly transported to a picturesque European locale. Song sequences are edited in such a manner that characters appear in a quick succession of costume changes from one location to another. During the course of a five- to seven-minute song, characters who are living in Bombay may be shown frolicking about in Swiss meadows, dancing in front of the Egyptian Pyramids, running along a Mauritian beach, and walking through an American mall.

Other features of popular Hindi cinema's visual style include the use of rapid camera movements such as zooms and pans for dramatic impact or to display heightened emotion. Sets are frequently grandiose and opulent and the emphasis of art direction is on larger-than-life spectacle. Hindi films are usually marked by bright lighting and richly saturated colors, which also serve a functional purpose. Without such brightness and saturation, films would be barely visible in smaller towns with poor projection equipment and dingy screens or rural areas where films may be projected on a bare wall or a sheet. Thus, one aspect of the visual style of popular Hindi cinema is a consequence of accommodating the diversity of viewing conditions within India.

The roots of Hindi cinema's visual style lie in a variety of popular visual art forms and practices from the nineteenth century such as Company School paintings – art made for British clients and Indian aristocracy, woodcut printmaking, cheaply produced watercolors, and mass-produced lithographs and oleographs. Scholars have described the aesthetic common to these various forms as "frontal" because of the disregard for the laws of perspective and a stylistic emphasis on the surface (Vasudevan 1990). This aesthetic of frontality was transposed on to new technologies such as photography, which in turn influenced early cinema. When photography was first introduced in 1840, Indians did not follow the standard "rules" of balance or symmetry practiced by European photographers. Instead, they took photos which were characterized by the use of flat planes, the elimination of middle distances, the absence of perspective, and the lack of a point of entry into the photograph. Items were frequently stuck directly on to the photograph, creating a collage effect. Scholars have characterized the viewer's experience of such photographs as a "frontal encounter" where a viewer's confrontation with the subject of the photograph is immediate and not shaped by depth or laws of perspective (Rajadhyaksha 1986).

In early Indian cinema, this frontal aesthetic is noticeable in the flat, tableau-like presentation of certain scenes where the characters are arrayed facing the camera as if performing for a live audience, or in the case of mythological films, as if in the presence of devotees or worshippers. Scholars have argued that this particular frontal aesthetic made the experience of early cinema less alienating and jarring as it allowed viewers to experience the new technology in familiar terms (Rajadhyaksha 1986). In contemporary Hindi cinema, the frontal aesthetic is still discernible in song sequences, but it is combined with other visual modes such as rapid editing and fluid camera movement, resulting in a hybrid visual style.

KEY FILMS

Note: The first two films, though from an earlier period, are included in this list as they have exerted a significant influence on post-independence Hindi cinema. Unless indicated as black and white (b&w), the films described are in color. Sources for this section include the *Encyclopaedia of Indian Cinema* (Rajadhyaksha and Willemen 1999).

Devdas (1935) b&w

Production Company: New Theatres; Director/Screenplay: P.C. Barua; Story: Saratchandra Chattopadhyay; Music: Rai Chand Boral, Pankaj Mullick; Lyrics: Kidar Sharma; Starring: K.L. Saigal, Jamuna, Rajkumari.

Based on the 1917 Bengali novel by Saratchandra Chattopadhyay, the film narrates the story of Devdas who falls in love with his childhood sweetheart, Paro, but is not allowed by his family to marry her because of the vast class differences between them. Devdas is the son of a wealthy landholder while Paro is the daughter of a much poorer neighbor. Unable to stand up to his family and heartbroken over Paro's marriage to a wealthy widower, Devdas escapes to Calcutta where he drowns his sorrows in alcohol in the presence of Chandramukhi, a dancing girl/prostitute, who falls in love with him. Her love is unrequited as Devdas cannot forget Paro. Overcome by his alcoholism and despair, Devdas eventually dies on Paro's doorstep.

A huge commercial success, the story of *Devdas* has been a favorite of Indian filmmakers; it was made as a silent film in 1928, remade in Hindi in 1955 and 2002, and made in a number of other Indian languages as well. The film introduced the figure of the tragic romantic hero into Hindi cinema and the term "Devdas" entered everyday parlance to refer to men pining for or melancholic about love.

Kismet (Fate; 1943) b&w

Production Company: Bombay Talkies; Director/Screenplay: Gyan Mukherjee; Story: P.L. Santoshi, Shaheed Latif; Music: Anil Biswas; Lyrics: Pradeep; Starring: Ashok Kumar, Mumtaz Shanti, Shah Nawaz, Moti, P.F. Pithawala.

Perhaps one of the earliest examples of the "lost and found" genre, *Kismet* is about a pickpocket, Shekhar, who is in love with a disabled singer, Rani. Rani works in a theater once owned by her father, but now owned by the villain Indrajit. Shekhar steals a valuable necklace belonging to Indrajit's wife, and when Rani unknowingly wears the necklace, she is arrested. Shekhar confesses to save Rani, but then escapes from the police after his arrest. Shekhar decides to burgle Indrajit's home to obtain the money needed to cure Rani's disability, but is caught once again. At this moment, it is revealed that Shekhar is Indrajit's long-lost son and the film ends happily with Shekhar reunited with his family and Rani accepted into their fold. The film was a major hit – running for three years consecutively in the same theater in Calcutta – influencing subsequent portrayals of heroes as romantic outlaws. The success of the film also generated a moral panic where the press criticized the film for glorifying crime and being a negative influence on youth.

Awara (Vagabond; 1951) b&w

Production Company: R.K. Films; Producer/Director: Raj Kapoor; Story: K.A. Abbas, V.P. Sathe; Screenplay: K.A. Abbas; Music: Shankar-Jaikishen; Lyrics: Hasrat Jaipuri, Shailendra; Starring: Raj Kapoor, Nargis, Prithviraj Kapoor, Leela Chitnis, K.N. Singh.

Essentially a discussion of nature vs nurture, *Awara* tells the story of Judge Raghunath's son Raju who grows up on the streets of Bombay since his father threw his pregnant mother out on the unfounded suspicion that she was unfaithful. Raju takes to a life of crime to support his poor, ailing mother and becomes a part of

FIGURE 4.1 **Raj Kapoor and Nargis in** *Awara*
Hyphen Films Collection, Courtesy R.K. Films

Jagga's gang. Raghunath had once convicted Jagga of a crime he did not commit because Jagga's father and grandfather were bandits, and "the son of a thief will always be a thief." Jagga sets out to disprove Raghunath's belief in hereditary status – "the son of a respectable man will always be respectable" – by turning Raju into a thief. Raju finally decides to change his criminal ways because of his love for his childhood sweetheart, Rita, now a lawyer. When Raju discovers the truth about Jagga and the circumstances around his mother's abandonment, he kills him and also tries to kill his father. The film unfolds in a flashback at Raju's trial with Rita as his defense lawyer and Raghunath initially ignorant of his relationship with the defendant. One of the musical and dramatic highlights of *Awara* is a nine-minute dream sequence that took three months to film. One of Hindi cinema's first global hits, *Awara* has had an enduring legacy on Hindi cinema in terms of its themes, characterizations, and moral conflicts.

CID (1956) b&w

Production Company: Guru Dutt Films; Director: Raj Khosla; Story/Screenplay: Inder Raj Anand; Music: O.P. Nayyar; Lyrics: Majrooh Sultanpuri, Jan Nissar Akhtar; Starring: Dev Anand, Shakila, Waheeda Rehman, Johnny Walker, K.N. Singh.

A hugely successful crime thriller with hit musical numbers, the film follows Bombay police inspector Shekhar's investigation of a newspaper editor's murder. During his investigation, Shekhar keeps running into a mysterious woman who tries to bribe him into releasing a prisoner. When the same prisoner is inexplicably killed in jail, Shekhar is accused of police brutality. He goes on the run, pursued by both the police and the murderer he was investigating. Shekhar eventually solves the case in the hospital. In addition to setting a trend for later films of this genre, *CID* is remembered for the spectacular debut of actress Waheeda Rehman (see chapter 3) who played the mysterious woman trying to entrap Shekhar.

FIGURE 4.2 Nargis in *Mother India*
Hyphen Films Collection, Courtesy Mehboob Productions Pvt. Ltd

Mother India (1957)

Production Company: Mehboob Productions; Producer/Director/ Story/Screenplay: Mehboob Khan; Music: Naushad; Lyrics; Shakeel Badayuni; Starring: Nargis, Raaj Kumar, Sunil Dutt, Rajendra Kumar, Kanhaiyalal.

Nominated for an Oscar and reputedly showing somewhere in India at any given time, *Mother India* has achieved a legendary status within Indian cinema akin to *Gone with the Wind* in American cinema. It narrates the story of Radha, a poor peasant woman, who has to raise two sons on her own after her husband whose arms were crushed in a farming accident abandons them. Though the lecherous moneylender is willing to absolve her debts if she becomes his mistress, Radha steadfastly maintains her virtue and dignity despite her abject poverty. Surviving drought, floods, and hunger, Radha manages to till her land and raise her sons into strapping young men. The village enters a prosperous phase in Radha's old age, but trouble keeps erupting in the form of her younger rebellious son, Birju, who cannot forget the moneylender's insult to his mother. Birju turns to a life of banditry and when attempting to kidnap the moneylender's daughter on her wedding day is shot dead by Radha. The film's plot and characters have had a lasting impact on Hindi cinema, providing a template for future films including *Gunga Jumna* and *Deewar*. The character of Birju can be seen as a precursor to the "angry young man" that emerged in Hindi cinema in the 1970s.

Pyaasa (Thirsty One; 1957) b&w

Production Company: Guru Dutt Films; Producer/Director: Guru Dutt; Story: Saratchandra Chattopadhyay; Screenplay: Abrar Alvi;

FIGURE 4.3 Guru Dutt in *Pyaasa*
Hyphen Films Collection, Courtesy Guru Dutt Films Pvt. Ltd

Music: S.D. Burman; Lyrics: Sahir Ludhianvi; Starring: Guru Dutt, Waheeda Rehman, Mala Sinha, Rehman, Johnny Walker.

Inspired by Saratchandra's novel *Srikanta*, *Pyaasa* examines the plight of the artist in a crassly commercial and insensitive world. Vijay is an unappreciated poet in Calcutta whose poems are sold by his brothers as waste paper. His college sweetheart marries an arrogant publisher for the comfort and security his wealth can offer. Unable to bear his family's disrespect for his poetry, Vijay chooses to live on the streets where a young prostitute, Gulab, falls in love with him. After a dead beggar wearing Vijay's coat is mistaken for him, Gulab uses her earnings to get Vijay's poetry published into a book. The book becomes a best seller and all those who had previously rejected Vijay gather to pay tribute to the dead poet. To the organizers' consternation, Vijay disrupts the event with a passionate song denouncing hypocrisy and calling for the violent destruction of a corrupt world. Not wanting to be a part of an opportunistic and materialistic world, Vijay leaves the city, walking off into the distance with Gulab at his side. Despite its dark and critical tone, the film was a box-office success as its bleakness was balanced by comic asides, popular songs, and rich cinematography.

Madhumati (1958) b&w

Production Company: Bimal Roy Productions; Producer/Director: Bimal Roy; Story/Screenplay: Ritwik Ghatak; Music: Salil Choudhury; Lyrics: Shailendra; Starring: Dilip Kumar, Vyjayanthimala, Johnny Walker, Pran.

One of the most famous examples of the reincarnation genre with its lead actors playing "double roles," (a term used when an actor plays two separate characters) *Madhumati* relates the love story of Anand, a plantation foreman, and Madhumati, a beautiful tribal woman from the nearby village. Their story unfolds in a flashback on a dark and stormy night when Devendra takes shelter in a deserted house and thinks he hears a woman crying. Wandering through the

FIGURE 4.4 Dilip Kumar and Vyjayanthimala in *Madhumati*
Hyphen Films Collection, Courtesy Bimal Roy Productions

house, he discovers a painting of the house's former owner, Raja Ugranarayan, which Devendra feels he had painted in a previous life as Anand. It is discovered that Madhumati had died escaping from the Raja's lecherous clutches and a plan is devised with Madhavi, who looks like the dead Madhumati and could be her reincarnation, to trap the Raja into confessing his crimes. The plot twist at the end adds to the sense of poetic justice. The film was a huge box-office success, and its songs have remained popular till today.

Mughal-e-azam (The Age of Mughals; 1960) b&w

Production Company: Sterling Investment Corporation; Producer/ Director: K. Asif; Screenplay: K. Asif, Aman; Music: Naushad; Lyrics: Shakeel Badayuni; Starring: Prithviraj Kapoor, Durga Khote, Dilip Kumar, Madhubala, Nigar Sultana, Ajit.

FIGURE 4.5 **Queen for a night** *Mughal-e-azam*
Hyphen Films Collection, Courtesy K. Asif Productions

The most expensive film of the time, which took 10 years to make, *Mughal-e-azam* is a grand historical epic set in the time of the Mughal emperor Akbar (1555–1605). The story, adapted from a play and rooted more in legend than in fact, revolves around Akbar's son, Prince Salim, and his romance with the beautiful court dancer, Anarkali. Furious that his son wants to make a commoner his queen and is ignoring his parent's entreaties, a frustrated Akbar wages and wins a war against Salim. Akbar orders Anarkali's execution, but as her dying wish she is allowed to spend one night with Salim as his queen. Unlike the original legend where Anarkali is walled in alive, the film shows Akbar sparing Anarkali's life without Salim's know-ledge. The most famous and stunning sequence of the film is Anarkali's dance performance in the palace of mirrors. This sequence, which was shot in color, is a cinematographic feat with the dancing Anarkali captured in the hundreds of fragmented mirrors covering the entire ceiling and walls of the set. The film is also remembered for its dialogues, its music, its scenes of confrontation between Akbar and Salim played by actors Prithviraj Kapoor and Dilip Kumar, and for actress Madhubala's performance.

Gunga-Jumna (1961)

Production Company: Citizens Films; Producer/Story/Screenplay: Dilip Kumar; Director: Nitin Bose; Music: Naushad; Lyrics: Shakeel Badayuni; Starring: Dilip Kumar, Vyjayanthimala, Nasir Khan, Anwar Hussain.

Notable for its use of the Bhojpuri dialect and its rustic setting, the film is about two brothers, Gunga and Jumna, growing up in a village controlled by an evil landlord. When Gunga is framed by the landlord for a crime he did not commit, he escapes to the mountains with his girfriend, Dhanno, and joins a band of dacoits (bandits). His younger brother, Jumna, is sent to the city for his education and becomes a police officer. Years later, when Gunga is about to become a father, he decides to return to the village to ask for forgiveness. However, Jumna wants him to surrender to the police for his crimes and when Gunga refuses and tries to leave, Jumna shoots him dead. Gunga's death is rendered more poignant by the fact that it was his money that paid for Jumna's education and allowed him to become a policeman. While *Gunga-Jumna*'s most immediate successor is *Deewar*, the story of two brothers (or father and son) on opposite sides of the law became a dominant narrative motif in Hindi cinema from the 1970s onward.

Guide (1965)

Production Company: Navketan Films; Director/Screenplay: Vijay Anand; Story: R.K. Narayan; Music: S.D. Burman; Lyrics: Shailendra; Starring: Dev Anand, Waheeda Rehman, Leela Chitnis, Kishore Sahu.

Adapted from an English novel of the same name, *Guide* is the story of a fast-talking, clever, opportunistic tour guide, Raju, and two

FIGURE 4.6 **Waheeda Rehman** in *Guide*
Hyphen Films Collection, Courtesy Navketan Films

distinct phases of his life. The first phase involves his relationship
with Rosie, a dancer, whom he seduces away from her cold, inat-
tentive, archaeologist husband. Raju helps Rosie to achieve her dream
of becoming a successful dancer and manages to become wealthy
himself by managing her career. Their relationship ends when Raju
is jailed for forging Rosie's signature on a check. After his release,
Raju becomes a wanderer and is mistaken for a holy man. Having
gained the trust of the villagers who had been providing him with
food and supplies where he had been staying, Raju has no choice but
to demonstrate his holy status during a drought by fasting for rain.
Though the rain arrives after 12 days, confirming Raju's status in the
eyes of the villagers, he dies of starvation. The film was a commercial success with major musical hits. A significantly altered, shorter,
two-hour English version directed by Tad Danielewski and co-
scripted by Danielewski and Pearl S. Buck was released in the U.S. in
the same year.

Aradhana (Worship; 1969)

Production Company: Shakti Films; Producer/Director: Shakti Samanta; Story/Screenplay: Sachin Bhaumick; Music: S.D. Burman; Lyrics: Anand Bakshi; Starring: Rajesh Khanna, Sharmila Tagore, Farida Jalal.

The film that made Rajesh Khanna (see chapter 3) into the superstar of his time, *Aradhana* is the love story of Vandana and Arun, an Air Force officer. The two get married secretly, but before they are able to notify their families, Arun dies in a plane crash. Arun's family rejects the now-pregnant Vandana as his legal wife. So that her son, Suraj, will not be considered a bastard, Vandana gives him up for adoption, but is involved in his upbringing by becoming his nanny. One day in the process of rescuing Vandana from the clutches of his lecherous adoptive uncle, Suraj accidentally kills him. To protect Suraj, Vandana takes responsibility for the killing and is sent to prison. Years later when Vandana is released from jail, she meets Suraj who has now become the spitting image of his father (also played by Khanna) and is also an Air Force pilot. By the end of the film, Suraj learns the truth about his identity, and mother and son are finally reunited. The film's music has remained incredibly popular and has been a fertile source for re-mixes.

Anand (1970)

Production Company: Rupam Chitra; Director/Story: Hrishikesh Mukherjee; Screenplay: Hrishikesh Mukherjee, Gulzar, Bimal Dutt, Yogesh Mukherjee; Music: Salil Choudhury; Lyrics: Gulzar, Yogesh; Starring: Rajesh Khanna, Amitabh Bachchan, Sumita Sanyal.

An immensely successful film about a man suffering from intestinal cancer, *Anand* popularized the genre of films where the protagonist suffers from a terminal illness. The film focuses on Anand and his friendship with Dr. Bhaskar who subsequently writes a book about him which wins a literary prize. Anand's story is narrated in flashback at the award ceremony. Communicating that life should be

FIGURE 4.7 **Amitabh Bachchan and Rajesh Khanna in** *Anand*
Hyphen Films Collection, Courtesy N.C. Sippy

grand rather than long, Anand confronts his impending death with good humor. His levity is contrasted with Bhaskar's more somber persona. Anand's cheerful disposition, sense of humor, and zest for life uplift the spirits of everyone around him. The reigning superstar Rajesh Khanna who played the title role won the Filmfare Award for Best Actor, while the newly discovered Amitabh Bachchan (see chapter 3) won the Best Supporting Actor Award in his role as Bhaskar. The film's music also contributed to its popularity.

Pakeezah (The Pure One; 1971)

Production Company: Mahal Pictures; Producer/Director/Story/ Screenplay: Kamal Amrohi; Music: Ghulam Mohammed, Naushad; Lyrics: Kamal Amrohi, Kaifi Bhopali, Majrooh Sultanpuri, Kaifi Azmi; Starring: Ashok Kumar, Meena Kumari, Raaj Kumar.

FIGURE 4.8 **Meena Kumari** in *Pakeezah*
Hyphen Films Collection, Courtesy Mahal Pictures

Set in turn-of-the-century Lucknow (Uttar Pradesh), the film depicts the desire of courtesans to escape their profession and find a place in respectable society. Nargis, after having been rejected by her husband's family, dies giving birth to their daughter Sahibjaan. Sahibjaan is brought up as a courtesan by her aunt who keeps her identity and existence a secret from her father, Shahabuddin. One day Sahibjaan falls in love with a mysterious stranger, Salim, who turns out to be her father's nephew. Salim's father forbids him to marry Sahibjaan, but he defiantly leaves with Sahibjaan and marries her even after she has revealed her profession. However, convinced that she is not worthy of his love, Sahibjaan leaves Salim. The film's climactic moments occur when Salim asks Sahibjaan to perform at his arranged wedding and his uncle, Shahabuddin, discovers her identity. He claims Sahibjaan as his daughter and she and Salim are married with the family's blessings. The climax where Sahibjaan dances barefoot on broken glass is referenced and recreated in a different context in the later film *Sholay*. *Pakeezah* had many famous songs which have been enduringly popular. The film took an inordinate amount of time to make it to the screen. It was launched in 1956 and started production in 1964, but was halted soon after when the star of the film, Meena Kumari, and her husband, the director, separated. Some years later, Kumari, who was suffering from alcoholism, agreed to complete the film. It was released on February 4, 1972, and after Kumari died on March 31, the film went on to become a big hit.

Bobby (1973)

Production Company: R.K. Films; Producer/Director: Raj Kapoor; Story: K.A. Abbas; Screenplay: K.A. Abbas, V.P. Sathe; Music: Laxmikant-Pyarelal; Lyrics: Anand Bakshi, Vithalbhai Patel, Inderjit Singh Tulsi; Starring: Rishi Kapoor, Dimple Kapadia, Pran, Prem Nath, Durga Khote, Prem Chopra.

An enormously successful film which established the genre of teenage love stories in Hindi cinema, *Bobby* also resurrected Raj Kapoor's career as a director. Raj, the neglected 18-year-old son of a wealthy Hindu businessman, falls in love with Bobby, the 16-year-old daughter of a prosperous but unrefined Catholic fisherman. Raj's family is unwilling to accept Bobby due to differences in class status. After many ordeals including one where Bobby is kidnapped, the families relent and the young lovers are united. *Bobby* marked the debut of Raj Kapoor's son, Rishi, as a leading man and of the young Dimple Kapadia who became a national sensation afterward. The film includes a recreation of Raj Kapoor's frequently recounted famous first meeting with the actress, Nargis: Raj's first glimpse of Bobby is when she answers the front door with flour on her hands, which she absentmindedly smears across her forehead. *Bobby*'s music also played a significant role in its commercial success.

FIGURE 4.9 **Dimple Kapadia and Prem Nath in** *Bobby*
Hyphen Films Collection, Courtesy R.K. Films

Deewar (Wall; 1975)

Production Company: Trimurti Films; Producer: Gulshan Rai; Director: Yash Chopra; Story/Screenplay: Salim Khan, Javed Akhtar; Music: R.D. Burman; Lyrics: Sahir Ludhianvi; Starring: Amitabh Bachchan, Shashi Kapoor, Nirupa Roy, Parveen Babi, Neetu Singh, Iftikhar.

The story of two brothers on opposite sides of the law, *Deewar* played a significant role in cementing Amitabh Bachchan's stardom and persona as an "angry young man." Bachchan's character, Vijay, is said to be partly modeled after the notorious Bombay smuggler, Haji Mastan Mirza. The film is narrated in one long flashback beginning with the brothers' childhood when their union leader father is blackmailed into breaking a strike and foregoing worker demands. Vijay's father, unable to bear the shame, abandons his family. Furious at their betrayal, some angry workers tatoo "My father is a thief" on Vijay's forearm. Vijay, his mother, and younger brother, Ravi, migrate to Bombay and struggle to survive. Vijay sacrifices his own education for the sake of his younger brother, working at many menial jobs to help pay for his brother's schooling. The two brothers grow up into very distinct personalities – Vijay, an intense, brooding dockworker whose tatoo is a constant reminder of his family's humiliation, eventually becomes the leader of a gang of smugglers; Ravi, a cheerful, clean-cut, college graduate, becomes a police officer. Ravi and his mother choose to live separately from Vijay once they learn the reality of his business. The "wall" of the title refers to the social and moral wall that has arisen between the two brothers. When Vijay decides to leave his life of crime, rival gang members murder his pregnant girlfriend and he loses control and goes on the rampage. On the run from the police, Vijay is shot by his brother and eventually dies in his mother's arms. A huge hit, *Deewar* is one of the few films in this list where music was not key to its success; With only three songs, the film is most remembered for its dialogues, action sequences, and Bachchan's performance.

Sholay (Flames; 1975)

Production Company: Sippy Films; Producer: G.P. Sippy; Director: Ramesh Sippy; Story/Screenplay: Salim Khan, Javed Akhtar; Music: R.D. Burman; Lyrics: Anand Bakshi; Starring: Amitabh Bachchan, Dharmendra, Sanjeev Kumar, Hema Malini, Jaya Bhaduri, Amjad Khan.

The phenomenally successful *Sholay* centers on the desire of a retired police inspector Thakur Baldev Singh, to wreak revenge on the dreaded bandit Gabbar Singh for massacring his family. Thakur hires two adventurous crooks – Veeru and Jai – whom he had once caught and imprisoned, to hunt down Gabbar Singh whose men periodically raid Thakur's village for grain and other supplies. Veeru and Jai are successful in protecting the village from the bandits and in the end capture Gabbar, but at the expense of Jai's life. The film is characterized by alternating sequences of drama, comedy, and action. *Sholay*, which ran for five consecutive years in Bombay and continues to be re-released to full houses, was the first Indian film produced in 70mm with stereophonic sound. It is significant not only for its tremendous commercial success, but also for its myth-ical status in the Bombay industry and among audiences as the pinnacle of filmmaking. Aside from ushering in a new era of film-making emphasizing action and violence, *Sholay*'s influence can still be felt today as its characters and dialogues are referenced and/or parodied in films and advertising. In fact, the film's dialogues became so popular – with audiences seeing the film repeatedly – that a cassette of dialogues was released, separate from the music. The experience of watching *Sholay* even today is marked by a high amount of viewer participation – people anticipating and reciting the dialogues with the characters on-screen.

Amar Akbar Anthony (1977)

Production Company: MKD Films; Producer/Director: Manmohan Desai; Story: Mrs. J.M. Desai; Screenplay: Prayag Raj; Music:

FIGURE 4.10 **Amitabh Bachchan as Anthony Gonsalves in** *Amar Akbar Anthony*
Hyphen Films Collection, Courtesy MKD Films

Laxmikant-Pyarelal; Lyrics: Anand Bakshi; Starring: Amitabh Bachchan, Vinod Khanna, Rishi Kapoor, Pran, Nirupa Roy, Parveen Babi, Shabana Azmi, Neetu Singh, Jeevan.

An exuberant example of the lost and found genre, the film narrates the story of how a poor driver named Kishenlal, his wife, and three young sons are separated due to a combination of fate and villainy. Each of the sons is found and raised by men of three different religions. Amar, the eldest, is brought up by a Hindu policeman; Akbar, the youngest, is raised by a Muslim tailor; and Anthony, the middle son, is looked after by a Catholic priest. The years pass, the brothers meet each other, become friends without realizing their true identities, and fall in love with women from their respective adoptive religions. Another series of events takes place which sets into motion the eventual unification of the family. Though a "multi-starrer," *Amar Akbar Anthony* is dominated by

Amitabh Bachchan who as the fast-talking, wise-cracking, comical Anthony plays a character very different from his dominant screen image at the time. The film was enormously successful and though heavily criticized at the time for its convoluted story, heavy reliance on coincidences, and many implausible moments, it is now considered a classic. Many of the younger members of the Bombay film industry list the film as among their all-time favorites.

Arth (Meaning; 1982)

Production Company: Anu Arts; Director/Story: Mahesh Bhatt; Screenplay: Mahesh Bhatt, Sujit Sen; Music: Jagjit and Chitra Singh; Lyrics: Kaifi Azmi; Starring: Shabana Azmi, Smita Patil, Kulbushan Kharbanda, Raj Kiran.

Arth is a film which explores the complexity of marital and extra-marital relationships. Inder Malhotra, an ambitious filmmaker, is married to Pooja but is having an affair with Kavita, a successful, but mentally unstable actress. When Pooja learns of the affair, she leaves Inder and manages after some difficulty to begin life anew. Kavita, suffering from schizophrenia, eventually leaves Inder who then tries to reconcile with Pooja, but is rejected. Even though Pooja has an ardent admirer, Raj, who wants to marry her, she decides that she is content to be single. The film garnered a great deal of publicity from gossip that it was autobiographical and from rumors about the rivalry between the two lead actresses. Although distributors were unwilling to purchase the film initially, *Arth* went on to become a critical and commercial success and made Bhatt into a director of standing in the film industry.

Parinda (Bird; 1989)

Production Company: Vidhu Vinod Chopra Films; Producer/Director/Story: Vidhu Vinod Chopra; Screenplay: Shivkumar; Music: R.D. Burman; Lyrics: Khursheed Hallauri; Starring: Anil Kapoor, Jackie Shroff, Nana Patekar, Anupam Kher, Madhuri Dixit.

FIGURE 4.11 **Anil Kapoor and Jackie Shroff as brothers in** *Parinda*
Courtesy Vinod Chopra Productions

Parinda is a gangster film that revisits the familiar trope of two brothers on different sides of the law. Kishen, the elder brother is involved in a life of crime to finance his younger brother Karan's education in the U.S. After his return, Karan witnesses the murder of his friend, Prakash, a policeman. Karan's desire to avenge his friend's death takes him into Bombay's criminal underworld where he discovers the truth about his brother's life. The film is notable for its shocking ending which deviates from the norms of popular cinema. Though not a commercial success, *Parinda* was a great critical success, winning multiple awards including the Filmfare and National Award for Best Film. Nana Patekar who played the ganglord, Anna, became a major star with this film. *Parinda*'s cinematography, editing, background music, characterizations, and narrative style influenced later films in the genre. A graduate of the Film and Television Institute of India, Vinod Chopra is regarded by scholars, the media, and other filmmakers as one of the most technically accomplished directors in the contemporary Bombay film industry.

Roja (1992)

Production Company: Kavithalaya Productions; Producer: K. Balachander; Director/Screenplay: Mani Rathnam; Story: Sujata; Music: A.R. Rehman. Original Tamil lyrics: Vaira Muthu; Starring: Arvind Swamy, Madhoo, Pankaj Kapoor, Nasser.

Originally made in Tamil and later dubbed into Hindi, *Roja* became the first dubbed film to achieve widespread national success. Inspired by an actual terrorist kidnapping of an Indian Oil official in conflict-ridden Kashmir, the film first depicts the halting love story of Roja and her husband Rishi Kumar, a cryptologist for the Indian government. Soon after the couple go to Kashmir because of Rishi's work, he is kidnapped by militants in retaliation for the army's capture of their leader, Wasim Khan. Roja, left alone and unable to communicate because she only speaks Tamil (a significant detail lost in the Hindi version when Roja's dialogues were dubbed into Hindi as well) befriends a temple caretaker who speaks both Tamil and Hindi. With his help, Roja doggedly works for her husband's release, including convincing a government official to release Khan in exchange for her husband. However, Rishi manages to escape with the help of two of his captors and he is reunited with his wife. The film's success brought director Mani Rathnam and music director, A.R. Rehman to national prominence, leading to their high standing within the Bombay film industry. The film's cinematography, lighting design, and song visualizations ushered in a new aesthetic regime in Hindi cinema. *Roja* was heavily criticized by many Indian intellectuals for its intense nationalism and depiction of Kashmiri militants and became the subject of a great deal of scholarly debate.

Aankhen (Eyes; 1993)

Production Company: Chiragdeep International; Producer: Pahlaj Nihalani; Director: David Dhawan; Story/Screenplay: Aneez Bazmee; Music: Bappi Lahiri; Lyrics: Indivar; Starring: Govinda, Chunky

Pandey, Raj Babbar, Shilpa Shirodkar, Rageshwari, Ritu Shivpuri, Kadar Khan, Shakti Kapoor, Sadashiv Amrapurkar, Gulshan Grover, Dina Pathak.

A slapstick, screwball comedy of errors that became an unexpected hit, *Aankhen* is the story of two rich, comical brothers, Munnu and Bunnu who get entangled in a plot to replace the Chief Minister of their state with a lookalike. Munnu subsequently gets kidnapped by criminals and develops amnesia. In the meantime, his country cousin who is his lookalike arrives in the city and is mistaken for Munnu. After a great deal of confusion and mistaken identities, the two brothers defeat the villains with the help of a policeman, and order is restored. The film's phenomenal success, breaking all previous box-office records, took the media and the film industry completely by surprise as the film did not have any major stars of the time and was directed by someone then regarded as B grade. *Aankhen*'s success reintroduced comedy as a viable genre and the figure of the comic hero into Hindi cinema after their long absence. Director David Dhawan and actor Govinda, went on to become a very successful combination, garnering hit after hit in the 1990s, and becoming a part of Bollywood's A-list.

Khalnayak (Villain; 1993)

Production Company: Mukta Arts; Producer/Director/Story: Subhash Ghai; Screenplay: Ram Kelkar; Music: Laxmikant-Pyarelal; Lyrics: Anand Bakshi; Starring: Sanjay Dutt, Jackie Shroff, Madhuri Dixit, Raakhee, Anupam Kher, Pramod Moutho.

A film that attracted controversy from the day it released, *Khalnayak* depicts how disillusioned youth can become vulnerable to antinational forces. Ballu (played by Dutt) is a gangster who is responsible for many political assassinations at the behest of his boss, Roshi Mahanta. Ballu is captured by Inspector Ramkumar Sinha but manages to escape from prison. In order to save his reputation, Sinha's girlfriend and fellow police officer, Ganga, decides to go

FIGURE 4.12 Madhuri Dixit and Sanjay Dutt in *Khalnayak*
Hyphen Films Collection, Courtesy Mukta Arts Ltd

undercover as a dancing girl and infiltrate Ballu's gang to bring about his recapture. Ballu falls in love with her despite knowing her true identity. When Ballu manages to escape once again from the police by using Ganga as a shield, she is accused of being Ballu's lover, harboring a fugitive, and betraying her duties as a police officer. At Ganga's trial which forms the climax of the film, Ballu shows up to vouch for Ganga's innocence, chastity, and loyalty to her duty and to Inspector Sinha. The film's success capitalized on two controversies surrounding the film. The first had to do with Sanjay Dutt's (Ballu) real-life arrest and imprisonment for his alleged involvement in the Bombay bomb blasts that happened earlier in the year. The second was the immense national uproar by the media, political leaders, and self-avowed "guardians of culture and taste" over the hit song, "*Choli ke peeche kya hai?*" (What's underneath the blouse?). While critics leveled charges of vulgarity against the song, others defended the song by invoking folk traditions.

Hum Aapke Hain Koun! (What Do I Mean to You? 1994)

Production Company: Rajshri Productions; Producer: Kamal Kumar Barjatya; Director/Screenplay: Sooraj Barjatya; Story: Keshav Prasad Mishra, S.H. Athavale; Music: Ramlaxman; Lyrics: Ravinder Rawal, Dev Kohli; Starring: Salman Khan, Madhuri Dixit, Mohnish Bahl, Renuka Shahane, Anupam Kher, Reema Lagoo, Alok Nath, Ajit Vachani, Laxmikant Berde, Satish Shah, Himani Shivpuri, Bindu.

Written off after preview screenings as one of the biggest flops waiting to happen, the film industry was stunned when *Hum Aapke Hain Koun!* (HAHK) went on to become the highest-grossing Indian film of all time, earning over 2 billion rupees world-wide. The film focuses on developing the clandestine romance between Nisha and Prem whose elder siblings, Pooja and Rajesh, are getting married to one another. When Pooja dies in an accident shortly after having given birth to a son, the elders of the two families, unaware of Nisha and Prem's relationship, decide that the widowed Rajesh should marry Nisha so that the baby will have a mother who loves him as her own. Instead of revealing their feelings, Nisha and Prem are willing to sacrifice their love for the sake of the family, but Rajesh learns of it just in time and Nisha and Prem get married. With its 14 songs, 195 minutes running time, minimal plot, absence of a villain, and lack of violence, HAHK broke with the dominant norms of filmmaking at the time and was dismissed by the industry as a "wedding video" because of its elaborate depiction of North Indian, Hindu wedding rituals. The film also presented a very different type of extended family – one free of conflict, tension, or jealousy. HAHK is filled with remarkably happy and jolly individuals. The film's tremendous success gave an enormous boost to the film industry and ushered in a new era of Hindi filmmaking focusing on wealthy, happy, extended families. After HAHK, songs against the backdrop of elaborate wedding celebrations became ubiquitous in Hindi films, as did extremely long titles that could be shortened into acronyms.

HAHK is also credited with "bringing audiences back" to the theaters – entire categories of viewers who had been "driven away" such as families, women, and members of the upper classes – and proving to the Bombay industry that "wholesome" family fare rather than sex and violence can also reap huge profits.

Dilwale Dulhaniya Le Jayenge (The One with a True Heart Will Win the Bride; 1995)

Production Company: Yashraj Films; Producer: Yash Chopra; Director/Story/Screenplay: Aditya Chopra; Music: Jatin-Lalit; Lyrics: Anand Bakshi; Starring: Shahrukh Khan, Kajol, Amrish Puri, Farida Jalal, Anupam Kher.

Following on the heels of HAHK, this film commonly referred to as DDLJ was also a huge box-office success and currently holds the title of longest-running Hindi film, playing for over five years (in

FIGURE 4.13 Kajol and Shahrukh Khan in *Dilwale Dulhaniya Le Jayenge*
Hyphen Films Collection, Courtesy Yashraj Films

matinee form) in Bombay. DDLJ depicts the love story of Simran and Raj, who have grown up in London and meet during a Eurail trip to Switzerland. Simran's father, Choudhury Baldev Singh, a strict patriarch nostalgic for his native Punjab, had promised his friend in India years ago that Simran would marry his son when the time was right. When Singh overhears Simran confessing her love for Raj to her mother, he uproots the family and returns to India immediately. Raj decides to follow and shows up in India promising to rescue Simran from her impending marriage. Although Simran's mother gives her blessing for the two to elope, Raj rejects the proposition stating that he will marry Simran only after they receive her father's blessing. Raj ingratiates himself with the entire family, but Baldev Singh's mind is not changed until the very end, after Raj has been violently beaten up by Simran's fiance and his friends. The film brought about a change in the representation of Indians settled in the West and led to the wealthy and culturally authentic "NRI" (non-resident Indian) character becoming a staple in contemporary Hindi cinema.

Satya (1998)

Production Company: Varma Corporation Ltd.; Producer/Director: Ram Gopal Varma; Screenplay: Anurag Kashyap, Saurabh Shukla; Music: Vishal; Lyrics: Gulzar; Starring: J.D. Chakravarthi, Urmila Matondkar, Manoj Bajpai, Shefali Chhaya, Saurabh Shukla, Govind Namdeo.

Hailed by Indian film critics as "India's first authentic gangster film," *Satya* offers a deglamorized and ethnically specific portrayal of the world of organized crime in Bombay. Though the Indian English-language press was hyperbolic in its assessment (there were older films that could be viewed as equally "authentic"), *Satya*'s cinematography, mise-en-scene, editing, lighting design, dialogues, characterizations, and depiction of violence established new norms for films of this genre. The film depicts how Satya, a young man who comes to Bombay in search of work, gets involved with the "underworld" – as organized crime is referred to in India. Unlike older films dealing with this topic, *Satya* offers no moral justification for the lead character getting into a life of crime. Satya is an orphan with no family to support and the film depicts his entry into the underworld as a matter of chance and a consequence of his temperament. The film portrays the connections between the Bombay underworld and the worlds of politics, filmmaking, and construction/real estate. The film humanizes gangsters and renders them more charismatic and sympathetic than the police. Satya and his gangster cronies are presented as a kind of family with its own hierarchy and code of morality. Though the film did well in the Bombay area, it was a greater critical success than a commercial success. Soon after *Satya*, a spate of films about the Bombay underworld ensued.

Lagaan (Land Tax; 2001)

Production Company: Aamir Khan Productions; Producer: Aamir Khan; Director/Story: Ashutosh Gowarikar; Screenplay: Ashutosh Gowarikar, Kumar Dave, Sanjay Dayma; Music: A.R. Rehman; Lyrics: Javed Akhtar; Starring: Aamir Khan, Gracy Singh, Rachel Shelley, Paul Blackthorne.

Hindi cinema's first cross-over success since *Awara*, *Lagaan* is a fictional tale set in the nineteenth century about a group of villagers in drought-stricken central India who take up a British officer's challenge to play cricket in order to get a reprieve from a crippling tax imposed by the colonial government. If the villagers beat the British team, they do not have to pay the tax for three years, but if they lose they have to pay triple the tax. The fact that the villagers have never played cricket and do not know the first thing about the game establishes the foundation of the film's narrative and dramatic structure. The British officer's sister takes pity on the villagers and secretly teaches them the game so that they have a fighting chance. The cricket match takes up the final hour of this nearly four-hour long

FIGURE 4.14 **Aamir Khan** in *Lagaan*
Kobal Collection

film and is marked by moments of comedy, drama, and suspense. The film was a phenomenal commercial and critical success both in India and abroad, breaking box-office records, earning accolades from Indian film critics, winning awards in European film festivals, and receiving an Oscar nomination for Best Foreign Film. A big-budget, lavishly produced film shot on location in the desert region of the western state of Gujarat, *Lagaan* is notable for being the first mainstream Hindi film to use synchronous sound. It is also perhaps many Americans' first encounter with "Bollywood" as *Lagaan*'s video and DVD became available through mainstream distribution outlets such as Blockbuster and Amazon.

5

REFLECTIONS AND PERSPECTIVES ON HINDI CINEMA BY CONTEMPORARY BOMBAY FILMMAKERS

HINDI CINEMA

Genre and narrative structure

Javed Akhtar, the co-writer of *Sholay* and *Deewar* (see chapter 4) reflects on the differences in narrative structure between Indian and Western films:

> We are, I feel, very . . . Victorian about the structure of the story. I'm not
> talking of content or the morality, but structure. If you take an average film
> from say America or Europe, in its structure, it is nearer to a short story. I
> mean there are films that are made on best-sellers, novels, like *Gone With
> the Wind*, *Ben Hur*, or *Spartacus*, or *Godfather*, leave aside those films, an
> average film will be nearer to a short story. But an average Indian film, again
> one is not talking of its intellectual level or aesthetics, strictly talking about
> the structure, an average mainstream commercial film is nearer to a novel.
> Now if we take traditional stories, even in the West, they're nearer to a
> novel. The short story is developed later. We have our own saga-like quality
> in our stories.

> On the other hand, parallel cinema or off-beat cinema is again nearer to a short story and perhaps that is why, it is one of the reasons that perhaps it doesn't work with the Indian masses. Indian masses somehow want a story that will engulf generations and eras, a larger period of time, and incidents, big influences on a larger spectrum. This is one major difference between the structure of a European or American film's screenplay and an Indian screenplay. You see a short story will have a beginning and an end, but these sagas have to have a beginning, a middle, and the end.
>
> (Interview with author, November 25, 1996)

Sutanu Gupta, a screenwriter since the late 1980s, discusses the challenges of writing a Hindi film given the narrative and generic structure:

> I personally feel Indian films are much more difficult to write than Hollywood films. Hollywood films can sustain interest, or can interest their audience with one track. You can have a bomb in a bus, a girl is driving the bus, and a man has to save the busdriver and the bus passengers. That is all! This is the whole film. We can't do a film like that. I wish we could – it's so straightforward! It can be one scene in a Hindi film, like the climax. It cannot be the whole film. These kinds of films will not run here.
>
> You see what happens here is, audiences have a very set belief that the kind of entertainment which is given in cinema should be containing everything – they should see part of family life; they should see romance; they should have songs; they want everything! Which becomes very difficult. At the same time they hate hodge-podge films. They want to know what is the emphasis – whether it's an action film, a thriller, a revenge, or a ghost story or a love story. It's amazing!
>
> And a particular artist does a particular kind of film, though his film has everything. Aamir Khan's film has everything that Sunny Deol's film has, has to have, at the same time, there has to be a change of emphasis. This is difficult to maintain. It's a massive balancing act, and when you're doing an Aamir Khan film, with the same ingredients, you are making a love story, but at the same time you have to have a certain kind of, some feel of an

action picture also. That's why we find it damn difficult to achieve success all the time.

(Interview with author, November 2, 1996)

Vikram Bhatt, a director since the early 1990s who has literally grown up in the film industry with a director grandfather and a cinematographer father, defines the term "story:"

> A story is nothing but a tool to generate a certain kind of emotion through a definite narrative. If it is a fairy tale, then it creates a certain excitement for children, but also in some ways leaves them with an emotion. The emotion that a story leaves you with could be of various sorts. You could feel sad, happy, vindicated, dissatisfied, but it is important to feel some emotion at the end of a film. If a film generates nothing but a headache then there is something wrong with the story. *Ghulam* [Slave] generated an elated feeling in the audience. *Deewar* made the audience very sad. *Kabhi Kabhie* [Sometimes] or DDLJ or any of the Yash Chopra films are called feel-good films because that is exactly the kind of feeling they generate. Any film that cannot draw any emotion out of you has a story problem or no story at all. It has no story at all because if you are left with no emotion at the end it obviously means that the story has not made you feel for its protagonists.
>
> (Email to author, November 13, 1998)

Rakesh Roshan, a producer/director since the 1980s, elaborates upon the dramatic arc of a Hindi film's narrative structure and relates it to screen time, pacing, background sound, and audience reaction:

> Once you position the hero, you have to establish the character, what is he? Where does he stay? Who are his mother and father? The principal actors you have to establish, what background they have. This takes about three–four reels, that's why you see normally in a film, for four–five reels nothing happens in the film. You're watching the film and the songs are coming and there's a comedian and when everything is established, in the sixth or seventh reel the story creeps in slowly. A man will come with secrets, and he'll disturb the whole family. So, the story starts. Actually it

should be like that – the story should start on the fourth or fifth reel, at least for that much period you can give them entertainment. And the interval point should be a turning point, so that when people come out they can say "What's going to happen now?" "This is going to happen." "No, this will happen!" When they discuss, then they're interested in the film.

Again, in the screenplay, there should be a lull, because even when you are recording, you are recording the whole film on one pitch. Okay? Before interval you bring the pitch down a little, and then you bring it up to the same level. You can't go higher. See this is the pitch line, for sound [Drawing a line on a piece of paper]. If you go higher, it'll burst. So what we do, we bring it down. Even for a screenplay it is like that. When you're making a screenplay, it's moving along, and when the climax is going to come, you have to bring your film down, make the pace slow, or give two–three scenes which are irritating, which are not gelling with the film, properly, and then pick up the film again. Even with the sound when we're re-recording, we bring the sound down. Because if we want to give a surprise, we have to bring it down and *dhup*! It comes, but that sound *dhup* is not above this [indicating to the line on the paper]. It is at the same level as this. You've brought it down. . . . You can't hear the background music, and suddenly *da-da-da-da* it'll come, and suddenly you'll hear and think, "Oh, what lovely background music the film has!" But this is because of re-recording the particular place where you want to heighten the scene.

Usually a film ends immediately after the climax. The villain is killed, and they [hero and heroine] unite and the film is over. After that we don't have anything to show. Also, here from the climax itself people start standing because they know the film is going to end. They'll start opening the doors and that creaking noise will begin.

(Interview with author, May 21, 1996)

Film music

Rumi Jaffrey, a screenwriter since the late 1980s who has worked a great deal with director David Dhawan (see chapter 3), reflects on why nearly all Hindi films contain songs:

> Music is such an integral part of our Indian culture; without music there is nothing. Music is a very necessary part of life – we sing when we worship; we sing when our children are born, we sing during weddings; even beggars sing when they beg. Music is such a part of our lives, that without music, our lives are empty. If you don't have songs in a film, the film doesn't run. Music is a very necessary part of India.
>
> (Interview with author, November 22, 1996)

Rakesh Roshan, whose father was a music director and whose younger brother is a music director, discusses the reason he is particular about music and the importance of creating just the right song situations in his films:

> I harp on [about] music a lot. It's not that I'm making musical films.[1] None of my films are musical films, but still music plays a very big part. Because only when the song situations are perfect, then can the music director give you a good song. If I just tell a music director "I want a song here, hero's walking and he sees the girl and starts singing a song." He won't know what to make. He can come up with a good number, but until you inspire them – this is the situation and this is how – even the song's lyric writer cannot come out with good words. It has to be a proper situation. People should feel "Yes, this is a situation for a song." Sometimes in our pictures one feels, "*arre yaar, gaana chaalu ho gaya*!" [Oh no, the song has started!] You know, something is going on, some serious thing is going on and the hero looks at the heroine and *phat*! [hits his desk] flash forward, *gaana* [song] starts – 100 girls are dancing behind. That should not happen. I try to avoid all those things. Songs should be a part of the story. It should move the story ahead. Even the lyrics and everything should move the story ahead.
>
> (Interview with author, May 21, 1996)

Anjum Rajabali, a screenwriter since the early 1990s, explains the narrative functions of songs in a screenplay and how he conceptualized the songs in *Ghulam* (Slave, 1998; dir: Vikram Bhatt) a film he had written starring Aamir Khan (see chapter 3):

> Once you really treat your own storytelling objectives and methods as part of a larger continuity of the story telling traditions in India, integrating songs becomes easier. In myths, legends, and their rendering in folk theatre, one finds lots of music. Where an emotion becomes intense, usually a song helps to underline it. It also cuts away the need for verbalisation through dialogue, and creates a mood that cues the viewer in to the state of mind of the character/s or the narrator. The most common emotion used is love. When the first "thunderbolt" strikes either, they express it through a song. When their love intensifies — usually the standard rain sequence — another song. If there is a breach or a tragedy in the relationship because of which they separate, we deal with it musically. So, extreme happiness, extreme love, extreme sadness, all of these qualify as song situations.
>
> In *Ghulam*, there is a long sequence of three scenes when the girl and boy meet for the first time. She is watching him, and he is very affected by her presence. In the third scene of this sequence he not only wins the race with the train, but also saves his rival from being run over. She notices this; he notices her noticing it — since in any case he had accepted the challenge only to impress her. After that, he saves her from the police and drops her home. The mutual exchange of looks says that there are strong stirrings of romance beginning here. As soon as he leaves her, music begins, leading to a song. She sings alone, he sings alone and each one fantasises about the other. Then, when love intensifies, mostly when it becomes physical, an accidental touch, both become conscious of it, physical stirrings, they break out into a song. Then, comes the breach. He accidentally has her brother killed; she rejects him. Both suffer; another song situation. This time a background song — non lip-sync — since I thought it looked awkward them singing this time. That is the romance part of *Ghulam* as I wrote it. But, then, and this frequently happens, the producer and the director came across a song which they thought was interesting and a hit. Someone showed it to them. So they thought, we should have this song in our film. Not terribly difficult in a Hindi film to do that. There was a sequence where

the hero and heroine speak about themselves to the other. At one point here, she is upset. Insert a scene, where to perk her up, he sings to her. Instant song situation.

The function of songs in screenplays has usually been to either take the narrative further – in the process of romance, the song tells the viewer that now this couple is deeply in love, so the story of the romance has moved ahead, or to intensify the feeling of the character – a luckless orphan comes across a child being pampered by his parents, he suddenly misses his own dead mother, breaks out into song expressing that feeling. It works, because we are used to this. We don't find it corny; it moves us to tears, genuinely. Or to create a mood – hero-heroine have just bought their dream house, they decorate it lovingly while singing. Mood: great happiness and anticipation of more happiness. Now, later if they get cheated out of their house, we feel their pain more, because of the song earlier.

See if you accept the dictum that songs are required almost invariably – all screenplays don't need them – then you keep that in mind while writing the screenplay. Every time you come to a point of intense feelings, you see if a song will convey it better. If you don't have enough situations for songs, then you have to create them. For example in *Mohra* [Pawn; 1994; dir: Rajiv Rai], Akshay Kumar and Raveena Tandon want to observe the villains doing a deal at a night club. Perfect place to insert a song: "*Tu cheez badi hai mast mast*" [You're a hot number]. This is loved by the producers for two reasons. First, the lyrics of the song don't have to mean anything to the narrative, so they can go around lifting potentially hit songs from their stocks, and secondly, it becomes an item, which brings me to an important development in the Hindi film industry. Film music has become very big business. Not only do you have to put catchy sounding numbers into your film, you also need situations where you can jazz up things visually. The *Mohra* example is very telling. Out of the blue, you have a very colourful stage and lights and the costumes and the works. It doesn't jar the narrative, because it is a night club anyway. The producer can show this song on TV in the countdown shows, and people run to see his film when it is released, because they already love the song.

(Email to author, April 9, 1998)

Sachin Bhaumick, a screenwriter since the late 1950s and the writer of *Aradhana* (see chapter 4), explains the structural placement of songs in a film's screenplay:

> In our lingo we say there should be a difference of 1,000 feet from one song to the next. It's a general rule of thumb. If a song happens and 300 feet later another song happens, people will say "What's this? We just saw a song!" So we use this technical term that there should be a 1,000-foot difference between songs. First half should be 7,000 or 8,000 feet, second half will be 6,000 or something – films are between 14–15,000 feet. And three songs must come in the first half, and three songs must be in the second half, but if it is necessary, four songs come in the first half, and three songs in the second half. There is more drama in the second half so there are less chances for song situations to arise.
>
> (Interview with author, October 15, 1996)

Visual style

Sharmishta Roy, an art director since the early 1990s who helped to redefine the visual style of Hindi cinema, describes the role of art direction and her method of designing the sets for a film:

> I think an art director's role is very important. Basically what an art director does is communicate to an audience where these people in the foreground are. Without them having to come on screen and say "I'm standing in so-in-so's house" or "I'm standing in the garden or ..." right? So what we're doing is communicating to the audience before any dialogue is even uttered. So it's as important as a dialogue, it's as important as the artist himself because the artist will look right or wrong in the backdrop. An art director could ruin a film because if he were to give a wrong ambience, everything that has been spoken would be a lie, or the background would be a lie. Either of them would have to be a lie, if they didn't match. It's like taking a very plump lady and saying she hasn't eaten for 10 days, you know, in the film. It doesn't work. If you are going to base your character, select

a character, select an artist, then the artist has to suit the character. Similarly you pick a background, it has to suit what is going on in the script. So to that extent the art director is very important.

The cinematographer also has a contribution in terms of the look of the space, and once we've decided what the look should be, the design should aid his lighting. So if I am designing a set and he can't light it up, or can't create source light, the design is a flop. So when he sees the design he says, "Look I think it would be better if you remove this wall because it facilitates shooting," crane movements and things like that. Or "I think you need to puncture this wall because I can get in a shaft of light from here." Or, "I think these colors are not going to look good with the kind of lighting I'm imagining." Right? Or if I have decided on a color, "I think this will look best with Tungsten lighting and not very bright light." So that's how the two of us would work.

Then we decide okay, that this is the color scheme and this is how we plan to light up the set, how we're going to light up the artists, what are the colors the artists should wear. Then the costume designer comes in, and he's been told, you know. Sometimes the costume designer decides that, if this is the mood, this is the color that she should wear, and if we don't think the set's going to work with the costume, we may change the color of the set.

I think any kind of texture looks good on screen, versus matte or dull finishes. Because they might be subtle and appealing to the naked eye, but when they go on screen they might just fall flat, and look like a mass of color, and had it been textured it would look that much better. Also what might look good in a house is a lot of patterned fabrics and things like that, which would look horrible on screen because it would compete all the time with the costumes, and take away from the person sitting on the − if you make a sofa which is very patterned, it will take away entirely from the person who is using it. And that shouldn't happen. That's something you also learn as you work.

I think I do a lot of things very instinctively. Quite honestly I don't know what I am going to pick up when I go out into the market. I have a very broad kind of idea as to what I want to do, but when I go into the market and when

I see things, things begin to fall into place. I know overall what I want – I want a subtle look or a very gaudy look or a glamorous look. I mean, on a broad scale I know what I want. When I go into the market I start seeing things and I start picking things and when I pick up one thing I try and coordinate it with another. Things fall into place like that for me. Which is why I can't hand over decoration to somebody, because that's something you have to do on your own. I can't leave the collection of fabrics to people, because if you make the wrong selection it would probably look wrong.

Knowing styles is important, whether you're doing Art Deco or you're doing Retro, or you're doing Renaissance or you're doing Baroque, it's important to know styles. It's important to read up on styles. Tapestries are different; all kinds of fabrics; the kind of detailing on cornices and vases are different, so if one knows the history behind every style of design, one can use that better. Not that our audience will notice it, not that it will make that much of a difference to what the people are doing. Also we are so eclectic in our style here. It's neither Indian nor Western. So it doesn't really matter that much, but knowing what you're doing is important, after that you can break the rules.

(Interview with author, October 26, 2000)

"Indianization"

Anjum Rajabali discusses the difference between Hollywood films and Hindi films and explains what is necessary to "Indianize" or adapt a Hollywood film:

Relationships! That seems to be the primary criteria when Indianising a subject. Lots of strong, close, intense relationships that will have interesting, moving stories/graphs of their own. Adding family is one important thing. That is why I think subjects like James Bond, detective stories, westerns and the like don't work as they are here. Who were James Bond's parents? Does Clint Eastwood of *The Good, Bad, & Ugly* love anyone? What about his brothers or sisters? The other thing is to make things more personal. Case in point: *Kiss Before Dying* was effectively remade as *Baazigar* [Player]. In the original, the hero's motive was to get rich by any means since he used to see the big company's train pass his house everyday and that made him envious and ambitious enough to end up killing all those girls. That was enough – his plain ambition. But, in *Baazigar*, that wouldn't have worked. Guy killing for ambition? No sympathy for him at all. But, if the guy had a back-story wherein his father was cheated by this company, and now the guy wants the company back as revenge and retribution for that. Okay, now he's my man. I can consider forgiving him all those killings. Not entirely of course, killing is killing, so he has to die himself in the end, but he will carry my sympathy with him. Or, *Deewar*, one of the best screenplays to have come out of India. The guy has a scarred childhood and that drives him remorselessly to coming up the violent way, eventually destroying his own self.

Hollywood films are considered "dry" here. That is, not enough emotions. When you Indianise a subject, you add emotions. Lots of them. Feelings like love, hate, sacrifice, of revenge, pangs of separation. But, in a Hollywood film if a hero and heroine were to separate and you had five scenes under-lining how they are suffering because they miss each other, people might find that soppy and corny too. Not here. Our mythology, our poetry, our liter-ature is full of situations where lovers pine for each other. Take the *Mahabharat* and you'll see what I mean. Every situation has feelings, dilemmas, other kinds of conflicts, confrontations, sacrifices, moral issues coming up all the time, etc. In a Hollywood film, James Bond kills on the job; here we need to justify it, because morality plays a more important part in our lives, because of our mythology, I suppose.

Recently I saw, *Murder in the First*. One brief flashback showed Kevin Bacon stealing bread for his sister and getting jailed, thus starting the whole story. In an Indian film, we'd have dwelt on that hugely, hugely. Really exploited that to underline the tragedy of the guy. Then, later Christian Slater brings Bacon's long lost sister along to convince Bacon to testify or something. Bacon is very uncomfortable with her, behaves very awkwardly with her, turns away finally and goes inside. After that scene, the sister doesn't feature in the film at all. It works, in the context of this film. But, Jesus, here the first thing that Bacon would've asked of Slater was "Bring my sister to me," and she'd have been the moving force of the film.

(Email to author, April 9, 1998)

BOMBAY FILM INDUSTRY

The Indian media landscape

Madhuri Dixit (see chapter 3) discusses the main change that has come about in filmmaking as a result of satellite television:

> There was a time you know when I started out, where content was given more importance. The packaging was not considered as a priority, it was secondary. What was concentrated on was the content of the film; what we're trying to say through the film, and technically we were not as aware as we are now at that point. So no one really took pains or utmost care, you know, about the film being glossy or giving it the right look. There used to be continuity lapses; it was taken into account – okay, as long as we have the content, nothing else matters. But today because of the satellite invasion and all the TV programs that people see, the MTV, the V-Channel, the Star Movies, the English films that are being dubbed, technical finesse has also become very, very important, because people have started getting used to seeing technically brilliant films. So today content is important, but how you present it is also very, very important today. That's the main change that I see in filmmaking. Also the readiness to experiment with something beyond just the usual Hindi film formula. I think people are more open to experimentation today than they were say 10 years back.
>
> (Interview with author, November 25, 1996)

Ravi Gupta, the CEO of B4U (Bollywood For You) a global satellite channel devoted to popular Hindi cinema, discusses the media scenario within India and the place of Hollywood and multinational media companies within it:

> In the Indian space we have ensured that we have given Hollywood a run for their money. In India today, not more than 5 percent of the market share is with Hollywood. No other country in the world can boast of that kind of situation in a free market economy. In India, there are no restrictions on Hollywood cinema being distributed; there are no restrictions on non-Indian

audio-visual media being freely distributed. There are a whole lot of channels around here, but you do find that despite all that, and mind you Hollywood cinema has been distributed in India for over 70 years, and despite that, the market share that they enjoy is just about 5 percent. They are trying all kinds of things including dubbing of movies and so on and so forth, but frankly it has not been able to make any noticeable inroads into the market share over here.

In fact what is interesting is that all those major overseas players who came to India wanting to make inroads here, ended up adapting themselves in the Indian marketplace. So you have for instance MTV starting over here as a purely international channel, but over a period of time they have become so Indian that today except for the name there is very little of MTV international left over here. The same happened with Sony when they first came in, they had a lot of non-Indian content, and a lot of dubbed serials and so on and so forth. They realized that in this marketplace what ticked was Bollywood. The same applied to Star. Star when it came in, Star Plus was largely a very non-Indian channel with a certain amount of Indian content, but over a period of time they realized they had to go all Indian if they wanted to be a significant player. The same applied to channel V for example. So you see that whether it was channels or whether it's in the movies, now you have a situation where Columbia Tri-Star has come into India to do distribution, not of foreign movies but also of Indian movies within India, and Sony is now thinking of distributing Indian movies overseas.

So these are some of the trends that you see, the recognition that Bollywood is a strong cinema, is possibly the major competitor and viable industry to Hollywood. Of course in terms of revenue it is no match for Hollywood, but in terms of numbers it is very important. You have to remember that over five billion tickets of Indian movies are sold every year, which possibly is at least as much as Hollywood.[2]

As far as Indians and South Asians are concerned, they will still continue to enjoy the typical dance and romance sequences, because we've all grown up on that. At the end of the day if India has been able to resist Hollywood's inroads, if you ask me, it's just that the Indian movie format is a totally different format. It's a totally escapist cinema, totally based on dance and music, and I think that is such a strong element of Indian cinema and particularly Bollywood cinema that I don't see a situation where Hollywood can start making movies that would appeal to Indian audiences, nor do I see a situation where India will start making movies that would appeal to Western audiences. Because the format which Hollywood has taken, and the format which Indian filmmakers have taken and which is what Indian consumers have been so used to, or the Western consumers have been so used to, are totally different.

(Interview with author, October 25, 2000)

Cosmopolitanism and diversity

Shammi Kapoor, a successful star of the 1960s and the younger brother of Raj Kapoor (see chapter 3) reflects on the polyglot nature of Bombay and the Hindi film industry and attributes the global popularity of Hindi films to the cosmopolitan environment which produces them:

We come from a very mixed society – a very cosmopolitan society, there are a lot of languages over here, there are a lot of people who work in different languages. I, for one, belong to Peshawar. I'm a Pathan. Someone from Pakistan sent me an email and they said, "How do you qualify as a Pathan? Pathans are only Muslims." So I'm writing to him that Pathan is not a religious group, but a community of people. I come from there. I was born in Bombay. I studied my junior schooling in Calcutta, in Bengali. Landed back in Bombay and I studied in a convent school – studied English. I finished my Matric [high school] in a Gujarati school at New Era over here. Went to college in a Marathi environment. What language do you want me to adhere to? This is what it's all about. Then it took me time, when I joined the theater to start learning – Mr. Amitabh Bachchan's father's books – they were more or less our syllabus in the theater. My father was very adamant about it: "You must all go through those books of his poetry, and learn the language. Hindi is very important." I have no pretensions of saying that I was good at it, but I made an effort, and that is very important. We're speaking all the time in English. I'm speaking to you in English. What is the native tongue over here in Bombay? I'd like to know that. What is the native tongue of the films? – we talk of money in Hindi, we receive checks in English.

In the South they're very particular. The Tamilians make their pictures in Tamil. They know their language; they know what they're doing. The Telugu [speakers] are different; the Canarese are different; the Malayalis are different; Bengalis are different; the Maharashtrians are very good. It's just the Bombay guy out over here who's suffering because he doesn't know whether he's speaking in Hindi, Urdu, Gujarati, English – what's he doing? He's having food at China Garden, having Chinese food, talking in Hindi, thinking in English, and flirting with a French girl for all you know. You see the whole thing is cosmopolitan as a word. The whole environment is such.

Don't you think that could be one of the major reasons why our movies are more articulate even abroad? That we are catering to a language which is now today understood all over. We are acting in a very common dialect – not of one particular language, but a dialect which is understood all over the world – we're speaking the language of love. Therefore you have a Bombay film industry picture which does fabulously well abroad also. You are in New York, but you understand what's happening out here. That comes out from Bombay, because the view is very broadened.

(Interview with author, July 18, 1996)

Women in the Bombay film industry

Ayesha Jhulka, an actress who made her debut in 1991, talks about the place of women within the industry and within Hindi cinema:

You have to accept the fact that it is a male-dominated industry. And you have to accept that basically heroes are given much more importance than the heroines, importance in the sense, because the film runs on them you know. That's an open fact which nobody can deny. So it's better to accept it and then carry on. You have your own place which nobody else can take.

What you can do, the heroes probably can't do. The whole team is required, heroines are also required. And a heroine is supposed to be basically a relief for the film, you know? She's supposed to be a relief for the audience. The audience, when they go to a theater, they should feel, "Oh she's my girlfriend" or "Oh, she's my wife." They must have that feeling and if they have that feeling then you're a successful heroine because they must want you. She has to be a good dancer, and she should be soothing. So a heroine is very, very important and I don't think a film can run without a heroine. There has to be a heroine in it. You can't really have a film just with heroes. It won't work.

(Interview with author May 28, 1996)

Punkej Kharabanda, who started off in the industry as an assistant director but then became a secretary or manager of a few stars, explains the difference between managing male and female stars and the importance of an actress's image for her fan following:

There's a lot of difference. First, while you're managing a heroine in Hindi films, you're managing her parents, and along with them, her boyfriend. That becomes a big pain. Then with the heroine, see films are basically hero-based and you're [actor] the first person to be signed. For a heroine, you're never the first person, you're always the second person to be signed, so it's a little more competitive. You got to select which film to do opposite which hero. And clothes are a big hassle; clothes, hair, a heroine must — like it's very easy to fix up a shooting for a guy — "Ok, tomorrow you shoot." But for a heroine, her clothes have to be ready, this has to be ready and stuff like that. Plus there's always a lot of interference which is there from the boyfriend, the family. The hero, at least they don't say anything — the family and the girlfriends — they don't interfere that much.

For a heroine it's very important what kind of an image she has. If I as an audience look up to a heroine, I'd look up to her as someone who I would like to be in love with, so if I hear about someone who's having affairs left, right, and center, it's not someone I would look up to. It's not that you stop your personal life, but make sure you manage your personal life so discreetly that the press never comes to know about it. That's one of the . . ., it's very difficult to tell today's kids — "Ok, do this, don't do that for your image," because they probably feel your ideas are too old-fashioned. It's after a couple of years they realize the worth of what you were telling them.

(Interview with author April 17, 1996)

Ritha Bhaduri who has played character roles such as mothers and sisters in a countless number of Hindi films asserts why character roles are preferable to the female lead:

At the moment, I think character roles have more to say than the female heroine, actress. Because in present day movies, heroines do what? Literally the myth that was there about Indian cinema, that they ran around trees and sang songs and things like that, that is what is happening. There are very few films that are women-oriented, or have a woman dominating the whole thing. Whereas the characters, character actors have at least, in three hours maybe, 20 minutes to themselves, maybe a good scene or two. Which, if the actor is good, will be remembered. But whereas the heroine, like today, all these are there, they're doing what? Six songs? Four scenes? Which they are not even good enough to portray it. So I think we are better off now.

(Interview with author, April 16, 1996)

Shabana Azmi, who has acted in mainstream Hindi cinema, art-house Indian cinema, and international English-language productions and has won numerous awards, discusses the portrayal of women within popular Hindi cinema:

The one thing however that hasn't changed, that has changed only super-ficially I think, is in its portrayal of women. Because earlier, in the 60s, there were women who were portrayed really in a stereotypical notion, of the forgiving mother, the all-suffering wife, the large-hearted sister, the sacri-ficing wife, etc. That changed and we had a whole spate of films in the mainstream commercial cinema which were basically just a cosmetic change in appearance. First we had Rambos, and now we had Rambolinas, who were basically women in drag wearing tight leather jeans and a gun in one hand, almost invariably seeking vengeance for some social injustice, largely rape. But what was happening was that they were taking on all the one dimensional characteristics that the men before them had done, and there wasn't anything particularly female, it was just a plain narrative where a woman was playing the part rather than a man.

And after that another change has occurred in recent times, . . . earlier we had very clear divisions between the vamp and the heroine. Because the vamp was always excluded from the field of domesticity, she was allowed to assert her sexuality. Whereas the heroine was cast in the chaste wife-mother mold, and so could never express her sexuality. Now the distinction between the vamp and the heroine is getting more and more blurred, so now we have the two-in-one heroine, who is this sultry sexy siren before marriage and then becomes the chaste wife after. That reveals the schizophrenia that we have in society.

Also another significant change that is occurring, a lot of people are saying that all the hue and cry about the obscenity that cinema is being allowed to express, comes because it is the heroine rather than the vamp who is asserting her sexuality. But that's not very true, because were that so, that would be healthy. But under the guise of sexually asserting herself, the woman is really surrendering herself to the male gaze. Because cinema is about images, and the way these images are constructed, a heaving bosom, a bare midriff, a shaking hip, the woman is really losing all autonomy over her whole body. She is becoming a subject of the male gaze, a victim of the male gaze, and there's much left to be desired there.

So although there's been a change, I think there is a lot of confusion about who this new woman should be. Society accepts that there is a new woman, but does not know how much "freedom," this woman should get before she threatens the very fabric of our society. So unless society can come to terms with who this new woman is, our new heroine will continue to be clouded in what is good or what is bad, because a heroine, a heroine or hero is somebody who is a personification of the morality and the aspirations of the society.

(Interview with author August 14, 1996)

Pooja Bhatt who made her acting debut in 1989 in a film directed by her father, Mahesh Bhatt (see chapter 3) and turned producer in 1996, discusses why she decided to start her own production company and the kind of films she hopes to produce:

My decision to become a producer was something that came out of, well I wouldn't say desperation, but it was quite close to that, because I was kind of tired of only going on to a film set and people ask me, "*Pooja-ji aap kya khayenge lunch break mein*" ya "*Aapka scene yeh hai, aapka costume yeh hai.*" [Pooja-ma'am, what will you eat for lunch? or This is your scene, this is your costume.] I wanted to do something more than just the usual heroine role, because unfortunately I think women in Hindi films don't really get that much to do. [The] maximum you have to do is six songs and probably four emotional-dramatic scenes and your role is complete. So I wanted to make films where women were shown in a very good light. I wanted to make heroine-oriented films in the sense, not the boring heroine-oriented films, but where the heroine and the hero were on par. They had equal roles, because all of the roles I had ever done in my life, my role was on par. I was quite tired of only doing what I have been doing. My decision to become a producer came from that, because I am basically from a film family where I've always been involved in every aspect of the film, not only coming on to the set and doing my bit and leaving. My uncle, Mukesh Bhatt, has been producing from a very long time; my father is a director, so actually this was the most natural step in the world for me to take. I wanted my own production company to promote new talent, to work with a lot of new people, with new ideas and fresh ideas and make different kinds of films.

I want to produce some good movies where the women in my films are going to be the women of today. They've got their own desires, and their own wants, and their own needs, and have no qualms about admitting it. I feel that women in Hindi films are very one-dimensional. The maximum a heroine says is "No, Dad, *main sirf isse shaadi karoongi, aur main usse shaadi nahi karoongi,*" [I'm going to marry only him and not him] and runs away from home. And we don't have much to do, that's quite unfortunate, because we have so many girls today, all of them, talented girls, very attractive, good-looking women, intelligent women who know their minds and speak their minds and basically can do so much more than what we're being offered. I think it's a waste if you don't offer them and give them roles that are on par with their hero. So I want to have my production company launch the careers of lots of new people in terms of technicians and actors and work with different actresses. I think that would be very interesting, and basically do films that are very pro-women. That should happen. Somebody's got to do that. No point in me complaining about the industry and saying that we don't get offered good roles when I have a chance, when I have the opportunity to make films.

(Interview with author, November 19, 1996)

HINDI CINEMA AND SOCIETY

Significance of Hindi cinema and of entertainment in India

Actor/producer Aamir Khan (see chapter 3) describes the cultural significance of Hindi cinema and relates his own relationship to Hindi cinema, specifically film music:

I think that Hindi cinema is very much part of the Indian culture; it has become part of the Indian culture. And over the last 50 years or so it has really grown in a big, in a sense that the people, maybe because it was one of the few modes of entertainment that it became such a big thing for an average Indian person and the majority of the population is viewing films. They're really hooked on to it. And they base a lot of their thoughts also on the films they see. And they base a lot of their morals perhaps, principles perhaps, on the way the heroes and heroines behave, the way certain characters in film behave.

Especially the songs, I think the songs are a definite part of the culture. Even somebody like me who as a child was not allowed to watch films by my parents, I used to watch a film maybe every three months, or maybe [every] six months. Till the age of about 15, I had barely watched any films at all you know and there wasn't any video and TV at that time. So I've watched very few films in my life, but Hindi film songs are still a part of me. They manage to change my moods. My favorite music which I listen to is old Hindi film songs. In terms of my reading, I've read very few Indian authors. Most of my reading, 99 percent of my reading has been books which are from the West, Russian authors maybe, British authors, American authors, French authors, European authors. My reading has been not Indian at all, but still film songs are something which are a part of me, are a part of my culture, and are a part of my romance. When I, when I think of the person I love, I sing a song in my mind about that person, it's like that you know. Songs are really a part of my culture, Hindi film songs. Somehow Western music has not influenced me so much.

(Interview with author, March 23, 1996)

Aditya Chopra, the director of *Dilwale Dulhaniya Le Jayenge* (see chapter 4) and Yash Chopra's (see chapter 3) son, discusses the significance of Hindi cinema as entertainment within India:

It's very significant, in India especially, because it's the cheapest form of entertainment in our country. So it can form a lot of opinions, it can change the way people think, definitely it can. So I feel that it does play a very, very important role. Because as I told you earlier I think we should be slightly more socially aware in our films than we are now, just slightly so, not even too much, because we shouldn't lose sight of the fact that we are here to entertain people. That should never be lost sight of I feel. But then also we shouldn't lose sight of the fact that we are dealing to a country which feeds on Hindi films, which breathes Hindi films, which does take its Hindi films very seriously, so we should not have things in our film which might have any negative influence on society.

What I mean is that for them Hindi films are a part of their culture. We don't have theater, or we're not into operas or stuff like that. Here, the common man, his ultimate dream, is escapism, is to watch films. He goes for three hours: he sees a world which he probably will never get, or he'll see women which he'll never meet or he'll see stuff where he's never gonna go to, and for him that's it. That's his ultimate, because you're dealing to a country of have-nots. So he takes his films seriously because it gives him an opportunity to . . ., it gives him a topic of conversation also, because in this country we don't have so many things besides politics and films. There are only two big things actually happening, and sometimes they connect. What else does the common man talk about? So films are his escapism; films also become a part of his conversation, part of his daily entertainment.

What everybody gets out of films I don't know, but I do know that they take their films seriously. Like they do feel cheated when you don't give them a good film, you know, because they put in so much money, that's why they take it seriously. For Indians, everything is money-oriented. Why? Because they're not, they don't have so much of it, so they can't afford to be casual about it. Like you go abroad and you see a flick and think, "Eh, it was okay, I didn't like it." You don't think of those four to five dollars that you spent on it. Here, you think about those 50 rupees, and you feel, "Oh God!". It feels that way because there are people here who work throughout the day, earn daily wages, and probably skip a meal to see a film! So he has the right to take his films very seriously and he does take his films very seriously, so that's why you need to take it very seriously.

You need to understand that there's a very big responsibility. More so, when your film does well, that means he's placed a certain faith in you and he's going to come on just that faith and you can't let him down. So that's why since they take it seriously, you have to entertain them because they've come here for entertainment and you cannot misuse that responsibility. You can't, just because you are in that position, or just because you are making films, you shouldn't use that as a platform to spread things which are undesirable.

(Interview with author, April 2, 1996)

Censorship

Producer/director Subhash Ghai (see chapter 3) asserts the necessity for censorship in India:

I think it's working all right. There's a lot of hue and cry about censors. I've been hearing for the last 30 years. I don't think you'll like a policeman stopping you on the road, but the policeman has to be there, the traffic cop has to be there. Nobody likes red lights, traffic lights, but you need to have them for the traffic to go smoothly for everybody. So you need a censor board for your society to go smoothly. Let them [society] develop themselves, if they want to develop their tastes, values, or change of fashions, let them change it and cinema will present and the Censor Board will also accept it.

You see, obscenity, when you define obscenity, it is very much relative to the aesthetic sense of the society. What is obscene for you may not be obscene for me? Like going into beaches with the swimming costume is quite obscene to the rural people of India. But it is a very healthy kind of thing in a Western country to go into beaches with swimming costumes. But then, if it is offensive to the mind of the people then it is obscene, that's how I define it. So the Censor Board does its job, okay, and it should be there and I don't agree with those people who say there should be no Censor Board. There has to be a law, and implementation of the law. There has to be, otherwise we will make pornos, nothing else. The people will go berserk.

(Interview with author December 10, 1996)

Director Ramesh Sippy (see chapter 3) expresses his ambivalence about film censorship:

There's always a hue and cry in this country about censorship. On the one hand, I don't think I would ever like to be a censor, on the board of the censors. The industry is always up in arms that they're over-doing their role, and there are critics who very strongly feel that they're not playing their role as strongly as required. I don't know, maybe that's healthy. Debate all the time on issues like this is probably healthy because if you go into an overdrive on censorship, you'll be curbing any creativity, there's no question about it. You'll be limiting the avenues and certainly curbing creativity. On the other hand if you give a total free hand, do we have a society mature enough to handle the kind of material that may be doled out in a totally free atmosphere? Personally I feel it's a constant change and therefore, one should view it with society's present view of things, ever-changing present view, it's always a changing view.

Ultimately, the audience themselves reject what is in excess and we have seen it time and again, an excess of sex and violence films have failed miserably at the box office. You will never find examples of sex and violence encouraging films to run. Because an action film will have action in it, you cannot prevent action, it's got to be an action film. But whenever it's in excess, people reject it — both sex and violence.

So the government on the censorship front also is in a peculiar spot. They have the Censor Board, and then they're called upon, questions are brought out in Parliament, and they're taken to task for not doing enough. I can see their predicament. When we have gone the democratic way, I think it would be wrong to start curbing anything — there is no censorship of books, there is no censorship in art or painting, now just to say that because the mass of audience does not see all that, and therefore a mass media should have censorship is not fair. But one can still understand the point that, one cannot allow it to go berserk either. Therefore of course, on the one hand you have a grading in censorship like they have in the West, a much wider grading — you have from a very general audience, universal audience to certificates of 12 years old, 15 years old, 18 years old, and X-rated films. Again for this unfortunately you need a more educated audience.

I think awareness should grow, people should be more exposed to, rather than kept away from aspects of life, which gives them an opportunity to build their own thinking process. Because we've lived in a society which is very isolated and sort of kept in wraps, you find a lot of issues never discussed, is that building a healthy society? In my opinion, no, on the other hand, aping the West or going entirely the other way is not necessarily the best alternative. [To say] you should be overclothed is as foolish as [to say you should be] unclothed. You can't say that on the other hand, if you have freedom, you go around naked, no that's not correct. That's equally wrong.

I think when you balance everything, what is decent behavior, what is behavior in public, these are such individual things, that the overall thing, in general to be kept in mind, is that it does not offend certain basic aesthetics of people, but at the same time the maker should not be denied an opportunity to present certain subjects when the overall, (the guideline is there in the censors), the overall impact of that particular film is to say something and therefore in that context, certain sequences which are shown are important.

This will be a continuous debate, it's a never-ending debate because everyday you are learning, becoming more aware, knowledgeable, changing values, and therefore films also, and their censorship also will have something to do with reflecting these changes. Cause if you make a film exactly as was made 50 years ago, it's not going to appeal to today's audience. I think the healthiest way is to have a good guideline and a certain criticism and if it goes out of hand, there's always a recall situation.

(Interview with author July 8, 1996)

Film audiences and fans

Actor/producer Shashi Kapoor, a leading star of the 1970s and 1980s and Raj Kapoor's younger brother, relates an anecdote about a particularly fervent viewer of *Bobby* (see chapter 4) directed by his elder brother:

I think *Bobby* was a sweet kind of film which was not different in its story, or unusual in its story, and yet it had a very unusual kind of effect on you. I remember I was the distributor of that film in Delhi, and it went on for years, and we realized that in one cinema, in the center of Delhi at Connaught Place, Regal Cinema, there was a member of the audience who had been seeing it right through the year, every day. He would come for his night show at 9:30, and the same seat had to be reserved for him, and he would sit, sometimes for an hour, sometimes for two hours, and then go away. He sat there for the whole year, and at the end of the year I asked the management of the cinema to go and find out why, because we did want to also honor him. But I wanted to know the reason, because when I told this to my brother Mr. Raj Kapoor, he said, "But why, why every day?" He said, in a very simple way, he was a Punjabi, and he was in his 60s, and he said in Punjabi, that it was so pleasing to the eyes. And maybe his mind and his health also, but he loved it. So after the entire day's work, and after

his meal, he would everyday go to the cinema, sit there, for a total relaxation for his entire self, and enjoy himself, and he did that for the whole
year. So we gave him an award.

(Interview with author August 8, 1996)

Aamir Khan discusses the relationship between an actor and the
audience:

On one level I feel that the relationship between an actor and an audience
is a very strange relationship. It's a very unfair relationship because what
happens is that as an audience you see various films of the actor. You see
him in various moods, you see him laughing, you see him crying, you see
him having fun, you see him brooding, you see him sulking, you see him in
pain. And you feel you know the person. You know [laughs], I feel I know
Bruce Willis. I haven't met him, but I think I know him. Actually I don't, okay?
[laughs]. The audience has an unfair advantage because they have seen
you, and they've seen how you smile, they know what your face looks like,

FIGURE 5.1   Aamir Khan signing autographs during a film shoot at the
Oshiwada Complex, Bombay
© Tejaswini Ganti, 1996

and they know a lot of things about you, they read a lot of things about you, and when they meet you, you don't know them at all. So you're looking at somebody who's a complete stranger and the person is, "Hi, how are you?" And you don't even know the person. So you find it difficult. You have to understand, "Oh one sec [second], he really knows me inside out; at least he thinks he knows me inside out." So there's a slight imbalance over there because the audiences have seen a lot of you and you haven't seen anything of the audience.

The other thing is, I think ultimately your character as a human being does seep in somewhere through your work. No matter how many different roles you play and different kinds of films you do, and you behave differently in all your various films, somewhere broadly speaking they get to know whether they like you or they don't like you, whether they respect you or they don't, how much they like you and how much they respect you, also they come to know. Somewhere that thing seeps through, whether they think you are a nice human being or not. And that is something which you can't control, you have no control over. What you are eventually seeps through in your work, and maybe that's true for every profession. In your work, your true self somewhere gets reflected, whether you're attempting or not attempting it. And so when an audience, when somebody from the audience sees me in real life – on the road or in my car or if I'm shooting someplace and if he comes to me or if she comes to me, the way they interact with me indicates how much they like me and how much respect they have for me. And I think that's important to me.

Hardcore fans have a heightened sensitivity towards their idols. They're extremely hurt if they see a film of yours which they don't like. They're extremely hurt if they see a film of yours which you haven't done well in, and stuff like that. And they are that much more excited than other people if your work is nice. They're like "Wow, see we always knew he was the best!" [laughs]. And then they get affected by what you say and how you behave and what you do . . . so when you meet a person who's just a normal audience who likes you and who's interacting with you it's different. When you meet a guy who's hyper about you, he may not show it, but when he's looking at you, and when he comes to say hi to you, he may be really hyper within himself. And at that point if you're not nice to him, it really hurts him.

But it's very difficult for an actor because what the audiences sometimes don't realize is that there are so many of them and there is only one of you. And there are times when you're trying to concentrate on your work; there are times when you're trying to be involved with what you're doing. Unfortunately our office space is everybody else's public space, you know [laughs]. Like they're shooting in this building now – this is my office, if 20 kids come and ask me for my autograph, what they are in fact doing is entering my office, opening my door, and while I am working, coming in and saying, "Sign those papers later, give that shot later, first we want our auto-graph." So that's a little unfair, I guess, sometimes you know; it's disturbing sometimes.

Sometimes, there's a lot of pressure on you, so it's not always possible to be absolutely polite to every person that you meet, but I try my level best to deal with each person that I meet on a one-to-one level. The person who is coming to meet me is a human being like me and I try my level best to interact as I would with any other human being, trying to put aside that I'm an actor, and that person feels I am special, though in fact, I am not you know, I am just like that person. It's just because a lot of people see me and I'm publicly visible that people sometimes think I am special. In fact I am not and if that person has liked my work, I must reciprocate in the appro-priate manner, I must behave myself properly, and basically I think that one must in life respect other human beings, whether you are an actor or not.

(Interview with author, March 23, 1996)

Madhuri Dixit talks about the relationship between stars and their fans and relays some anecdotes about her encounters with fans:

I have always been fascinated by the concept of fans because I've always wondered at the mystery of this whole phenomenon, that a person watches me or any other person playing some third person on the screen and they get so carried away or so impressed by that, that if they're old women, they start feeling, "This is my daughter." If they're very young kids, they start feel-ing, "This should be my sister." What is this phenomenon? That's why whenever I meet my fans, it's with a great deal of respect because they are what make us. You know we cannot survive on our own; we need them to survive. Also I have this feeling, what are they missing that they find so attractive in me? Or what are they searching for? You know? It's that kind of a thing.

Like I came to know about this little girl who was 7 years old, she used to go to school, and once they had a parent day meeting. She lives abroad in the U.S., so she went to her school and her teacher started talking to the mother and said, "Is there any tension in your family, is there something wrong?" She [the mother] said, "No, why do you ask?" "Well she keeps referring to someone in India who's her mother and she says she's got two mothers." So this lady was flabbergasted and said, "What?" "Yeah, she talks about sisters being there and she's dying to meet her mother." So the mother asked her daughter, "What is this? What have you been telling at school?" First she got scared and then they cajoled her into saying, "Yeah, I have another mother there." "Who's that?" "Madhuri Dixit" [laughing]. So you know sometimes, their fantasy carries them to such an extent.

And of course there are fans who I don't know, they think that you're something beyond life, or you're not human probably, you're made up of something else or I don't know what it is. Once we were shooting in Jaipur and there's this fan who walked up, "Can I have an autograph?" And I gave him an autograph, and he said, "Can I ask you a question?" I said, "Yeah sure." He says, "Is this your original face?" [laughs]. I said, "What do you mean? Is this my original face?" And I still don't know what he meant – did he mean that do you look like this in your real life too, or do you look like this everyday, or what is it? It's always fascinating to meet fans.

(Interview with author, November 25, 1996)

Actor/producer Shahrukh Khan (see chapter 3) discusses how audiences are generally perceived by the film industry and then explains his views about film audiences:

I think the Indian audience is the most developed, most intelligent, most open audience that the world has. Filmmakers, when we do a film, they say "Audience will not understand." That means, you are essentially making a film thinking that your audience are fools. And then, on the other hand, the dichotomy or the irony is that, you keep saying, "I make films only for the audience." You have to understand, that an audience, logical things even a kid will understand. You know, A is equal to B, B is equal to C, that's why A is equal to C. A plus B, or C plus A plus T is equal to a CAT. Now, I'm showing the audience that there is a man who's jumping from 100 feet, on to the back of a horse, and nothing happens to him or his genitals, and he rides off very happily on this horse and goes and saves the princess. They *know* it is unreal! You know, there's a level of intelligence which 100 percent understands it's unreal, *but*, you are sitting there, you say "I forgive that, *yaar*! I know it's unreal *yaar*!" Now if you have a guy who says, "That doesn't happen in that way! Come on, you can't be like this!" I think his level of intelligence is really low.

We *know* we can't be like this! We know everything. People don't fly. But, unless you accept these things, and dream about them, they will never become reality. If there was, I mean, I think those people who are elitist and talk lowly about the audience, they are the people who didn't believe that man will reach the moon. They are the same people who did not believe that man can fly; they are the same people who believe that there can't be a heart transplant.

And it is the normal person, who is − you know, I have a line which I tell everyone, "That it is not special to be special, it is special to be ordinary." And our audience is ordinary. You know, I have a lot of money, a lot of fame, and I get up in the morning when I feel like, I go for my shooting. I come back and relax. I sit down with my friends; I play on my computer; I have video games; I have access to every place in the world; I fly down with my wife; I have a very good time and come back, *but*, that same guy, in the morning, at six o'clock in the morning he gets up to reach a place, which [he'll reach by] is ten o'clock. Four hours he travels in a train. He is pushed around. He goes back there, gets his 30 rupees, gets back home, plays with his children, and he still celebrates Diwali[3] with more happiness, a simpler Diwali with more happiness. I have to have a party. I have to have a drink to enjoy myself. I have to call friends. I have to get the high society people attending my party. I'm so bloody bothered about, "Will this guy come, won't he?" Because my party won't happen otherwise. That guy doesn't give a damn. He's got his four children. He's got his wife who fights with him, but he really has a good time!

The ability to really have a good time in less, is what makes you special. Not if you're going to find happiness in specialties, that is nothing special. So it is special to be ordinary, and if you are ordinary, I believe, that anyone who's special looks down upon, obviously they will look down upon the ordinary. Because somewhere along the line, they are *very envious* of the fact that they can't enjoy a simpler Diwali, like that ordinary man can. And that is why, to make themselves feel better, they want to demean the status of someone who they already think is less. So you have to keep reminding yourself, you're not reminding him, you're reminding yourself of *your* greatness by looking at somebody else's lessness. And, I think, that is why they look down upon the audience.

I think the Indian audience is the most intelligent, most open – they let anyone come into the industry. A guy who's, I think that I in no parlance could I have been hero material, but they accept me. I'm not a great looker; I'm not very tall; I don't have a fantastic persona; I don't talk very well; I don't have a great voice; I don't have a fantastic physique; I don't dance like a Govinda; I don't fight like Bruce Lee. I don't even act like Robert DeNiro. But, they accept me. They've given me so much. That *means*, to be able to accept, is much greater than to be able to criticize and not accept. I mean, a guy who's really big will accept even an idiot. He'll say, "Okay, he's not bad, he's okay." So they accept idiots like me, and I don't have to prove to him that okay, I'm great. He already knows. He's paid 20 rupees, "You're great, come, show me good fun. That's all!"

So I'd rather be liking the person who accepts me as I am, instead of the person whose attitude is, "Shit, look at Shahrukh. He comes to a party in blue jeans and a white shirt." I was never invited for big parties when I came down. Everybody found, all the elite people found my hair wrong, my dialogue delivery wrong. I would never dress up and go for parties because I don't believe in that. People used to make comments about the fact that, "Oh, look at the way he's dressed." Some people have told me also, "Shahrukh, dress up properly and come to a party." I wouldn't go there.

Today they all call me, and my, "slobbiness," or sloppiness, has been now converted into a more intellectual word, "eccentricity." And I'm accepted at the biggest of parties, and people love to have me there, so basically what they're going for, is just the name. While the audience accepted me with my bad jeans, wrong hair, wrong dialogue, and they love me. So I know, they're much more open; they are much more loving. And if you are much more loving, then you are much better than the elite.

(Interview with author, March 15, 1996)

6

SIGNIFICANT DATES AND EVENTS IN THE HISTORY OF INDIAN CINEMA

Sources for this chronology include *Indian Film* (Barnouw and Krishnaswamy 1980) and the *Encyclopaedia of Indian Cinema* (Rajadhyaksha and Willemen 1999).

1896   First screening of motion pictures in India – the Lumière cinematographe takes place at the Watson's Hotel in Bombay on July 7.

1897   Harischandra S. Bhatvedekar, a photographer, imports a motion picture camera and starts filming short subjects.

1898   Short films are being shown in theaters and tents set up on fair grounds in Bombay, Calcutta, and Madras.

1902   J.F. Madan launches regular bioscope showings in a tent in Calcutta's Maidan (fair grounds), thus laying the foundation of an extensive exhibition and distribution network that dominated silent Indian, Burmese, and Sri Lankan cinemas.

1906   "Picture palaces" start becoming a feature of major cities in India.

1910   Dadasaheb Phalke sees *The Life of Christ* at the America-India Cinema in Bombay.

1911   George V's visit to Delhi and his grand Durbar (public meeting) is the first extensively filmed public event in India.

1912   *Pundalik*, a stage play, is filmed and can be considered the first Indian feature film.

1913   *Raja Harischandra*, a feature-length film by Phalke opens at the Coronation Theatre in Bombay on May 3.

   Phalke's second feature, *Mohini Bhasmasur* (The Legend of Bhasmasur) is the first Indian film to use an actress.

1914   Phalke shows his first three features, *Raja Harischandra*, *Mohini Bhasmasur*, and *Satyavan Savitri* in London.

1916   Universal Pictures becomes the first American company to establish an agent in India.

1917   Phalke releases a documentary, *How Films Are Made*, to educate audiences about the filmmaking process.

1918   The Indian Cinematograph Act establishes censorship and a theater-licensing system.

   The Hindustan Film Company is formed by Phalke and financial backers.

1920   Gandhi launches non-cooperation movement against British rule calling for "the defiance of every state-made law."

   Film censor boards are set up in Bombay, Calcutta, Madras.

   Nala Damayanti, an Indian-Italian project, produced by Madan Theatres is the first international co-production involving India.

1921   Kohinoor Studios' *Bhakta Vidur* (Vidur's Devotion), banned in Madras and Sindh becomes Indian cinema's first censorship controversy.

1922   Entertainment tax on film exhibition is levied in Calcutta.

1923   Entertainment tax of 12.5 percent is levied in Bombay.

1925   *The Light of Asia*, an Indo-German co-production directed by Franz Osten, begins a series of international ventures between him and Himansu Rai who also starred in the feature.

The first Indian woman producer and director, Fatma Begum, starts her production company and debuts as director with her film *Bulbul-e-Parastan* (Fairy) released in 1926.

1926 Imperial Films is founded by Ardeshir Irani who later makes India's first sound film.

85 percent of the films shown in India are foreign, mainly American.

1927 The Indian Cinematograph Committee is formed to study the cinema in India, and the feasibility of furthering "empire films" to counter American dominance.

1928 The Indian Cinematograph Committee publishes its report. Rather than recommending preferential treatment for British films, the Report proposes a series of measures to promote Indian films instead. The British administration ignores it.

1929 Many important studios are founded such as Prabhat Film Company in Kolhapur and Ranjit Movietone in Bombay.

Universal's *Melody of Love* initiates the sound film era in India at Madan's Elphinstone Picture Palace, Calcutta.

Universal negotiates for purchase of the Madan chain, but negotiations end due to the Wall Street crash and the beginning of the world-wide economic depression.

1930 Many Indian silent film companies collapse.

Colonial government begins to ban all newsreels on Gandhi's activities and demonstrations.

1931 *Alam Ara* – the first sound film in India is released in the Hindi language, directed by Ardeshir Irani, and produced by Imperial Films.

In the same year, the first sound features in Tamil, Telugu, and Bengali are produced.

New Theatres is founded by B.N. Sircar in Calcutta.

1932 The first sound features in Gujarati and Marathi are produced.

The Motion Picture Society of India is established to represent the Indian film industry.

1933   75 Hindi films are produced, all with songs and dances.

Wadia Movietone is founded and begins to specialize in "stunt films" and establishes them as a respectable, big-budget genre with *Hunterwali* (Whip; 1935).

Prabhat Studios' *Sairandhri*, processed and printed in Germany, becomes India's first color film.

1934   Bombay Talkies is established by Himansu Rai.

First sound features in the Oriya and Kannada languages.

Toofan Mail produced by Ranjit Studios is Hindi cinema's first major success in the "stunt film" genre.

1935   India produces 228 features.

The playback singer becomes a permanent fixture in Indian film production with the film, *Dhoop Chaon* produced by New Theatres.

The Bengali and Hindi versions of P.C. Barua's *Devdas* are extremely successful, leading to the popularity of the theme of the tragic, love-lorn hero.

First sound features in Punjabi and Assamese.

1936   All India Radio is started.

1937   Prabhat's *Sant Tukaram* (Saint Tukaram) wins a special jury mention at the Venice Film Festival, the first Indian film to do so.

The first indigenously made color film is *Kisan Kanya* using the Cinecolor process acquired by Imperial Films.

Phalke makes his last film, *Gangatavaran* (Descent of Ganga).

Indian Motion Pictures Producers Association (IMPPA) is established in Bombay.

1938   The Indian Film Industry celebrates its twenty-fifth anniversary (using Phalke's *Raja Harischandra* as a starting point).

First feature film in Malayalam.

1939   British government declares war on Germany in the name of India. Nehru protests, as do other nationalist leaders.

1940   The Film Advisory Board is set up by the colonial government and is granted monopoly over raw stock.

Censorship of films likely to support the independence movement with images or words intensifies.

1942   The Quit India movement is launched and widescale unrest and violent confrontation between the colonial regime and Indian subjects follows.

Censors remove portraits of Gandhi and Nehru along with Congress songs and symbols from feature films.

Filmistan Studios is founded by a splinter group from Bombay Talkies led by S. Mukherjee and Ashok Kumar.

V. Shantaram starts the Rajkamal Kalamandir Studio on the former Wadia Movietone premises.

Mehboob Khan starts his own production company which becomes a studio in 1952.

1943   *Kismet*, one of the biggest hits in Indian film history, is released.

Rajkamal Kalamandir's debut film, *Shakuntala*, is a major hit.

The English version of *Raj Nartaki* – Court Dancer – is released in the U.S. in a few theaters.

The Indian Peoples' Theatre Association (IPTA) puts on its first production.

1944   The government appoints a Film Advisory Committee.

Entertainment tax is increased in the United Provinces, Central Provinces, Bombay and Madras Presidencies.

Dadasaheb Phalke dies, forgotten and destitute.

1945   The government withdraws state control on raw stock distribution.

1947   India wins its independence from Britain but is partitioned into India and Pakistan.

V. Shantaram's *Shakuntala* becomes the first Indian feature to be shown in a U.S. theater.

1948   Mahatma Gandhi is assassinated by a Hindu extremist, upset by the Partition of the subcontinent.

Raj Kapoor starts R.K. films, building his studio in 1950.

Prime Minister Nehru announces a freeze on the construction of movie theaters.

India and Pakistan go to war over Kashmir.

1949   Protesting taxation, the film industry stages an All India Protest Day. In response, the government forms a Film Enquiry Committee that includes members of the industry.

Dharti Ke Lal (Children of the Earth – produced in 1946 by IPTA) becomes the first Indian film to receive widespread distribution in the Soviet Union.

Cinematograph Act of 1918 is amended.

Entertainment tax rates increase to 50 percent in Central India and to 75 percent in West Bengal. Protesting these increases, theaters in these regions go on strike.

Brothers Chetan and Dev Anand start Navketan Productions in Bombay, which becomes one of the main avenues for IPTA members to enter Hindi cinema.

1950   The Dravidian Forward Movement (DMK), closely linked to Tamil film interests and the struggle against Hindi as a national language, gains further strength in southern India.

The Pakistani government initiates a tax of one rupee per foot on all imported Indian films.

1951   The Report of the Film Enquiry Committee (appointed in 1949) is released: it urges the creation of a Film Finance Corporation, an Institute of Film Art as a training school, and an Export Corporation to promote foreign markets.

Film censorship is centralized under a Central Board of Film Censors located in Bombay.

The Film Federation of India is formed – joining together all sectors of the industry.

1952   The First International Film Festival of India is held in Bombay, Madras, and Calcutta. The films of Italian neo-realist Vittorio De Sica have a great impact.

Bimal Roy moves to Bombay from Calcutta and starts his production company.

The Indian Cinematograph Act of 1952 is passed replacing the 1918 Act but makes few changes.

Bombay Talkies ceases production.

Film producers end their agreement with All India Radio (AIR) to broadcast film songs because AIR refuses to name producers or the film titles.

West Pakistan bans the import of Indian films.

An Indian film delegation visits Hollywood on invitation from the Motion Picture Association of America.

1953   Prabhat Film Company ends production, effectively ending the studio era in India.

Filmfare magazine inaugurates its annual awards for the best in Hindi cinema.

1954   Raj Kapoor's *Awara* is a huge success in the Soviet Union.

Bimal Roy's *Do Bigha Zamin* is given a special mention at the Cannes Film Festival and wins the Social Progress Award at the Karlovy Vary film festival.

National Awards for films are instituted.

Indian film delegations visit the Middle East and the Soviet Union.

1955   Nehru inaugurates the Non-Aligned Movement in a cold war context.

Satyajit Ray's Bengali film, *Pather Panchali* (Song of the Road) has its world premiere at the Museum of Modern Art in New York. It makes money for the West Bengal State government which partially financed the film; this in turn helps to persuade the central government to set up the Film Finance Corporation in 1960. Ray is celebrated by the Western media for representing "authentic Indian realities." His work is held up as achieving a standard that most Hindi filmmakers do not meet.

Festivals of Indian cinema take place in Beijing and London.

1956   The States Reorganization Bill is passed and the map of India is redrawn resulting in linguistically organized states.

Language riots take place in Ahmedabad over the proposed division of Bombay state into the states of Maharashtra and Gujarat.

The freeze on the construction of new cinemas in Bombay is lifted.

Indian films are shown at the Edinburgh, Karlovy Vary, and Berlin film festivals.

1957   Raj Kapoor's *Jagte Raho* (Keep Awake) wins first prize in Karlovy Vary.

Satyajit Ray's *Aparajito* wins first prize at the Venice Film Festival.

Bimal Roy's *Kabuliwala* (The Man from Kabul) wins a special mention for music at the Berlin Film Festival.

K.A. Abbas produces *Pardesi* (Foreigner) in collaboration with Mosfilm, and becomes the first Indo-Soviet co-production.

Raw stock is declared an essential commodity and its import is centrally controlled.

1959   Television arrives in India as a weekly half-hour service with a range of 40 kms around Delhi.

Guru Dutt makes the first Indian CinemaScope film, *Kaagaz ke Phool*.

V. Shantaram's *Do Aankhen Baara Haath* (Two Eyes, Twelve Hands) is shown in Berlin and wins the Hollywood Foreign Press Association and Samuel Goldwyn awards for Best Foreign Film.

1960   Bombay State is divided into the states of Maharashtra and Gujarat.

The Film Finance Corporation (FFC) is formed by the government to give low-interest loans to selected projects. During the late 1960s, the FFC emphasizes the financing of the independent sector.

The Film Institute of India is established at Pune in the old Prabhat Studios.

Mughal-e-azam, the most expensive feature to date is completed.

1961   The import of raw film stock is drastically reduced.

Gunga Jumna promotes the use of regional dialects in the mainstream Hindi film.

1962   India engages in a border war with China in the North and Northeast.

Pakistan bans Indian films in its eastern, Bengali-speaking half, which has negative repercussions for the production of Bengali cinema in Calcutta as the industry loses 40 percent of its audience.

As All India Radio concentrates on popularizing classical music, Radio Ceylon begins its broadcast of Hindi film songs and film-based programs, thereby capturing India's commercial radio audience.

1963   The Indian Motion Picture Export Corporation is formed.

1964   Prime Minister Nehru dies.

The National Film Archive of India is established at Pune under the Ministry of Information and Broadcasting.

1965   India and Pakistan engage in a second war over Kashmir's borders.

Major language riots take place in South India over the adoption of Hindi as the "link" language.

Television becomes a daily service of one hour restricted to Delhi.

1966   Indira Gandhi, Nehru's daughter, becomes Prime Minister after the sudden death of Nehru's successor, Lal Bahadur Shastri.

The Dadasaheb Phalke Lifetime Achievement Awards are established to honor Indian film pioneers.

1967   Hindustan Photo Films makes India self-sufficient in black and white film and sound negative film. All color stock however is still imported, but locally perforated.

The first 70-mm wide-screen film is screened in India.

1968   The G.D. Khosla Committee publishes its Report on Film Censorship, criticizing the censor guidelines, asserting that if followed closely, not a single film would be certified.

        K.A. Abbas' independent short film, *Char Shaher Ek Kahani* (Four Cities, One Story), initiates a major controversy by implying that censorship violates the constitutional right to free speech.

        Filmmakers Mrinal Sen and Arun Kaul issue a manifesto for a New Indian Cinema movement advocating a state-sponsored alternative to commercial cinema.

1969   *Bhuvan Shome* and *Uski Roti* (His Bread) financed by the Film Finance Corporation initiate "New Indian Cinema" – a movement rejecting the style and substance of the Bombay film industry.

        The tremendous success of *Aradhana* makes Rajesh Khanna a nation-wide sensation.

1970   The publication of the English-language magazine *Stardust*, focusing on gossip and scandal, transforms the concept of the film magazine.

        The centennial anniversary of Dadasaheb Phalke's birth is celebrated and a street is named after him in Bombay.

1971   India produces 433 feature films making it the largest film producer in the world.

        The agreement between the Indian government and the Motion Picture Export Association of America (MPEAA) is allowed to expire. The number of foreign films censored drops from 114 in 1972 to 38 in 1973 and 26 in 1974.

1972   Television starts in Bombay.

        First art-house cinema is opened by the Film Finance Corporation.

1973   The Film Finance Corporation becomes the regulating agency for the import of raw stock. A 250 percent import duty on raw stock is imposed.

Zanjeer starring Amitabh Bachchan is released and is a huge success – launching the "angry young man" genre, which has a lasting impact on Indian cinema.

1974 A 'peaceful' nuclear blast demonstrates India's nuclear capability.

The Film and Television Institute of India – the preeminent film training school – is formed with the merger of the Film Institute of India and the TV Training Centre.

The International Film Festival of India becomes an annual event.

Shyam Benegal's *Ankur* (Seedling) does well commercially and gives a boost to "alternative cinema."

1975 Ramesh Sippy's *Sholay* is released and is an enormous box-office success. A new agreement with the MPEAA signals that films can once again be imported from the U.S.

Prime Minister Indira Gandhi declares the Emergency.

The state television network, Doordarshan, expands its number of terrestrial stations.

1976 Film Finance Corporation's art-film policy is attacked.

The negative of Amrit Nahata's *Kissa Kursi Ka* (Episode about a Chair), a satire on Emergency Rule, is destroyed by Sanjay Gandhi's representatives.

1977 Indira Gandhi is defeated in national elections and a coalition of different opposition groups form the government. The Emergency is withdrawn.

M.G. Ramachandran, an extremely popular star of Tamil films, becomes the chief minister of Tamil Nadu. He introduces programs to assist the Tamil film industry including government subsidies – film production goes up substantially.

1978 A number of state governments (Orissa, Andhra Pradesh, Tamil Nadu) adopt programs ranging from financing schemes to directly building (state-owned) movie theaters in rural and semi-urban areas.

1979 Malayalam film production reaches 123 exceeding Hindi cinema, partly because of the Kerala government's subsidies, but mostly due to the influx of money remitted by Malayali workers in the Middle East.

1980 Doordarshan has its first color telecast on July 18.

The Information and Broadcasting Minister makes color television one of the Congress (I) party's main election promises.

The Film Finance Corporation merges with the Indian Motion Picture Export Corporation to become the National Film Development Corporation (NFDC).

The Report of the Working Group on National Film Policy is published, but all of its recommendations are ignored by the government.

1981 The short-lived Indian Academy of Motion Picture Arts and Sciences celebrates 50 years of Indian cinema (using 1931 as a point of reference).

India borrows $5 billion from the IMF, the biggest such loan in history.

1982 INSAT 1-A (a satellite) is launched from Cape Canaveral, inaugurating a national television program.

The Ninth Asian Games held in New Delhi provide the first nation-wide color broadcasts.

1984 The worst industrial disaster of the twentieth century takes place at the Union Carbide plant in Bhopal where deadly emissions kill nearly 4,000 people and injure half a million people.

Prime Minister Indira Gandhi is assassinated by her security guards in retaliation for her ordering the army to attack the Golden Temple in Amritsar – the most sacred of Sikh shrines – to hunt down Sikh separatists. Her death sets off wide-scale riots in Delhi where over 2,700 people, mostly Sikhs, are killed.

Doordarshan starts a second channel from Delhi.

Cable television begins unofficially, spreading from tourist hotels to apartment blocks and individual households. These networks are initially fed by videocassette players, linked centrally to the cable network.

1985   Doordarshan becomes fully commercial by selling advertising slots to private sponsors.

The first successful series sponsored by Colgate-Palmolive and Nestlé, is *Humlog* (We, the people), modeled on the Mexican concept of the "development" soap opera.

Several privately-made television series follow as TV ownership increases from 2.7 million in 1984 to 12.5 million in 1986.

1987   The *Ramayan* television serial based on the Hindu epic becomes Indian television's first major hit.

1989   The Soviet Union withdraws from Afghanistan leading the U.S. to end its financial and military support to Pakistan as its ally against communism in the region. As a result, the insurgency in Kashmir flares up since the region is flooded with arms and mercenaries, who were originally focused on the fight against the Soviets.

Hindi filmmakers are unable to shoot in Kashmir – one of their favorite locations – due to the ensuing violence and curfews.

1990   3,450 cable TV networks exist in India, divided between the four major metropolitan areas of Bombay, Delhi, Calcutta, and Madras.

The U.S., U.K., and their allies go to war against Iraq for its invasion of Kuwait.

1991   Cable networks become equipped with satellite dishes and start broadcasting CNN, BBC, and STAR TV reports of the Persian Gulf War.

Former Prime Minister Rajiv Gandhi is assassinated by a suicide bomber, suspected to be a member of the LTTE

(Liberation Tamil Tigers of Eelam) who have been fighting for a separate Tamil homeland in Sri Lanka since 1983.

Indian government takes a loan from the International Monetary Fund (IMF) for $1.8 billion in January and another one later in the year. These loans are accompanied by conditions that initiate a policy of economic reform which is popularly referred to as "liberalization."

1992   The sixteenth-century Babri Masjid (mosque) in Ayodhya, Uttar Pradesh, is destroyed by mobs of "volunteers" organized and mobilized by Hindu chauvinist organizations. While large-scale riots break out all over the country, the violence is particularly severe in Bombay.

Rupert Murdoch's STAR TV starts its telecasts into India.

Zee TV – India's first private Hindi-language satellite channel – is launched.

1993   Further riots and violence break out in Bombay in January, as the death toll in the city in the aftermath of the Babri Masjid's demolition rises to nearly 800.

A series of 10 bombs explode through key areas of Bombay including the stock exchange, leaving 317 dead.

Movie star Sanjay Dutt is arrested under the TADA (Terrorists and Disruptive Activities Prevention) Act for possessing an illegal AK-56 assault rifle.

Subhash Ghai's *Khalnayak* starring Sanjay Dutt releases and a nation-wide controversy ensues over its song, *Choli ke peeche*.

1994   *Jurassic Park* is dubbed into Hindi and grosses 120 million rupees. Shortly after, a whole spate of Hollywood films are dubbed into Hindi and released, but none repeat the success of *Jurassic Park*.

Hum Aapke Hain Kaun! is declared the biggest hit in the history of Indian cinema – estimating a total gross of 2 billion rupees world-wide.

Shekar Kapur's *Bandit Queen* about infamous outlaw Phoolan Devi is virtually banned by the Censor Board.

1995   NFDC launches its celebrations of the centenary year of cinema.

1996   *Bandit Queen* is released in January, but is banned in March by the Delhi High Court ruling in favor of a defamation suit brought against the film by a member of the Gujjar community claiming the film was excessively derogatory. The Supreme Court lifts the ban in May.

   The hundredth anniversary of the Lumière screenings are celebrated by the state government of Maharashtra in Bombay with a parade, a reception, screenings, a photography exhibit, and a plaque affixed to the building that was the site of the first screenings.

1997   Gulshan Kumar, owner of the T-series music label and responsible for breaking HMV's monopoly over recorded music by marketing and manufacturing cheap audiocassettes, is murdered in broad daylight. Leading Hindi music director Nadeem is accused of murder and of acting in collusion with Dubai-based gangster, Dawood Ibrahim. Much is written in the Indian press about the "nexus" between the "underworld" and the Bombay film industry.

1998   The Hindu nationalist Bharatiya Janata Party (BJP) comes to power for the first time in a coalition government.
   Explosions of nuclear devices, first by India and followed by Pakistan, confirm long-held suspicions about both countries' nuclear weapons capabilities.
   Filmmaking is granted official industry status by the government, thus opening the way for bank and corporate finance. Hindi films start appearing regularly on the weekly top 10 box-office charts in the U.K.

1999   Subhash Ghai's *Taal*, debuts on *Variety*'s weekly domestic box-office report as the twentieth highest-grossing film in the U.S. It performs better overseas than in India. The overseas market becomes a coveted territory for Hindi filmmakers.

First Annual Bollywood Awards are held in New York City. Organized by a South Asian businessman, the awards are based on popular choice – people vote online – to represent the South Asian diaspora's point of view on Hindi films.

2000 A wax statue of Amitabh Bachchan is installed at Madame Tussaud's Museum in London.

First International Indian Film Academy Awards are held at the Millenium Dome in London. The Academy is formed by prominent members of the Bombay film industry to help promote Indian cinema globally and to capitalize on the popularity of Hindi cinema among the South Asian diaspora. It becomes an annual event taking place in different foreign venues such as Malaysia and South Africa.

Small-time Hindi film producer Nazim Rizvi is arrested by the Bombay police for his links with Karachi-based gangsters. Police seize the negatives of his big-budget, star-cast film, *Chori Chori Chupke Chupke* (CCCC; Secretly and Quietly), thus delaying its release. Once again, much is written in the Indian press about the "nexus" between the "underworld" and the Bombay film industry.

2001 Diamond merchant Bharat Shah who became the Bombay industry's most prominent and powerful financier in the past decade is arrested by the Bombay police for his alleged business links with organized crime in connection with his financing of CCCC.

CCCC is released in March through a court-appointed receiver. Bombay High Court orders that its box-office earnings be given to the Government of India.

Lagaan – directed by Ashutosh Gowariker and produced by Aamir Khan – is nominated for an Academy Award for Best Foreign Film. Only the second time that a film from the Bombay film industry is nominated, the previous one being *Mother India* (1957).

Phoolan Devi, an ex-outlaw and Member of Parliament, upon whose life the film *Bandit Queen* was based, is gunned down and killed in front of her home in Delhi.

2002   *Devdas* – directed by Sanjay Leela Bhansali – is the first commercial Hindi film to premiere at the Cannes Film Festival.

Andrew Lloyd Webber's Hindi cinema inspired musical, *Bombay Dreams*, opens in London's Apollo Victoria Theatre.

An exhibition detailing the history of Hindi film posters entitled "Cinema India: The Art of Bollywood" is held at London's Victoria & Albert Museum.

Selfridge's, a chain of department stores in England, stages a "Bollywood season" at one of its London stores, converting the premises into a celebration of Hindi cinema culture. Entire film sets are recreated in the store as is actress Dimple Kapadia's entire Bombay home.

The British Film Institute organizes "ImagineAsia," an eight-month festival of South Asian cinema.

2003   Hindi actress, Aishwarya Rai and one of the stars of *Devdas*, is asked to be on the jury at the Cannes Film Festival.

Turner Classic Movies has a month-long festival of "Bollywood" films on its cable channel in the United States.

SUGGESTIONS FOR FURTHER READING

General reference

Rajadhyaksha, A. and Willemen, Paul (eds) (1999) *Encyclopaedia of Indian Cinema*, London: British Film Institute.

Thoraval, Y. (2000) *The Cinemas of India*, New Delhi: Macmillan.

Broad historical surveys

Barnouw, E. and Krishnaswamy, S. (1980) *Indian Film*, New York: Oxford University Press.

Garga, B.D. (1996) *So Many Cinemas: The Motion Picture in India*, Mumbai: Eminence Designs.

Specific film history

Bandyopadhyay, S. (ed.) (1993) *Indian Cinema: Contemporary Perceptions from the Thirties*, Jamshedpur: Celluloid Chapter.

Kaul, G. (1998) *Cinema and the Indian Freedom Struggle*, New Delhi: Sterling.

Shoesmith, B. (1988) "Swadeshi Cinema: Cinema, Politics and Culture: The Writings of D.G. Phalke," *Continuum* 2(1): 44–73.
—— (1987) "From Monopoly to Commodity: The Bombay Studios in the 1930s," in T. O'Regan and B. Shoesmith (eds) *History On/And/In Film: Selected Papers from the 3rd Australian History and Film Conference*, Perth: History and Film Association of Australia.

Censorship

Vasudev, A. (1978) *Liberty and Licence in the Indian Cinema*, New Delhi: Vikas.

Film industry's perspective

Baghdadi, R. and Rao, R. (eds) (1995) *Talking Films*, New Delhi: Indus.
Kabir, N.M. (1999) *Talking Films: Conversations on Hindi Cinema with Javed Akhtar*, New Delhi: Oxford University Press.
Manto, S.H. (1998) *Stars From Another Sky*, New Delhi: Penguin.

Individual films and directors

Chatterjee, G. (2002) *Mother India*, London: British Film Institute.
—— (1992) *Awara*, New Delhi: Wiley Eastern.
Chopra, A. (2003) *Dilwale Dulhaniya Le Jayenge*, London: British Film Institute.
—— (2000) *Sholay: The Making of a Classic*, New Delhi: Penguin.
Dwyer, R. (2002) *Yash Chopra*, London: British Film Institute.
Kabir, N.M. (1996) *Guru Dutt: A Life in Cinema*, New Delhi: Oxford University Press.
Thomas, R. (1989) "Sanctity and Scandal: The Mythologization of Mother India," *Quarterly Review of Film and Video* 11(3): 11–30.

Formal/textual analysis

Mishra, V. (2002) *Bollywood Cinema: Temples of Desire*, New York: Routledge.

Prasad, M. (1998) *Ideology of the Hindi Film: A Historical Construction*, New Delhi: Oxford University Press.

Vasudevan, R. (ed.) (2000) *Making Meaning in Indian Cinema*, New Delhi: Oxford University Press.

Narrative style

Gopalan, L. (2002) *Cinema of Interruptions: Action Genres in Contemporary Indian Cinema*, London: British Film Institute.

Thomas, R. (1995) "Melodrama and the Negotiation of Morality in Mainstream Hindi Film," in C.A. Breckenridge (ed.) *Consuming Modernity: Public Culture in a South Asian World*, Minneapolis: University of Minnesota Press.

Vasudevan, R. (1995) "Addressing the Spectator of a 'Third World' National Cinema: the Bombay 'Social' Film of the 1940s and 1950s," *Screen* 36(4): 305–34.

—— (1989) "The Melodramatic Mode and the Commercial Hindi Cinema: Notes on Film History, Narrative and Performance," *Screen* 30(3): 29–50.

Visual style

Dwyer, R. and Patel, D. (2002) *Cinema India: The Visual Culture of Hindi Film*, New Brunswick, NJ: Rutgers University Press.

Rajadhyaksha, Ashish (1993) "The Phalke Era: Conflict of Traditional Form and Modern Technology," in T. Niranjana, P. Sudhir, and V. Dhareshwar (eds) *Interrogating Modernity: Culture and Colonialism in India*, Calcutta: Seagull.

Vinnels, D. and Skelly, B. (2002) *Bollywood Showplaces: Cinema Theatres in India*, London: Decorum Books.

Social and cultural analyses

Brosius, C. and Butcher, M. (eds) (1999) *Image Journeys: Audio-Visual Media and Cultural Change in India*, New Delhi: Sage.

Dwyer, R. and Pinney, C. (eds) (2001) *Pleasure and the Nation: The History, Politics and Consumption of Popular Culture in India*, New Delhi: Oxford University Press.

Ganti, T. (2002) "'And Yet My Heart Is Still Indian:' The Bombay Film Industry and the (H)Indianization of Hollywood," in F. Ginsburg, L. Abu-Lughod, and B. Larkin (eds) *Media Worlds: Anthropology on New Terrain*, Berkeley: University of California Press.

—— (1998) "Centenary Commemorations or Centenary Contestations? – Celebrating a Hundred Years of Cinema in Bombay," *Visual Anthropology* 11(4): 399–419.

Nandy, A. (ed.) (1998) *The Secret Politics of Our Desires: Innocence, Culpability and Indian Popular Cinema*, New Delhi: Oxford University Press.

Nation and nationalism

Chakravarty, S. (2000) "Fragmenting the Nation: Images of Terrorism in Indian Popular Cinema," in M. Hjort and S. MacKenzie (eds) *Cinema and Nation*, London: Routledge.

—— (1993) *National Identity in Indian Popular Cinema 1947–1987*, Austin: University of Texas Press.

Niranjana, T. (1994) "Integrating Whose Nation? Tourists and Terrorists in *Roja*," *Economic and Political Weekly* (29)3: 79–82.

Virdi, J. (2003) *The Cinematic Imagination: Indian Popular Films as Social History*, New Brunswick, NJ: Rutgers University Press.

Global circulation

Larkin, B. (1997) "Indian Films and Nigerian Lovers: Media and the Creation of Parallel Modernities," *Africa* 67(3): 406–40.

Pendakur, M. and Subramanyam, R. (1996) "Indian Cinema Beyond National Borders," in J. Sinclair, E. Jacka, and S. Cunningham (eds) *New Patterns in Global Television*, New York: Oxford University Press.

Tyrell, H. (1999) "Bollywood versus Hollywood: Battle of the Dream Factories," in T. Skelton and T. Allen (eds) *Culture and Global Change*, London: Routledge.

—— (1998) "Bollywood in Britain," *Sight and Sound* 8(8): 20–2.

NOTES

1 Introduction

1   This episode is from March 1996, and the film under production was the Hindi film *Duplicate*, starring Shahrukh Khan and Juhi Chawla, directed by Mahesh Bhatt, which was released in May 1998. The man in the chef's uniform was the star of the film, Shahrukh Khan, and the woman instructing him was Farah Khan, the film's choreographer who in Indian cinema parlance is referred to as the "dance director." Research in Bombay was supported by the American Institute of Indian Studies Junior Fellowship for dissertation research.

2   References to Luhrmann's film *Moulin Rouge*; Webber's musical *Bombay Dreams*; Channel Four's yearly season of Hindi films and documentaries about the Bombay film industry; Turner Classic Movies "Hooray for Bollywood" festival of Hindi films in June 2003; Macy's Bollywood window display in their flagship store in New York City in 1999; Selfridge's "Bollywood Season" in one of their London stores in 2002; Oscar nomination of *Lagaan* for best foreign film of 2001; World premiere of *Devdas* at the

Cannes Film Festival in 2002; Philips TV commercial for their televisions aired in the late 1990s which featured a spoof of Hindi films; Verizon TV commercial for their international calling plan aired in 2002 referred to India by stating, "Find out what's new in Bollywood."

3 Output has decreased since 1990. For example, 948 films were produced in 1990 out of which 200 were in Hindi, while 693 films were produced in 1998 out of which 153 were Hindi films. See Rajadhyaksha and Willemen 1999 for production figures from 1931–95 and Thoraval 2000 for figures from 1990–9.

4 Readers interested in the colonial period should consult the following: Bandyopadhyay 1993; Barnouw and Krishnaswamy 1980; Garga 1996; Kaul 1998; Shoesmith 1987, 1988; Rajadhyaksha and Willemen 1999; Thoraval 2000.

5 Sources for this section include: Barnouw and Krishnaswamy 1980; Chakravarty 1993; Dwivedi and Mehrotra 1995; Gangar 1995; Garga 1996; Oldenburg 1991; Patel and Thorner 1995a; Rajadhyaksha and Willemen 1999; Shoesmith 1987, 1988.

6 The date is not exactly clear – Chakravarty (1993) states 1896, Barnouw and Krishnaswamy (1980) state 1897, and Rajadhyaksha and Willemen (1999) state 1899. The confusion about dates is testament to the incomplete nature of the historiography of early Indian cinema. Much more research needs to be done. That the earliest films no longer exist adds to the difficulty.

7 The name Bombay is derived from the Portugese phrase, *bom bahia*, meaning the good bay. Originally an archipelago of seven islands, the Bombay islands were gifted by the King of Portugal in 1661 to King Charles II of England when he married the Portugese princess, Catherine of Braganza. The British Crown handed over the islands to the East India Company in 1668 for a rent of 10 pounds per year (Dwivedi and Mehrotra 1995). Although Bombay was officially renamed its Marathi equivalent "Mumbai" in 1995 and the print and broadcast media use the new name, the city is still referred to by its former name in daily

parlance by the vast majority of Indians, especially filmmakers. My choice to use "Bombay" rather than "Mumbai" throughout the book reflects this usage, but is also driven by a distaste for the nativist politics represented by the name change. The change was effected by the Shiv Sena, a Hindu and Marathi chauvinist political party, soon after they came to power in 1995, as an attempt to alter the diverse and cosmopolitan character of the city. For more about the cultural politics of the Shiv Sena see Ganti 1998.

8　The current Parsi community is miniscule with the largest concentration in Bombay. According to the 1991 Census of India, there were 76,382 Parsis in India, with 53,794 based in Greater Bombay. Another 40,000 are spread out throughout the world (in Luhrmann 1996: 31).

9　In 1970, during the celebrations of the birth centennial of Phalke, the main road in one of Bombay's suburbs – Dadar – was renamed Dadasaheb Phalke Road.

10　Navyug was a popular monthly cultural journal founded by Gavesh Vitthal Kulkarni in 1913. It published new writers on new subjects. It was part of a group of publications which advocated for complete independence from British rule (Shoesmith 1988).

11　There are 18 official languages in India and thousands of dialects. No one language is spoken by a majority of the population. Hindi is spoken by a plurality which means that it is the language spoken by the largest percentage of the population – close to 40 percent. However, this figure is calculated by counting a variety of dialects as well as languages that are similar to Hindi as Hindi. There is a standardized form of Hindi which is taught in schools and used in state television and radio broadcasts.

12　Urdu is a language originating and spoken in northern India with its roots in Persian and Arabic, and using an Arabic script. At the level of colloquial speech, Hindi (derived from Sanskrit and sharing its Devanagari script) and Urdu are mutually intelligible and interchangeable.

13 They did, however, change their names to appear more "Indian," so that Renee Smith became Sita Devi, Ruby Meyers became Sulochana, Effie Hippolet became Indira Devi, Bonnie Bird – Lalita Devi, Beryl Claesen – Madhuri, Winnie Stewart – Manorama, and Iris Gasper became Sabita Devi (Barnouw and Krishnaswamy 1980: 170).

14 Of course, readers should remember that a majority implies the presence of others so that a Muslim majority region means that Hindus and perhaps other religious communities also exist in that area and vice-versa for a Hindu majority region. In pre-Partition South Asia, it would have been difficult to find a religiously homogenous region.

15 The irony is that Urdu is not native to the regions which eventually became Pakistan. The dominant languages were Punjabi, Sindhi, Bengali, Baluchi, Pashtu, Multani, and Kutchi. Muslims who migrated from northern and central India to Pakistan were the initial community of Urdu speakers. The imposition of Urdu as the national language bred its own forms of resentment, especially in the eastern wing which spoke Bengali.

16 The British colonial government's obsession with orderly classifications and categorizations led them to reduce and essentialize many of the complex cultural, social, and religious institutions and practices in the subcontinent. Language was one of them, where through the censuses and other forms of bureaucratic discourse, the British along with Hindu chauvinists played an important role in delineating Hindi as "Hindu" and Urdu as "Muslim," which is a completely artificial distinction.

17 This total includes touring cinemas which comprise almost a quarter of the theaters, so in terms of actual permanent theatres, there are less than 10,000 screens. Movie theaters are unevenly distributed throughout the country, with many more in the southern states of Andhra Pradesh and Tamil Nadu than in the northern and most populous states of Uttar Pradesh and Bihar.

The U.S. which has a much smaller theater-going population (1.63 billion tickets sold in 2002) had 35,804 movie screens in 2002 (National Association of Theatre Owners 2003).

18 However, the number of screens can be misleading since the seating capacities of movie theaters in India are much larger than the U.S. Seating capacities range anywhere between 600–2,500 for a single screen, and 150–300 in "mini-theaters." A true comparison would be possible only by comparing the number of theater seats across different national contexts.

19 Although the Indian Constitution has an elaborate doctrine of fundamental rights and freedoms, it also has a provision that allows for a state of emergency and the suspension of those rights during situations where the security of India is seemingly threatened by war, "external aggression," or "internal disturbance." Though a state of emergency had been declared twice before – in response to the Chinese invasion in 1962 and the 1971 war with Pakistan, it was the first time that this measure was being imposed in response to domestic turmoil and unrest.

20 The first phase of economic liberalization began in 1985 under Prime Minister Rajiv Gandhi's government, focusing on exports and the import of some consumer goods and reducing some of the red tape required for such activities. Rajiv Gandhi had campaigned as a new kind of politician and leader capable of "leading India into the twenty-first century" and doing away with the "licence raj," referring to the extensive bureaucracy that had emerged over the years to the frustration of entrepreneurs and business leaders.

21 Since 1986, India has ranked as the one of the world's largest arms importers; the U.S. is the world's largest arms exporter.

22 Currency devaluation hurts domestic consumers, however, as it drives up prices.

23 Diaspora refers to a population that has dispersed from a common origin. South Asia comprises the countries of India,

Pakistan, Bangladesh, Nepal, Sri Lanka, Afghanistan, and Bhutan. South Asian diaspora refers to the communities from the afore-mentioned countries who have settled elsewhere.

24 A joint family is where at least two adult generations of a family reside together in the same household. The most common depiction in films is of three generations living together under one roof: a married couple, their unmarried daughters, their sons and daughters-in-law, and their grandchildren.

25 For example in 1998, West Bengal's tax rate of the box-office gross was 41 percent for non-Bengali films and 16 percent for Bengali films. In Karnataka, the entertainment tax rate on non-Kannada films was 52 percent while no tax was levied on Kannada films.

26 English language films released in these states would also be taxed at a higher rate.

27 *Swadeshi* was a principle articulated by Indian nationalists with respect to imported goods, especially mill-made cloth. The call by Gandhi and others to reject foreign goods and use only indigenously produced goods culminated in a movement where a form of protest against colonial rule was to burn British cloth.

28 The committee established by the colonial government focused on production, distribution, exhibition, import, censorship, taxation, and regulation and its report is the main source of information about cinema in India in the silent era.

29 Made during his speech of welcome at the Symposium on Cinema in Developing Countries, organized by the Indian Institute of Mass Communication and the Directorate of Film Festivals from January 9–11, 1979, in conjunction with the Seventh International Film Festival of India in New Delhi.

30 Although New Cinema generated its own stars, specifically Shabana Azmi, Smita Patil, Naseerudin Shah, and Om Puri who appeared in film after film.

2 The production and distribution of popular Hindi cinema

1 Vertical integration means that the production, distribution, and exhibition of films are controlled by the same company. This was the pattern of the Hollywood studios in their heyday in the 1920s and 1930s before they were broken up by American anti-trust legislation, but has increasingly become the trend with large mergers such as AOL-Time Warner which provides content as well as the means to disseminate it. Horizontal integration refers to one sector being controlled by one or a few companies. In the U.S. theatrical exhibition is basically controlled by a few large companies.

2 Official exchange rates for 2001 peg the dollar to be equal to 47.19 rupees. Currently, the exchange rate fluctuates between 47–50 rupees to a dollar. Exchange rates however do not accurately reflect the purchasing power or value of a particular currency. Purchasing power parity (PPP) is a better indicator of currency value and in 2002, $1 = Rs. 9 which means that $1 and Rs. 9 were able to purchase the same amount of goods and services (World Bank 2003). Therefore, using the PPP rate to convert rupees into dollars, budgets for Hindi films range from approximately $1.6–72 million. An average big-budget film ranges from $16–22 million. Top male stars earn between $1.1–3.3 million per film and female stars, $800,000–1.6 million per film. I thank Richard Ball for calculating the PPP conversion rate from rupees to dollars.

3 These are 1) Bombay 2) Delhi/U.P. 3) East Punjab 4) West Bengal or Eastern 5) Bihar/Nepal 6) Assam 7) Orissa 8) C.P.(Central Province)/Berar 9) C.I. (Central India) 10) Rajasthan 11) Nizam 12) Mysore 13) Andhra 14) South or Tamil Nadu/Kerala.

4 *Mahurat* is derived from the Sanskrit *muhurtha* which literally means "moment." The most common use of the concept is during Hindu wedding ceremonies.

5 This is markedly different from Hollywood, where revenues from the domestic theatrical release have currently become the smallest source of revenue for a film, as compared to the revenues generated from cable, video, television rights, licensing, merchandising, and overseas theatrical release.

6 This is known as "advance booking" – people reserve and buy movie tickets beforehand for a specific day and time, sometimes a few weeks before a movie's release. Advance booking is one way for producers, distributors, and exhibitors to gauge the initial interest in a film as well as predict its opening weekend.

7 See note 4 above.

8 Sometimes films are not completed because producers run out of finance or stars are no longer available. Even after films are produced, many may not find distributors willing to buy them or may not find distribution all over India.

9 Telugu and Tamil are the languages spoken in the South Indian states of Andhra Pradesh and Tamil Nadu respectively. Both are home to film industries equally and sometimes more prolific than Bombay's.

10 Since the mid-1990s, connected to the growing number of music-oriented satellite television channels and music-based programs, there have been a growing number of recording artists, singing mostly in the Hindi language who have been labeled as "pop" or "Indi-pop" artists.

11 By this time, HMV was no longer a subsidiary of the multinational company but a part of the Goenka group of companies, an Indian industrialist/business family. Everyone still referred to the music company as HMV, and the cassettes and compact discs would still carry the HMV logo along with the RPG logo of the Goenka group.

3 Key figures in the Bombay film industry

1 In addition to these three, Indian filmmaking is divided into the following main categories: lyric writing, story/screenplay writing, dialogue writing, playback singing, choreography ("dance direction"), stunts/action ("fight direction"), costume design, art direction, cinematography, editing, and post-production sound which includes dubbing and sound mixing.

2 Additionally, readers may be interested in viewing films by the following directors: Abbas-Mastan (director duo), Mukul Anand, Shyam Benegal, Sanjay Leela Bhansali, Vikram Bhatt, Tanuja Chandra, Basu Chatterjee, Aditya Chopra, Vidhu Vinod Chopra, J.P. Dutta, Gulzar, Nasir Hussain, Karan Johar, Feroz Khan, Mansoor Khan, Raj Khosla, Indra Kumar, Manoj Kumar, Prakash Mehra, Aziz Mirza, Govind Nihalani, Mani Rathnam, Rakesh Roshan, Shakti Samanta, Rajkumar Santoshi, Kundan Shah, and V. Shantaram.

3 The oldest system of awards dating back to 1953 for Hindi films, instituted by the English-language film magazine, *Filmfare*, published by the *Times of India* Group.

4 Instituted in 1969 to mark the centennial year of Phalke's birth, the Dadasaheb Phalke Award is the highest honor specific to filmmaking bestowed by the Indian government. It is presented annually to one individual during the National Film Awards to recognize his or her lifetime contributions and achievements in the field of cinema.

5 The Indian government instituted a series of civilian awards in 1954 to recognize the achievements of individuals in the arts, literature, science, performance, research, scholarship, social service, politics, government service, entrepreneurship, etc. The four levels of awards listed in descending order are Bharat Ratna, Padma Vibhushan, Padma Bhushan, and Padma Shri.

6 No relationship to Mehboob Khan's *Andaz* starring Raj Kapoor, Nargis, and Dilip Kumar and released in 1949. Hindi film titles

are registered for a period of 10 years and are then in the public domain unless the producer continues to register them. Therefore, many titles are recycled and the films bear no relationship to one other. For example *Andaz*, has been the title for four different films, in 1949, 1971, 1994 and 2003.

7 For example, Waheeda Rehman who starred as Amitabh Bachchan's wife in two films in 1976 (*Adalat, Kabhi Kabhie*), played his mother in *Trishul* in 1978. Raakhee, who played Bachchan's heroine in a number of films including the hit *Barsaat ki ek Raat* in 1981, played his mother the next year in *Shakti*.

8 Pooja Bhatt formed her own production company in 1996 while Juhi Chawla started a production company with Shahrukh Khan in 1999. Other actresses such as Sri Devi, Manisha Koirala, Aishwarya Rai, and Raveena Tandon produced their first films between 2001–3.

9 The antecedents for this character, however, already existed in Ashok Kumar's character in *Kismet*, Raj Kapoor's in *Awara*, and Sunil Dutt's in *Mother India*.

10 Anecdotes abound about Bachchan's popularity in Egypt, Morocco, Tanzania, Trinidad, Afghanistan, etc. According to one anecdote relayed to me by an Indian journalist, during a trip to Cairo, the crowds at the airport hoping to get a glimpse of Bachchan were so large that he had to undergo customs clearance in his hotel.

11 Kapoor was already married when he met Nargis. Throughout his career he was linked romantically with a few of his co-stars, but he never left his wife.

12 The first is Vyjayanthimala, also from Madras, and the second is Waheeda Rehman from Hyderabad.

13 She starred opposite Khanna in 1974 (*Prem Nagar*) when his career was on the downturn, although their film together was a hit, and she was already a major star when Bachchan had his first success. Though she starred opposite Bachchan in 1974 in *Kasauti*, they did not do so again until 1981 in *Naseeb*. When they

were in films together, it was with other romantic leads, i.e., *Sholay*.

4 Key films of post-independence Hindi cinema

1   Melodrama literally means "play with music" and originated in the late eighteenth century in Europe.
2   For example, if a character appears in the left side of the frame and walks toward a tree at the right side of the frame, the 180-degree axis would be broken if the next frame showed the same character on the right walking toward the tree on the left side of the frame.

5 Reflections and perspectives on Hindi cinema by Bombay filmmakers

1   See chapter 4 for what Hindi filmmakers mean by a "musical."
2   Five billion tickets are sold in India alone annually, therefore the number of tickets sold world-wide would be greater than this figure. However, this figure accounts for all films in India which would include tickets sold for films in languages other than Hindi.
3   Diwali or the festival of lights is a very important Hindu festival that takes place in the lunar month of *Karthik* and falls between late October and early November.

BIBLIOGRAPHY

Arthur Andersen (2000) *The Indian Entertainment Industry: Strategy & Vision*, New Delhi: Federation of Indian Chambers of Commerce and Industry (FICCI).

Bamzai, K. and Unnithan, S. (2003) "Show Business," *India Today*, February 24: 48–51.

Bandyopadhyay, S. (ed.) (1993) *Indian Cinema: Contemporary Perceptions from the Thirties*, Jamshedpur: Celluloid Chapter.

Barnouw, E. and Krishnaswamy, S. (1980) *Indian Film*, New York: Oxford University Press.

Bordwell, D. and Thompson, K. (1993) *Film Art: An Introduction*, New York: McGraw Hill.

Chakravarty, S. (1993) *National Identity in Indian Popular Cinema 1947–1987*, Austin: University of Texas Press.

Chaya, R.B. (1996) "Discordant Notes," *Screen* (Bombay), November 15: 39.

Das Sharma, B. (1993) "Indian Cinema and National Leadership," in S. Bandyopadhyay (ed.) *Indian Cinema: Contemporary Perceptions from the Thirties*, Jamshedpur: Celluloid Chapter.

Dayal, J. (1983) "The Role of the Government: Story of an Uneasy Truce," in A. Vasudev and P. Lenglet (eds) Indian Cinema Superbazaar, New Delhi: Vikas.

Dwivedi, S. and Mehrotra, R. (1995) Bombay: The Cities Within, Bombay: India Book House.

Ganapati, P. (2002) "Lights, Camera, War!" Mumbai: rediff.com. Online. Available HTTP: http://www.rediff.com/entertai/2002/oct24main.htm (accessed June 27, 2003).

Gangar, A. (1995) "Films from the City of Dreams," in S. Patel and A. Thorner (eds) Bombay: Mosaic of Modern Culture, Bombay: Oxford University Press.

Ganti, T. (2002) "'And Yet My Heart Is Still Indian:' The Bombay Film Industry and the (H)Indianization of Hollywood," in F. Ginsburg, L. Abu-Lughod, and B. Larkin (eds) Media Worlds: Anthropology on New Terrain, Berkeley: University of California Press.

—— (2000) "Casting Culture: The Social Life of Hindi Film Production in Contemporary India," unpublished PhD dissertation, New York University.

—— (1998) "Centenary Commemorations or Centenary Contestations? – Celebrating a Hundred Years of Cinema in Bombay," Visual Anthropology 11(4): 399–419.

Garga, B.D. (1996) So Many Cinemas: The Motion Picture in India, Mumbai: Eminence Designs.

Gopakumar, K.M and Unni, V.K. (2003) "Perspectives on Copyright: The 'Karishma' Controversy," Economic & Political Weekly, July 12: 2935–6.

Gopalan, L. (2002) Cinema of Interruptions: Action Genres in Contemporary Indian Cinema, London: British Film Institute.

Hardgrave, R. L. and Kochanek, S. (1970; 4th edn 1986) India: Government and Politics in a Developing Nation, San Diego: Harcourt Brace Jovanovich.

Kaul, G. (1998) Cinema and the Indian Freedom Struggle, New Delhi: Sterling.

Luhrmann, T.M. (1996) *The Good Parsi: The Fate of a Colonial Elite in a Postcolonial Society*. Cambridge, MA: Harvard University Press.

Miller, T. (1998) "Hollywood and the World," in J. Hill and P.C. Gibson (eds) *The Oxford Guide to Film Studies*, Oxford: Oxford University Press.

Ministry of Information and Broadcasting (1992) *The Cinematograph Act, 1952* (As Modified up to May 1, 1984), New Delhi: Directorate of Advertising and Visual Publicity.

National Association of Theatre Owners (2003) "Number of U.S. Movie Screens," Online. Available HTTP: http://www.nato online.org/statisticsscreens.htm (accessed September 15, 2003).

Neale, S. (1990) "Questions of Genre," *Screen* 31(1): 45–66.

Ninan, S. (1995) *Through the Magic Window: Television and Change in India*, New Delhi: Penguin.

Oldenburg, V.T. (1991) "Lifestyle as Resistance: The Case of the Courtesans of Lucknow," in D. Haynes and G. Prakash (eds) *Contesting Power: Resistance and Everyday Social Relations in South Asia*, Berkeley: University of California Press.

Patel, S. and Thorner, A. (eds) (1995a) *Bombay: Metaphor for Modern India*, Bombay: Oxford University Press.

—— (1995b) *Bombay: Mosaic of Modern Culture*, Bombay: Oxford University Press.

Pingle, V. (1999) *Rethinking the Developmental State: India's Industry in Comparative Perspective*, New York: St. Martin's Press.

Prakash, S. (1983) "Music, Dance and the Popular Films: Indian Fantasies, Indian Repressions," in A. Vasudev and P. Lenglet (eds) *Indian Cinema Superbazaar*, New Delhi: Vikas.

Raheja, D. and Kothari, J. (1996) *The Hundred Luminaries of Hindi Cinema*, Bombay: India Book House.

Rajadhyaksha, A. (1986) "Neo-Traditionalism: Film as Popular Art in India," *Framework* 32/33: 20–67.

Rajadhyaksha, A. and Willemen, Paul (eds) (1999) *Encyclopaedia of Indian Cinema*, London: British Film Institute.

Ray, M. and Jacka, E. (1996) "Indian Television: An Emerging Regional Force," in J. Sinclair, E. Jacka, and S. Cunningham (eds) *New Patterns in Global Television*, New York: Oxford University Press.

Shoesmith, B. (1988) "Swadeshi Cinema: Cinema, Politics and Culture: The Writings of D.G. Phalke," *Continuum* 2(1): 44–73.

—— (1987) "From Monopoly to Commodity: The Bombay Studios in the 1930s," in T. O'Regan and B. Shoesmith (eds) *History On/And/In Film: Selected Papers from the 3rd Australian History and Film Conference*, Perth: History and Film Association of Australia.

Thoraval, Y. (2000) *The Cinemas of India*, New Delhi: Macmillan.

Vasudevan, R. (1995) "Addressing the Spectator of a 'Third World' National Cinema: the Bombay 'Social' Film of the 1940s and 1950s," *Screen* 36(4): 305–34.

—— (1990) "Indian Commercial Cinema," *Screen* 31(4): 446–53.

—— (1989) "The Melodramatic Mode and the Commercial Hindi Cinema: Notes on Film History, Narrative and Performance," *Screen* 30(3): 29–50.

World Bank (2003) *World Development Indicators*, Online. Available HTTP: http://www.worldbank.org/data/onlinedatabases/online databases.html (accessed September 26, 2003).

INDEX

Gupta, Ravi 184–6
Gupta, Sutanu 174–5

Hallauri, Khursheed 163
Hamrahi (film) 96–7
Hare Rama Hare Krishna (film) 118,
    131
He Ping 113
Hema-Malini 129–31
Hindi film industry: artistic debate
    50; categories of jobs 235n;
    cosmopolitanism of 92;
    decentralized structure 53–6;
    defined 2–4; diversity of 54–6,
    66–7, 91–5; early infrastructure
    11; economics of 25–7, 33–5,
    43–5; effect of partition 22–3;
    effect of television 36–7;
    internationalization 37–40, 51–2,
    58, 219–21; male dominance of
    94–5; Mrs Gandhi's era and 30–3;
    "national" character 12; output
    per year 3; place in Indian culture
    192–4; post-independence period
    23–30; pre-war era 15–19, 208;
    production values 37; recognition
    as 'industry' 50; silent era 8–11,
    205–7; state attitudes towards
    46–52; studio era 208–11; World
    War II and 19–20
Hindi language 186–7, 229n;
    dubbing process 73; effect of
    partition 22–3; first film in 207;
    "Hinglish" 69; Imperial Films 16;
    industry standard 3; large market
    for 11–12; regional dialects 213;
    state economic incentives and 45;
    struggle against 210 *see also* Hindi
    film industry
Hinduism: chauvinism 22, 24;
    Diwali 237n; *mahurat* 70; Phalke's
    "mythologicals" 9, 10
Hindustan Cinema Films Company
    10
Hindustan Film Company 206
Hindustan Photo Films 213

Hindustani language 12, 23
Hollywood: character of films
    182–3; market shares 184–6;
    remakes and adaptations 75–8;
    vertical integration 233n
Hollywood Foreign Press Association
    212
House Number 44 (film) 118
How Films Are Made (documentary)
    206
Hulchul (film) 131
Hum Aapke Hain Koun! (film) 39, 86,
    107, 135, 168–9, 218
Hum Ek Hain (film) 118
Hum Log (television) 116, 217
The Hundred Luminaries of Hindi Cinema
    (Raheja and Kothari) 91
Hunterwali (film) 208
Husain, M. F. 86, 135
Hussain, Anwar 153
Hussain, Nasir 122
Hussain, Tahir 122
Hyderabad 3

Idiot (film) 124
Iftikhar 160
Ilzaam (film) 127
Imperial Films Company 16, 207
India: colonial era 43, 230n;
    cosmopolitanism of 186–7;
    diaspora 38, 231–2n; films in
    culture 192–4; independence
    20, 209; legal provision for
    emergencies 231n; levels of
    awards 235n; map redrawn
    211; under Mrs Gandhi 30–3;
    nationalism 41–3; non-aligned
    movement 211; nuclear power
    51, 215, 219; partition 20–3,
    209; patriotism 29; state
    attitudes towards films 45–52;
    war over Kashmir 210, 213
Indian Cinematography Committee
    46, 207
Indian Film (Barnouw and
    Krishnaswamy) 205